This is number two hundred and thirty in the
second numbered series of the
Miegunyah Volumes
made possible by the
Miegunyah Fund
established by bequests
under the wills of
Sir Russell and Lady Grimwade.

'Miegunyah' was Russell Grimwade's home
from 1911 to 1955
and Mab Grimwade's home
from 1911 to 1973.

Beyond the Meeting of the Waters

A Yorta Yorta Life Story

Dr Wayne Atkinson
Catherine Guinness

THE MIEGUNYAH PRESS

We dedicate our story to the Yorta Yorta fighters for justice,
who inspired us to pass on the power of the voice and
the spear of the pen to future generations.

~

Melbourne University Publishing acknowledges the traditional owners of the unceded land on which we work, learn and live: the Wurundjeri Woiwurrung peoples of the Kulin Nation. We pay respect to elders and acknowledge the importance of Indigenous knowledge.

Aboriginal and Torres Strait Islander peoples are respectfully advised that this publication contains images of people who are deceased.

A Miegunyah Indigenous title
THE MIEGUNYAH PRESS
An imprint of Melbourne University Publishing Limited
Level 1, 715 Swanston Street, Carlton, Victoria 3053, Australia
mup-contact@unimelb.edu.au
www.mup.com.au

First published 2025

Cover design by Pfisterer + Freeman
Typeset in 11.25/15pt Adobe Caslon Pro by Cannon Typesetting
Printed in China by 1010 Printing Asia International Ltd

NATIONAL LIBRARY OF AUSTRALIA
A catalogue record for this book is available from the National Library of Australia

9780522881011 (hardback)
9780522881028 (ebook)

Contents

Keywords from Yorta Yorta Language

Alcheringa: the Dreaming; title of Uncle Bill Onus's 1960s television show

Algabonyah: grassy plain on Dungula downstream from Moira Lake; word for handsome, good-looking (see Ronald Morgan's memoir)

apical: at the top, or apex, of a family tree

Baala wala: Broken River

Barmah, parma: home of the plover

Barmah Moira Forest: Original name of Barmah–Millewa Forest wetlands

batjelan: money

bayadherra: long-neck turtle, totem of Yorta Yorta

bitja: word for fire management, called cultural burning, of Barmah National Park

bitjau: firestick

biyala: river red gum

bloodline: connection to ancestors and land

borpa: freshwater crayfish

burnanga: Murray cod

Coranderrk: Aboriginal reserve near Healesville, 1863–1924

Country: used by Aboriginal people to describe the lands and waterways to which they are connected as an inherent right through their ancestors

Cummeragunja, Cummera: Our home; Aboriginal settlement on the NSW side of the Murray River near Barmah, 1882 to present

Cummeragunja walk-off: action of over 200 residents who walked off Cummeragunja Station in 1939 in protest at their living conditions and denial of their human rights

dhama winyarr: woman elder

dhamangalnya: senior male elder

dhangan: damper

dharnya: red-gum trees

djitiga: meat

Dungula: Murray River; the town name Tongala is an anglicised version

Dungula watjerrupna: Murray River short-necked turtle

Dunguma wala: big flood

dyiuman: afraid

galnyan yakurrumdja: respect

gammin: fake, not fair dinkum fella

gane: Great Rainbow Serpent

gangupka: Murray perch (yellow belly)

Garradha mowla: Yorta Yorta occupation site in Barmah National Park

golyinan: angry, aggravated

goolin: person upset about something

goopna ngarwu: deep listening, used in teaching/yarning/healing circle goopri: grog

gowala: kind, kindly

gubbah: white Australian

Gulpa Gaka: Welcome

Gulpa Gaka Yorta Yorta Woka: Welcome to Yorta Yorta Country

Gunbungwerro: Dja Dja Wurrung and Baraba Baraba name for Loddon River

gurranyin: eagle

guthup: person who is too flash

identified ancestors: Yorta Yorta Nations term for original ancestors who were on Country when British sovereignty was imposed; alternative name is apical or principal ancestors

Itchica: meeting of the waters; Echuca

jiliwa: toilet

Kanyapella: big wetlands

Kaiela: Goulburn River

Kolety: Wamba Wamba name for Edward River

Koori: name for themselves used by Aboriginal people in Victoria and New South Wales

Kotopna, kootoopna: deep waterhole, name of a district

Kyabram: thick forest; name of a town

lotjpa yapaneyepuk: speak together

Maloga Mission: Aboriginal mission station, 1874–88; 'maloga' means sand or sugar

mar-noo, mia mia: camp, bark hut

Millewa: name of region in north-western Victoria; called 'Pama Narrows' by Yorta Yorta

Moama: burial ground, place of the dead; name of a town

Moira: lake connected to Barmah Lake; protected by Ramsar Convention

Moira Station: NSW pastoral station adjoining Moira Forest

moom: bottom

Mooroopna: name of a town, from mirrapoona, meaning deep waterhole

mulana: spirit

ngalnya nginak: kind regards

Ngarrindjeri: people of the lower Murray region in South Australia

nurtja: forest

Nunga: name for Aboriginal people in southern parts of South Australia

Nyoongar: name for Aboriginal people in south-west Western Australia

Tatura: small lagoon; name of a town

tiddas: sisters

Tongala: name of a town; anglicised version of Dungula

wakeda: wild about something

wala: water

winyarrn mana: woman's camp

Woka: Country; the lands and waterways to which Yorta Yorta are connected as an inherent right through their ancestors

wudjelas: white people in South Australia

wulumburra: communal fire

wuta yapaneyepuk: all together

yakai: goodness gracious

Yakoa wala: Campaspe River

yalca: meat, tea and damper

yama muttar: bark canoe cut from river eucalypt trees

yamyabuk yepuc: walking together

yanagai: go away

yenbenon: our people

yillita: letters, message stick

yoorrook: 'truth' in Wamba Wamba language

Yorta Yorta Nation: First Nations Peoples of the Dungula, Baala, Yakoa, Kaiela (Murray, Broken, Campaspe and Goulburn rivers)

Family Trees

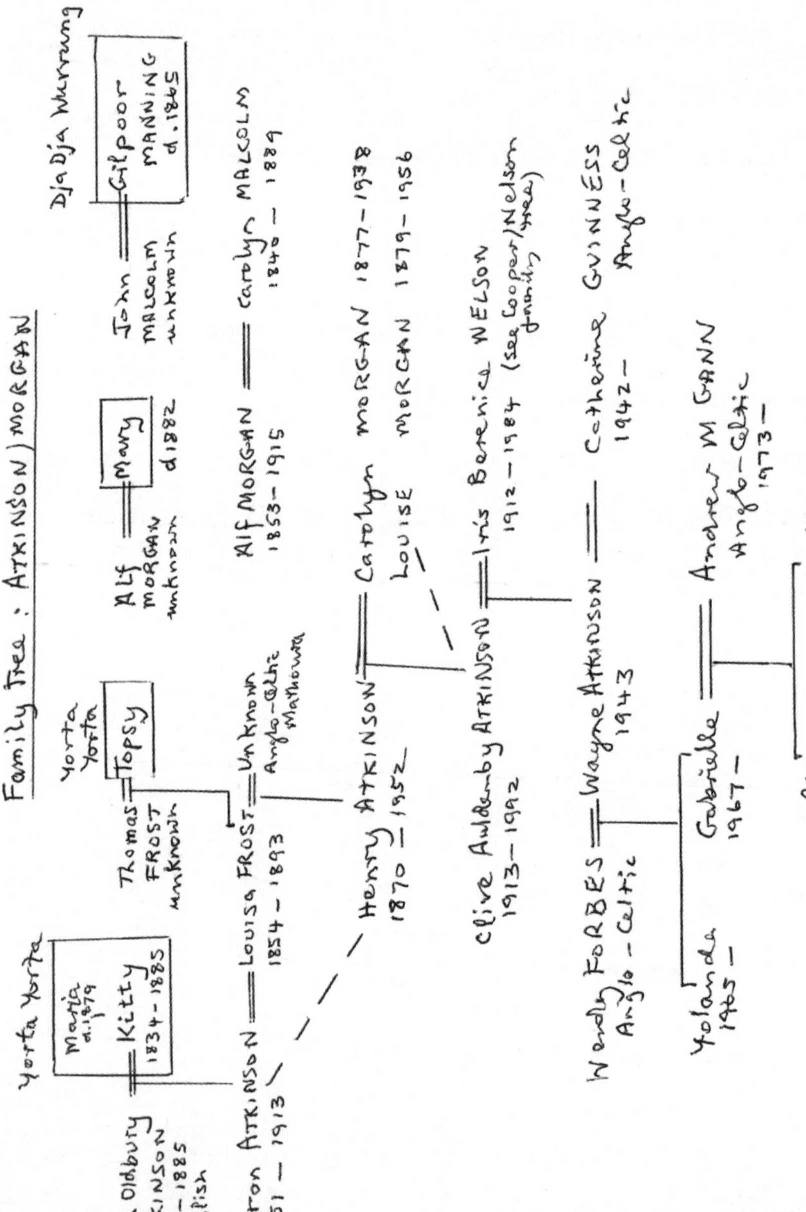

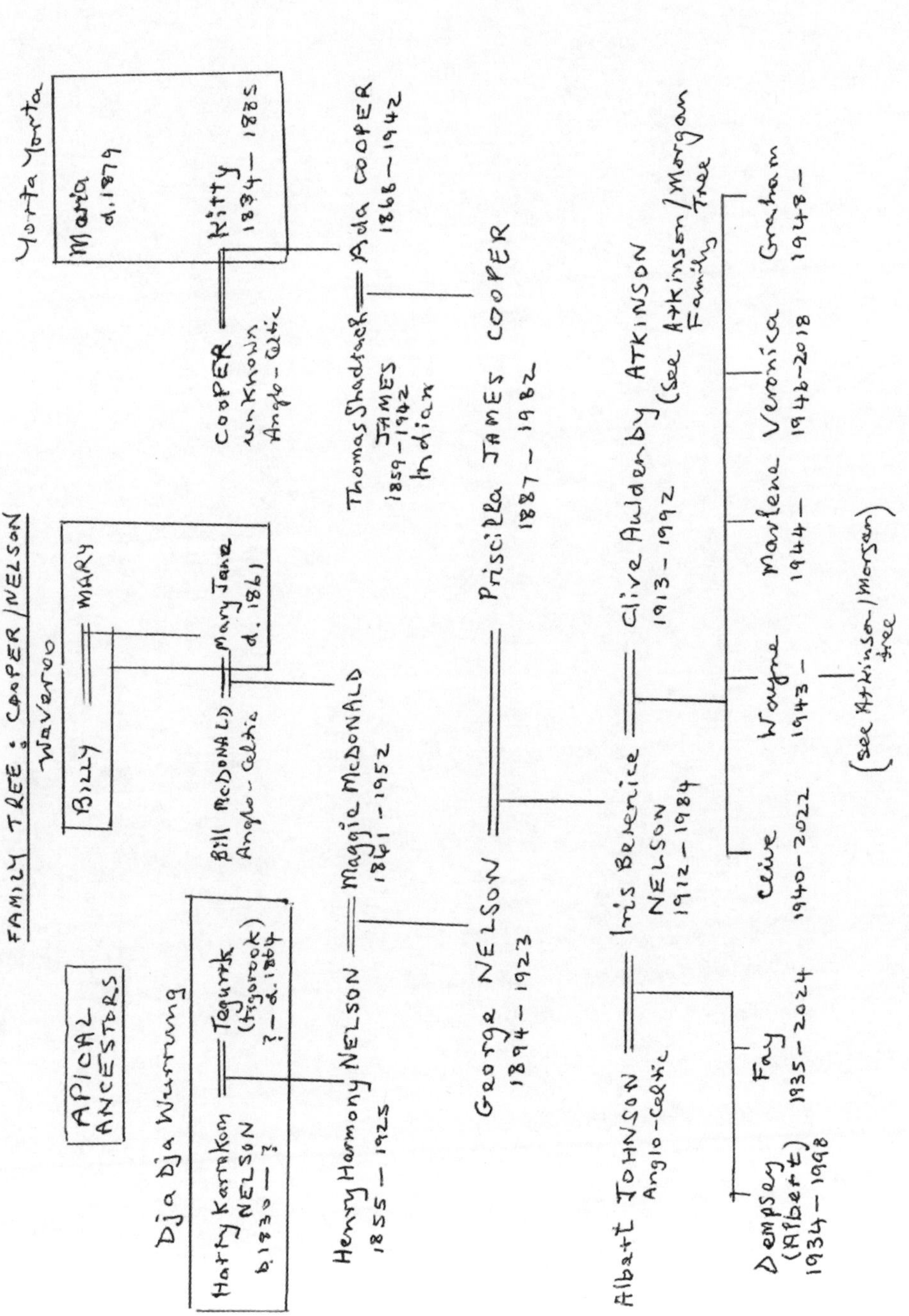
FAMILY TREE: COOPER/NELSON
APICAL ANCESTORS
Dja Dja Wurrung
Harry Karrakom NELSON b.1830 – ?
Tegurrk (Ascgorook) ? – d.1864
Waveroo
BILLY
MARY
Bill McDONALD Anglo-Celtic
Mary Jane d.1861
Yorta Yorta
Maria d.1879
Kitty 1834 – 1885
COOPER unknown Anglo-Celtic
Henry Harmony NELSON 1855 – 1925
Maggie McDONALD 1861 – 1952
Thomas Shadrach JAMES 1859 – 1942 Indian
Ada COOPER 1868 – 1942
George NELSON 1894 – 1923
Priscilla JAMES COOPER 1887 – 1982
Albert JOHNSON Anglo-Celtic
Iris Berenice NELSON 1912 – 1984
Clive Aulden by ATKINSON 1913 – 1992
(see Atkinson/Morgan Family Tree)
Dempsey (Albert) 1934 – 1998
Fay 1935 – 2024
Clive 1940 – 2022
Wayne 1943 –
Marlene 1944 –
Veronica 1946 – 2018
Graham 1948 –
(see Atkinson/Morgan tree)

Introduction: Gulpa Gaka Yorta Yorta Woka

Welcome to Yorta Yorta Country.

As I sit in my study reflecting on life as a senior Yorta Yorta elder (dhumangalnya), I look around at the photos of my ancestors on the wall. They stretch back over many generations to the Yorta Yorta, Dja Dja Wurrung and Waveroo Traditional Owners. These are featured in the family tree and throughout the book.

Granny Kitty, an apical ancestor of the Yorta Yorta Nation, had eight children and they flourished, becoming a large family group living at Maloga and Cummeragunja on the Murray River. Her children and grandchildren became outstanding leaders of the Aboriginal community in Victoria and New South Wales. Our native title land claim from 1994 to 2022 verified our bloodline connections to these elders and, through them, to the original ancestors who lived on Country since creation. This was long before the British came and imposed their law over the original Indigenous lore and sovereign ownership of the territorial land and waters. (The term 'lore' is used to denote the oldest and original First Peoples law, tradition and knowledge that preceded the import of English law.)

I look at the photos of our sacred rivers and the rich forest wetlands. Just recently a new bridge was built over the Murray River at Echuca and was named Dungula. My brother Clive, his wife Judy Atkinson, and the Yorta Yorta Nation proposed this name to honour the Yorta Yorta ancestral connections and name for the Murray. It is a fine example of how the broader community is gradually recognising our proud

Yorta Yorta language and heritage. Much of the language used in this book is drawn from Yorta Yorta speakers and our comprehensive online database and dictionary.

Our history is long and enduring. It tells us that we are of the land and the rivers that flow through Yorta Yorta Country. Our land abounds in rich river systems, intersecting and spreading out to replenish and create rich alluvial soils, grasslands and forest wetlands. Most of the food resources in Yorta Yorta Country came from water-based activities like canoeing, shell fishing, making fish traps to store food, spearfishing, and collecting food from the lagoon systems. The traditional hunting and fishing practices continue today in adapted forms, keeping our connections to Country going for future generations.

The title of this book, *Beyond the Meeting of the Waters*, takes readers directly to my home in Echuca. In Yorta Yorta language we call it Itchica, which means 'meeting of the waters'. We are river-based wala (water) people. This is my ancestral place from where I have travelled beyond the meeting of the waters. My journey of learning has come full circle and will one day return to Itchica, the eternal resting place. It is a sacred homeland that calls us at the end of all journeys so that the spirit is free to rest in peace in the eternal Dreaming.

Our storylines draw on much of the traditional language, which is woven together with English. Indigenous Australia is one of the most linguistically diverse countries in the world. The Australian Institute of Aboriginal and Torres Strait Islander Studies (AIATSIS) map of Indigenous Australia provides an overview of the location of territorial groups and languages spoken—languages that precede the advent of English. They seek to be treated as distinct and equally valued linguistic traditions. They evolved over time immemorial and, in the words of my niece and linguistic scholar Dr Lou Bennett, 'our language is efficient. It stands firm in its own right without being measured by outside sources'.[1]

AIATSIS has identified over 250 Indigenous languages, including 800 dialects, that were once spoken across the length and breadth of the country. Much language was affected by the impact of colonisation, and since the 1980s there has been a concerted effort to restore it through language retrieval processes. We are seeing a paradigm shift in the inclusion of Indigenous languages in schools, music, theatre, media and Welcome to Country ceremonies, and in the traditional naming of Australian capital cities and regional areas. In the words of Indigenous early education specialist Deborah Hoger for Community Early Learning Australia:

> Replacing European names, which more often than not, reflect a painful colonial past, can be a wonderfully positive move forward in terms of building on reconciliation. Using traditional First Nations names for places both acknowledges and celebrates the connection of First Nations people to those places; long-lasting connections which span tens and tens of thousands of years …
>
> Returning the official name of a place to its original name then, is a powerful reminder to all that we are living within a cultural landscape; we are and always have been, living on Aboriginal land.[2]

English has left a permanent mark on the landscape, devising and choosing names for sites and places within Yorta Yorta land. Many place names are anglicised versions of the original names. Tongala is based on the Dungula River, and Mooroopna comes from our word mirrapoona, meaning deep waterhole. Names of other towns in the area are also derived from the Yorta Yorta language. Fortunately, the imbalance in language representation is changing through the efforts of the revival process. The Yorta Yorta language used in this book comes from sources including the Wiradjuri Condobolin Corporation (WCC) Language Program's Yorta Yorta Dictionary app, missionary Daniel Matthews' diaries, and Yorta Yorta speakers.

The Yorta Yorta Nation uses the terms 'identified' and 'principal' ancestors to denote the original ancestors who were on Country when British sovereignty was imposed. The term 'bloodline' is used to explain connections to the original ancestors, who are called 'apical' ancestors. These are the original ancestors from whom Yorta Yorta bloodline connections are validated. Colonisation did not extinguish the sovereignty of the Traditional Owners. Their sovereignty has never been ceded to the Crown by way of a treaty, compact or any formal agreement.

Language is always changing in how we talk about Indigenous culture and land relations. Terms like First Peoples, First Nations Peoples, Traditional Owners, and apical, principal and identified ancestors are used to describe tribal group identity and territorial connections. The way I talk about knowledge of identity and connection to Country is drawn from language used in our Yorta Yorta native title case (see Part IV). Since our storylines draw on traditional Yorta Yorta language woven together with English, I have tried to find a balance between older and newer versions of terminology throughout this book. The list of keywords at the start of the book will help you learn some of our traditional words. It is also important to acknowledge that there is a distinct Yorta Yorta English that we call the Cummera drawl, a dialect that grew out of the Cummeragunja Reserve history. It is a dialect of English that contains values and concepts of Aboriginal culture, some traditional words and non-verbal communication, and is still a key language of communication within our communities today.

My journey is long and winding, covering my life from the Mooroopna riverbank to Itchica (Echuca), Adelaide, Melbourne and overseas. It is a lifetime journey with my partner, Cathy Guinness. We have written this book together, blending both our stories into one narrative. Hopefully, it will find its place as a legacy of our adventures and as a family history for future generations, friends and the broader community.

Much material on our lives is located on my website (http://waynera.wordpress.com/). I now have time to reflect on those stories with the advantage of a broader knowledge base, new experiences and different perceptions. This allows me to focus on the profound changes and issues that have influenced and shaped my life from its beginnings on the riverbank to Itchica and beyond.

I hope my contribution adds further value to the broader Indigenous narrative. My Yorta Yorta worldview has been enriched by studies and knowledge accumulated from a lifetime of work experience and education. It provides an opportunity for me to reposition myself within our own ways of being and seeing things, and through our own ways of teaching. In claiming that space, I draw largely on the rich oral tradition of my people's cultural history and survival. That is the basis of the identity I have been brought up to follow as a proud Yorta Yorta man. My life has been guided by values that have inspired us to walk tall and proud wherever we may choose to go. This inspiration comes from the admirable leadership, wisdom and knowledge that we have been privileged to inherit from our ancestors. I share how this has shaped Yorta Yorta thinking and Yorta Yorta lives.

Part I of the book introduces my ancestors and looks at the impact of colonisation on our people, and three places that were important after colonisation: Moira Station, Maloga Mission and Cummeragunja Reserve. When I was in my late thirties I recorded the stories of the elders in my oral history project *A Picture from the Other Side.* The account of the life and times of my people before I was born that you read in this book is based on these stories.[3]

Part II deals with the first thirty years of my life, in the Aboriginal community on the Flat at Mooroopna and then in the town of Itchica. I share my experience of education, race relations and friendships made along the way. This includes the valued cultural learning I got from my elders, which takes my story to 1974.

Part III is about the opportunity to return to study, which was a major turning point in my life. I want to share the knowledge and wisdom I have gained from education, teaching, oral history projects and participation in the struggle for justice.

Part IV explains how my path in education culminated in a PhD while I also worked on the Yorta Yorta land claim between 1994 and 2002. Our native title claim is a story of sharing knowledge, hard work, denial of rights and then bouncing back to base-camp politics.

Part V comes from my experience of teaching the Oncountry Learning program at the University of Melbourne. This is a community-based education program I was privileged to teach in Yorta Yorta Country for nearly two decades, from 2003 to 2019.

Part V includes discussion of the racial vilification case involving News Limited journalist Andrew Bolt. I also talk about how global travels with Cathy have added to our story: her Irish connections and Anglo-Celtic heritage enrich the storylines as we trace the impact of British colonisation and the origins of the reserve system our people were forced to live under for so long. In Part VI, the impact of colonisation comes back to revisit the First Peoples of Victoria with the establishment of the Yoorrook Justice Commission from 2021 to 2025. In the final chapter, I analyse and reflect on the changes in government policy that continue to impact and shape our lives as First Nations Peoples.

The impact of the racial ideology that drove colonisation and continues to manifest itself in our everyday lives is a significant part of the book. Indigenous people have stories to tell of the way racism has affected us and our families, and how it remains a systemic barrier to equality and human dignity in our lives today. Dealing with racism at the individual and community level is critically examined, and we see how governments have struggled to deal with it as it continues to raise its ugly head. I discuss racism in my life experiences from the riverbank to schooling, on the sporting field, and in public life generally. As an agent of reform, I reflect on what changes have been achieved through government, and people's actions to deconstruct racial barriers.

The calls for justice through the Anglo legal system are ongoing, and the sparsity of outcomes has taken a heavy toll on the social and emotional wellbeing of my people. The victories along the way have been minimal. They are important milestones, however, in balancing the justice scales. The Bolt case is an example of persistence, courage and determination to seek fair and just outcomes for the effects of racial vilification. Courage is also about standing one's ground against prejudice and the ongoing practices of racial vilification, witnessed in the Stan Grant, Adam Goodes, Tanya Day and Veronica Nelson cases.

In measuring the gains achieved on the justice front in my lifetime, I draw on the 'chipping-away' philosophy, which has helped me find some serenity and inner resolve against adversity and negativity. For me, it is rejoicing in the big chips gained that helps to restore your passion for justice when the odds are continually stacked against you. They are minimal gains, but they help to restore hope and inspire you to keep fighting. 'The struggle continues' is language that constantly reminds us of the daunting reality First Nations Peoples are faced with. Small gains are better than none, and while bigger ones may be elusive, they are achievable with the power of the voice and collective solidarity. I reflect on ideas like these, drawing on the political philosophy and strategies for change advocated by our admirable leaders.

Our struggle for Indigenous-based human rights has been extensive. How rights are reflected in First Peoples sovereignty, land justice, heritage and self-determination is a major focus of the book. The Voice referendum of October 2023 was divisive in its representation, becoming a political football in similar fashion to the land rights debate that culminated in the Yorta Yorta native title fiasco. I devote much attention to these matters in the book.

The storylines in this book have a strong cultural context. They are like a large river red gum with interconnecting branches that are grounded in our ancestral lands, waters and creation stories. All of these experiences and events have had a profound effect on my life and my sense of being as a Yorta Yorta man. By sharing my journey through the storylines approach, I hope to inspire our next generation as I have been inspired by my ancestors.

PART I

Who's Your Mob?

1
My Mob, Our Country

One of the first questions we ask when we meet other First Peoples is 'Who's your mob?' We use this as a cultural protocol to establish identity connections in the Koori world. Indeed, it is a mandatory requirement.

To me, this question has a much deeper and broader meaning. It is grounded in traditional lore and validated by our bloodline connections with the original (apical) ancestors. The language used about identity comes from traditional ways of knowing and being. The question of who you are and what tribal mob you are from is customary cultural protocol. In using this question to confirm identity, we can then start talking and find out more about each other.

Two important aspects of your identity need to be known. Firstly, for me, my main mob is Yorta Yorta. Secondly, and equally important, is the place where your ancestors come from. It is about ancestral lands as well as the reserve or mission station your people lived on. Knowing your mob and your connections to Country are a guiding framework that you carry with you forever. It's like a road map that guides your life journey, wherever you may travel in Indigenous Australia.

My wife, Cathy, is familiar with the notion of 'Who's your mob?' from the exchanges that often happen when she is with me. If we're in Melbourne, for instance, and I see someone who looks familiar, I approach them respectfully by using the word 'Koori' to get their attention. This usually evokes a quick eye-contact response that leads to communication. Recently at Preston Market, I approached someone who looked familiar. He quickly replied, 'Yes, I'm Yorta Yorta.'

I responded with delight, saying, 'Hey, that's my mob too.' This takes us to the next step in the kinship process, where I ask, 'Who's your family group?'

The person might reply, 'Ahh, I'm an Atkinson.' An immediate bond brings us together with the same tribal group and bloodline connections. We keep talking about kinship relations and usually end with a Koori handshake of solidarity.

Cultural exchanges like this become news items to take home and share with family: 'Oh, I met a Koori fella today at the market who is a grandson of Dad's first cousin.' We grow our knowledge base and learn about each other through our mob and where we're from.

The deeper levels of knowing and family connections can take you to broader kinship relations. The connections between the reserves and mission stations are reflected in our oral histories. For instance, when I say I'm Yorta Yorta it directly relates me to the Dungula, Kaiela, Yakoa and Baala rivers and to the reserves where my ancestors lived. They lived at Cummeragunja from 1889 until the walk-off in 1939; before that, from 1874 to 1888, they lived on the mission station of Maloga, and earlier still, they lived in the bush or on Moira Station and other squatters' stations. This opens further dialogue on the names of family groups who lived on the reserves and the migrations and intermarriages that took place before and after colonisation. We are now drawn into the broader intricacies of migration patterns and kinship relations.

It usually turns out you're related at different levels to other people through the cultural relationships that evolved in time and place. Once contact is made and your mob is identified, it engages other storylines. A person may say, for example, that their aunty or uncle married someone from Cummera or lived at Coranderrk or Lake Tyers and married into the community. Or they may talk about an ancestor who is buried at a particular reserve. In most cases you are related as cousins, which engages the 'Hey cuz, we're related' saying. This is a bonding experience that unites your bloodline connections. It extends your kinship connections to other distant family groups and also gives you a sense of cultural security to know that you have relatives spread far and wide. Indeed, it is common for these kinship connections to extend across Australia: I've found this in my own travels.

The question of Aboriginal identity and sense of place is explained more clearly in an oral history interview I did with a Cummeragunja elder some forty years ago. Uncle Bevan Nicholls' take on the matter is most enlightening when he says:

> There's been a lot of changes for us as far as a race of people goes. But we'll never change our identity. We've changed in a lot of other ways but the people who have left Cummera still call it their 'home' even though they might live in Melbourne or Sydney. It's something that always crops up when someone who lived on Cummera has to give their place of birth, or their children want to know where their parents were born. Then there are [the younger ones] who are always curious to find out about Cummera. I've seen it happen a lot. I've met people that didn't know their background and then all of a sudden 'Goodness gracious', they find out they're Aboriginal and the next thing they want to do is check out their origin, which will bring them back to Cummera. It's a good thing too, because I wouldn't like to see our people lose their identity and origins. After all it goes back for 1000s of years and that's something we must be proud of.[1]

From my research, I have found that these migration and intermarriage patterns go back much further than the reserve system. They come from pre-invasion times and continue through the reserves that were established in First Peoples Country.

Watching and being part of cultural protocols like 'Who's your mob?' is something that Cathy regularly experiences:

> What amazes me is how people know all these names and connections. Wayne's memory is prodigious, extending back and forth over five generations to his great-great-great-grandmother Maria. She survived the killing times and visited Maloga Mission in 1874. Then he knows all his cousins, their parents and grandparents and their children. Then he knows the families they married into. Then he knows the main family groups from the reserves around Victoria and in New South Wales so that he can often place a person's mob from their family name and even their looks. Of course, they also talk about what this one or that one is doing, and now we are elders, always about those who are sick or have passed. These connections are the main conversation point. They can literally go on for hours twisting and turning with

many jokes along the way. I am just left listening as I have found it impossible to remember all these relationships. It is one of the many cross-cultural differences between Koori and non-Koori ways. To me it is distinctly a Koori cultural way of knowing.

'Who's your mob?' is the culturally proper way of establishing your Indigenous identity and bloodline connections with the original ancestors. It's a complex process that needs explaining and makes a mockery of the fraudulent 'tick the box' and gammin processes used today to circumvent the proper way of identity proof.

~

My ancestors lived on the traditional lands of the Dja Dja Wurrung and Yorta Yorta before the British invasion of Yorta Yorta lands in the 1830s. In genealogies and land claims, these people are called apical ancestors—that is, they are at the top of our family trees. It is from them that we inherit our identity and bloodline connections.

My parents are Clive Atkinson and Iris Nelson. My mother's bloodline connections come from two apical ancestors of the Dja Dja Wurrung and Yorta Yorta Nations, and her people are of the Dungula, Kaiela, Yakoa, Baala and Gunbungwerro rivers in north-central Victoria and southern New South Wales. Our ancestors had traditional linguistic and territorial boundaries that evolved over time immemorial. They precede the way the government decided in 1851 to use Dungula as the political boundary between Victoria and New South Wales. Before that it wasn't a political boundary, which is why the names of many of the groups along the rivers repeat themselves, indicating that they occupied both sides of the river. A good example as we travel downstream from Yorta Yorta is Barapa Barapa, Mutti Mutti, Latji Latji and Wamba Wamba of the Edwards River, which is called Kolety in Wamba Wamba language.

My mother's Dja Dja Wurrung connections come through her grandfather, Henry Nelson, who was born in 1855 in Dja Dja Wurrung Country at Majorca, near Maryborough. His parents are recorded as Gorrakkum Nelson and Tgorook/Teurrk. Henry married Margaret (Maggie) Stone/McDonald at Coranderrk in 1880, and they later moved to Cummeragunja. Maggie was born in Waveroo Country on the Little River near Kiewa in eastern Victoria. Her mother is Mary Jane and her grandfather is Billy, who is an apical ancestor of the Waveroo people. After Henry passed in 1924, Maggie stayed on Cummera where she ran a small grocery shop. She then moved to Itchica and lived with our family until she passed away in 1952; she is buried in Echuca Cemetery.[2]

On the Yorta Yorta side, my mother's bloodline connections come from the Cooper family line. She is the granddaughter of Ada Cooper, who lived between 1868 and 1942. Ada was a daughter of Granny Kitty and granddaughter of Old Maria. Maria and Kitty are the two apical ancestors who were born in Yorta Yorta Country and lived in the Moira Forest, which covers both sides of Dungula. Maria is assumed to have died at Maloga in 1879; Kitty died in 1885. Both are buried with sixty other ancestors, including some of missionary Daniel Matthews' children, in unmarked graves in the old Maloga cemetery. Sadly, there is no official acknowledgement or memorial at the gravesite. Such sacrilege and lack of respect for our ancestors, who lack a proper cemetery to protect their graves, remains unresolved business for our people today.

My father, Clive Atkinson, also has Yorta Yorta and Dja Dja Wurrung bloodline connections. His father is Henry (Puppa) Atkinson, whose parents are Aaron Atkinson and Louise Frost. Louise was born at Mathoura near Moira Station in 1858 and had three children before she married Aaron in 1873. One of these was Puppa Henry. His white father is unknown, but Aaron Atkinson, the second son of Granny Kitty, was his cultural father who raised him.

My father's mother, Caroline Morgan, is the granddaughter of Gilpoor Mauning, an apical ancestor of the Dja Dja Wurrung. While Caroline is my father's mother, he was reared by Caroline's sister Louise Morgan of the Dja Dja Wurrung at Cummeragunja. Caroline died at Coranderrk in 1933 at the age of forty-four. She is the daughter of Caroline Malcolm nee Morgan, who married Alfred Mur-terrin Morgan. Alfred was born at Wharparilla in Yorta Yorta Country in 1855.

Louise Morgan had a younger brother who carried the Alf Morgan name. He died in 1949 and is buried in the same grave as Nanny Lou and Puppa Henry in Echuca Cemetery. It gets a bit complicated here given that there are three Alf Morgans and another Yorta Yorta apical ancestor called Bagot Morgan. As far as I know there is no relationship between the Dja Dja Wurrung Morgan and the Yorta Yorta Morgan at the apical ancestral level.

Louise, or Nanny Lou as we call her, married Puppa Henry Atkinson in Moama, New South Wales in 1898. Puppa Henry and Nanny Lou reared me in their home in 37 Hovell Street, Echuca East, where they moved from Cummeragunja following the walk-off. Puppa Henry died in 1952 and I stayed with Nanny Lou until she died in 1956. I returned to my family home in Echuca South when I was thirteen to be with my brothers and sisters. Often, we had other extended-family relatives from the Nelson and Atkinson family line living with us.

It is significant that my parents, all my grandparents and most of my great-grandparents lived at Cummeragunja. My Aboriginality flows to me from these identified ancestors. Through them and as an extended family group, we trace our bloodline connections to Country. Our bloodlines go back to the original ancestors who have been on Country since time immemorial and have been buried on Country since creation. In Chapter 3 I return to the question of the Anglo names that we carry from the assumed fathers who had relations with Yorta Yorta women during the history of invasion and the pastoral stations.

~

'Gulpa Gaka Yorta Yorta Woka' is a Welcome to Country message of the Yorta Yorta Nation. We are a proud river people. Our relationship with the rivers and forest wetlands is a spiritual and sacred one. The majority of Yorta Yorta live in the towns now known as Echuca, Moama, Shepparton, Mooroopna, Cummeragunja, Barmah, Nathalia, Cobram, Kyabram, Wangaratta and Mathoura, and other smaller centres within the traditional lands. Some live nearby at Albury, Wodonga, Deniliquin, Kerang, Barham and Swan Hill. Others have moved to the cities to pursue education and economic interests, but most of them still visit the area regularly to maintain social and cultural links.

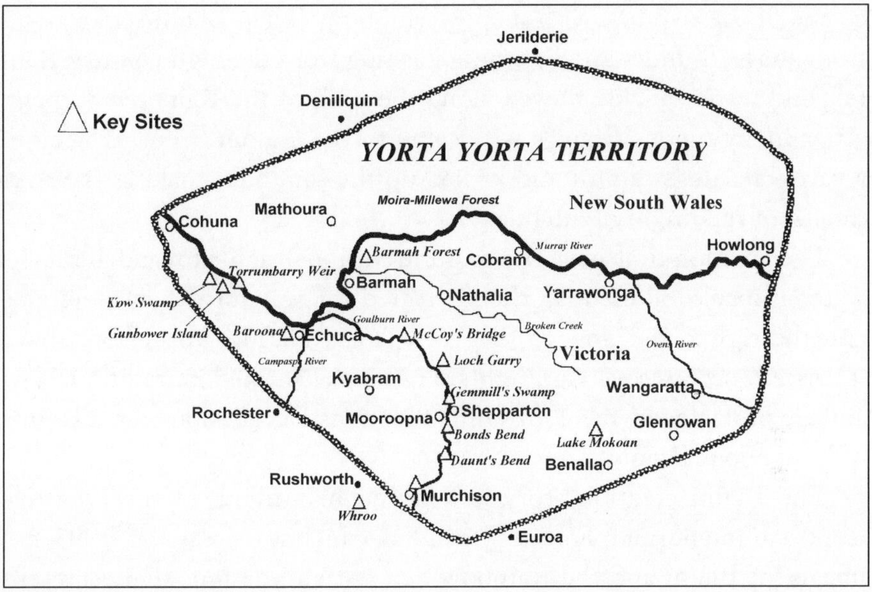

Traditional Yorta Yorta Land and Waters comprising 200,000 square kilometres. *Courtesy the author.*

I grew up camped beside Kaiela in Mooroopna, drawing our household water from the river. When I was seven, I moved with my family to Itchica close to the Yakoa, Kaiela and Dungula rivers. We fished, swam and explored and watched the wala replenish the forest wetlands that link us with our ancestors. My great-great-great-grandmother Maria and her people travelled in bark canoes and lived on both sides of these ancestral rivers flowing through Yorta Yorta Country.

On Country I often dream of the campfires at night as my people cooked food and shared stories of the spirit ancestors and their creations. Our creation story goes back so far it cannot be dated, and it lives within us as the eternal Dreaming.

Biami created Dungula by sending his wife down from the high country. With her dogs and yam stick she journeyed across the flat and waterless plain. As she travelled, Biami sent his giant snake along to watch over and protect her. She walked for many miles, drawing a line in the sand behind her with her digging stick. The giant snake followed, weaving and turning as it meandered through the land, creating the curves of the riverbed with its powerful body. Then Biami spoke aloud from above, thunder and lightning flashing from the high country. Rain fell, and water quickly flowed along the path of the Rainbow Serpent. After many moons Biami's wife came to the sea and went to sleep in a cave. Her dogs ran off and kicked up the sandhills, making the river mouth of the mighty Dungula.

The creation time gave rise to our traditional rights to land, heritage, water and cultural identity. Biami created the way for the river systems and the rights that flow to the Yorta Yorta Nation. Yorta Yorta have inherited these as sovereign rights. They are enshrined in traditional law and are protected by the 2007 United Nations Declaration on the Rights of Indigenous Peoples.

The Biami creation story is featured in a mural at the Dharnya Centre in the Barmah Forest. The mural, which was created in 1985, has images of Biami and the Rainbow Serpent and designs that represent the totemic beings in our creation story. It is a powerful display of Yorta Yorta artistic expression by Yorta Yorta artist Robin Bailey Cooper. Our totems are binding elements of Aboriginal religion, a sacred link between humans and all living beings in nature and the Dreaming. Our connections were handed down by the Dreamtime ancestors as the lore of the land when caring for Country.

The extensive river networks were major focal points for food collection and community life. Throughout Yorta Yorta occupation there have been constant natural and cultural changes. Yorta Yorta people adapted and continued their culture despite adversity. I have learned to respect these stories as I travel through the Barmah–Millewa Forest.

Barmah and Moira are the names of the two forests that evolved on both sides of Dungula over time immemorial.[3] They are one ecosystem that took different names when the Murray River became the political boundary between Victoria and New South Wales in 1851. Since then the names have changed, with Barmah keeping its given name and 'Moira' being replaced by 'Millewa'. For administrative purposes they are now referred to as Barmah–Millewa. Given that the Moira Forest and wetlands were a significant part of the traditional lands of the Yorta Yorta Nation, the area is still called Moira Country in our language. Both the forests and the lakes are the heartland of Yorta Yorta territory, abounding in evidence of Yorta Yorta occupation. Like many other cross-border issues between the two state jurisdictions, these are matters that the Yorta Yorta Nation had to deal with after Dungula became a political boundary.

Once you learn to see the evidence, you can appreciate the land's long history. The forest wetlands are rich in water-based resources, and there are hundreds of scarred trees from which bark has been removed. The smaller scars tell of coolamons cut to carry babies, food and water, while the large scars were for bark canoes. The trees themselves live on to tell the story today. The bark was removed with stone axes traded from as far away as Mount William, Mount Camel and Dookie stone quarries. Stone was traded in exchange for our hardy reed spears.

The Yorta Yorta were at the cutting edge of developing stone-tool technology. They adapted their technology as it progressed to more sophisticated levels, such as using ground-stone tool technology for cutting and crafting implements. Ground-stone tools like axes, scrapers and cutting tools continue to be exposed today by erosion and land development. A lot of the stone tools that were part of the traditional portable toolkit were buried with people when they died. It was a sacred part of their personal property that was protected under tribal law.

Growing up, I learned about this sacred river Country of ours. Uncle Bill Onus took us young fellas into the bush to teach us our cultural traditions (see Chapter 7). As an adult, with my cousin Gary I surveyed the Barmah and Moira forests in search of our heritage. We found evidence of Yorta Yorta occupation in scarred trees, cooking mounds, burial grounds and fish-trap systems. In our ways of yarning, Gary and I called ourselves the dirt scratchers because we spent so much time on our knees in the dirt finding evidence of our ancestors. We uncovered stone tools, shell middens, bones and older artefacts. What we found strengthened our identity and connections with Country.

I love reflecting on Gary's and my journey through the forest wetlands and learning how our ancestors collected their food. While we searched, we saw turtles in the shallow water of the forest floods. We thought of our long-neck turtle totem and my grandfather's favourite food, the short-neck turtle. We came across dozens of cooking mounds full of calcinated clay balls about the size of your fist. These clay balls were placed in the fire and used as heat retainers for cooking food. After each cook-up they became part of the mound, which built up over thousands of years. As we examined the surface and uncovered the dark soil blackened by fire, we found the clay balls. Some of them still had the fingerprints of their makers in the clay, a tangible link with our ancestors. Animal bones showed what sort of meat was eaten. The mound ovens were used for cooking kangaroo, possum, emu and fish, and damper made from grass seed. The mounds themselves indicate traditional conservation practices of keeping all discarded food and materials in one compost heap. Along the river we found heaps of shell middens—thousands of years of discarded shells from mussels and other shellfish. What a rich diet our ancestors enjoyed. As we canoed down the river, we could see evidence of fish traps made of branches at the junctions of the creeks as they flowed into the river.

Our explorations showed us how our ancestors lived, and our journeys were like a magnet that pulled us into deeper levels of knowing. Our hunger for more knowledge would take us to other sources.

In 2002 at Melbourne University, I developed the concept of Oncountry Learning. I wanted to share not only what I had learned as a youngster but also the rich oral and written learning available. In those courses I started my teaching at the cultural mounds in the Barmah Forest that were created over 6000 years ago, a time in world history when all human societies were regarded as hunters, collectors and fishing peoples. This is relatively recent in the timeline of Yorta Yorta occupation. Indigenous occupation of Australia is put at 60,000–120,000 BP (Before Present). The 60,000 BP figure comes from dating timelines at Lake Mungo in the Murray-Darling Basin. It is still debated by scientists and Traditional Owners. While Australia is still a relatively young country in archaeological methods, there is every likelihood that more timelines of Indigenous occupation will be uncovered in the future. Other dates, taken from prior vegetation pollen samples at Lake George near Canberra, indicate that fire was used by Indigenous people for land management and food production around 120,000 BP.[4] The coastal midden site of Moyjil (Point Ritchie) near Warrnambool in Gunditjmara Country, still undergoing scientific analysis, is estimated to be 120,000 BP.[5]

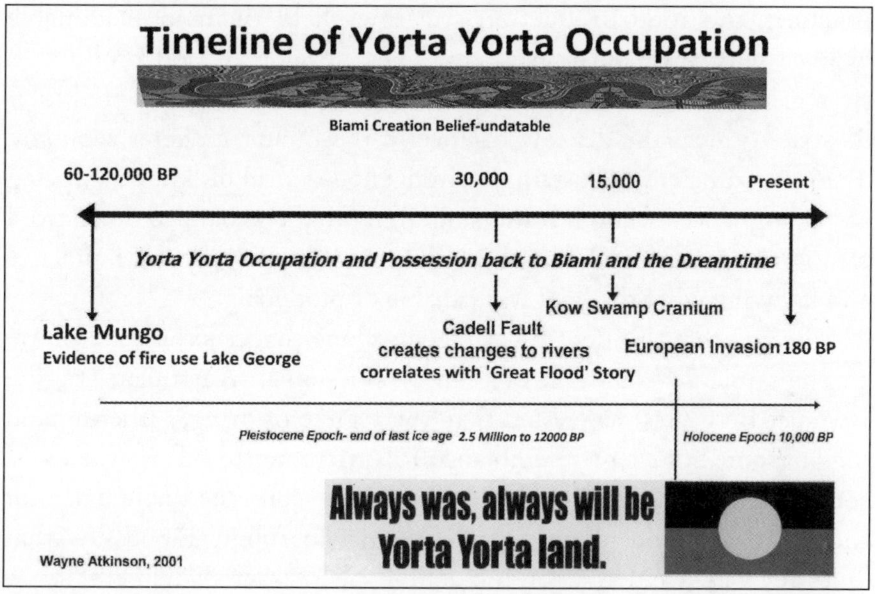

We can compare what was happening for Yorta Yorta people at the cultural mounds with other world events of that time, which takes us back beyond the pyramids of Egypt and Stonehenge in England. The date of 6000 BP is estimated for the mound culture that evolved in the Murray Valley, which is long before any other known dates for religious belief systems in the Middle East and Central Asia. While there were no central places of worship in Aboriginal society, religious observance was practised and lived in everyday life on Country. It was a holistic religion in which the sacred lore of the land, spirituality and totemic relationships helped life and culture continue through practice and ceremony. There is no equivalent dating system for Aboriginal spirituality and belief in the Dreaming. It is something that is said to be timeless and ever-present in the Aboriginal worldview, an intellectual achievement still to be fully recognised for its theological strength and teachings.[6]

In my teaching of Indigenous Studies, I am often asked why Aboriginal people did not make the transition from hunting/fishing to farming. The answer comes from the path they chose to take in the food production process. Really, they didn't have to become farmers, because they were able to keep their culture and lifestyle going at the hunting/collecting and fishing level. Their religious duties, land management practices and food production strategies held them in sustainable balance with the land's resources. They developed food production strategies long before the idea of farming happened, and adapted their lifestyle to meet the delicate balance of the hunter-gatherer economy. This was sufficient to sustain the Indigenous world of 'knowing, being and doing' since creation. It was something that was handed down from creation and developed over thousands of years of observance, practice and knowing what the land was capable of producing.[7]

The fact that this debate has raged so long suggests there are shortcomings in how we think of food production in Australian studies. Botanist Beth Gott suggested that 'the regime of firing, gathering and digging bore sufficient resemblance to agriculture to be regarded as a sort of natural gardening which ensured the continued abundance of the important food plants'.[8] Archaeologist Josephine Flood says that 'nothing was accidental or incidental: people acted deliberately to improve quality of food yield', adding that 'people were so affluent they didn't need to change'.[9] Historian Bill Gammage dedicates a chapter of his book *The Biggest Estate on Earth*, 'Farms Without Fences', to the question, saying 'there was no need for fences' in the food production strategies used: 'People civilised all the land, without fences, making farming and wilderness one.'[10] And so the debate continues.

In teaching Oncountry Learning, I encourage students to come with an open mind and a willingness to learn from the Yorta Yorta worldview. As we look around us and learn about the forest and river wetlands, I invite the students to draw their own conclusions from the knowledge presented. The Indigenous worldview is explained by visiting Country and seeing the tangible evidence. It is about cultural continuity, keeping life going and adapting to changes as they arise. Our culture is strong and claims its own space in the global story. These are some of the messages that come out of the Oncountry teaching program.

We can see that Indigenous uses of the land were certainly different from those of Europe, but they were not frozen in time and place, unyielding to change. Rather, they developed along different paths and continued to evolve and be refined over time. Aboriginal people took their own pathway and were unique in the way they provided for themselves. One can project what could have been but for the impact of colonisation, a relatively recent event on the Indigenous timeline. The journey of learning towards what First Peoples of the land could have achieved, if left alone to pursue their own ends, is a continuous process.

~

Yorta Yorta people adapted traditional land management practices and technology over time. They used sophisticated practices that varied from simply managing existing resources to cleverly manipulating the environment for sustainable returns. Our people learned how to nurture the environment to produce food and to avoid overexploiting the resource. This required a delicate balance between food extraction and what the land was able to produce.

Our ancestors had diverse ways of managing the rich resources of the rivers and forest wetlands. Making elaborate fish-trap systems is one way the Yorta Yorta were able to make their fishing practices more efficient and less labour-intensive. Yorta Yorta people observed the river flows and fish migrations during replenishment times. They utilised boughs and brambles to construct elaborate fish traps across the mouth of the river channels that replenished the forest wetlands. As the floodwaters flowed back into the river, the fish were trapped in backwater storage pools for easy taking. This clever strategy allowed our people to store food for longer periods with minimum effort. You can see these natural depressions along the riverbanks, accompanied by the build-up of shell middens. The visibility of middens along the riverbanks are evidence of the abundant fish, crustaceans and freshwater mussels that were cooked and eaten at the site.

Yorta Yorta elders told me about other clever ways of getting food. The story of the duck hawk is an example of how advanced traditional society was in its intimate relationship with the land and its diversity of plant and animal life.

The duck hawk was a natural predator of the wild duck. It had a special whistle as it hovered over the ducks when they were in flight. When the ducks heard the sharp whistle, they would quickly descend to the water level for protection, flying just above the surface of rivers and creeks, flapping their wings on the water to deter the duck hawk. The duck hawk avoided getting too close to the water, which enabled the ducks to evade being attacked—a natural defence in the hunter-versus-hunted strategy.

Over time our ancestors learned to be astute watchers and listeners of wildlife behaviour, and this is where the story reaches its pinnacle. The skilled hunters learned to imitate the duck-hawk whistle, then made a net to catch the ducks as they retreated along the creeks for protection. The net was strung across the creek while one of the group hid in the bush and imitated the duck hawk whistle. This would bring the wild ducks down to the water's surface. As they flew along the creek the net would be pulled as a capture trap. Many ducks would be caught, providing a rich food source for the community. I was told they could catch over a dozen ducks in one haul, thank you very much.

They made the nets from a plant called typha that grows in the forest wetlands. The roots are chewed into fibre to make nets and other items like baskets and carry bags. My grandmother Priscilla used to weave the gill nets that my grandfather George Nelson used for fishing. They camped at the Barmah Lakes where the fish were plentiful and would pack what they caught and sell to the market. Grandfather George was a man of the wala, continuing the old ways and adapting new methods to his bag of tricks.

If our ancestors could get a reliable food source from the whistle of a duck hawk, why stop your hunter-gatherer ways when the land, rivers and forest wetlands are your haven?

Daniel Matthews was aware of the plentiful resources of the Moira and Barmah Lakes when he established the Maloga Mission in 1874. On 7 July 1887, he applied to the Victorian Board of Land to establish a fishing reserve for the Yorta Yorta at the Barmah Lakes. The application was refused by the Board, which said it could not 'see its way clear to carrying out your suggestion of forming or assisting to form a fishing station at Lake Moira'.[11]

The potential of establishing fishing as a commercial enterprise for the Traditional Owners followed the lines of Joseph Rice's Murray River fishing enterprise. In 1855 Rice and his workers set themselves up in huts near the lakes, eager to make big money from the market conditions in Bendigo. The story goes that this enabled them to make huge profits by exploiting the skills of Aboriginal fishers, whose labour, it is said, was 'paid for in grog'.[12] As well as making big money, the fishing and timber camps brought with them other undesirable elements that confronted the Traditional Owners and Matthews' missionary venture.

The storylines show that Aboriginal culture and lifestyle took their own pathway. It made graduations along the hunter-gatherer continuum, but the people were able to keep it going at the hunting/fishing level. There was no need to make the full transition to farming. Our ancestors had sophisticated food production strategies that allowed more quality time for leisure, cultural development, the maintenance of kinship systems, tribal business, and the management and care of Country. It is estimated that our ancestors would have spent around three-and-a-half to four hours a day on the food quest. The rest of their day was quality culture time. When compared with today's workloads, stress levels and rising mental health problems, why would you change such a lifestyle when it worked so well? It's an idealistic proposition, but one worth considering when faced with the toll that climate change, environmental destruction and land and water degradation has taken.

~

On the cultural side of Yorta Yorta life, Uncle Ronald Morgan shared stories about cultural matters and ceremonial grounds like the Algabonyah plain in his 1952 book, *Reminiscences of the Aboriginal Station at Cummeragunja and Its Aboriginal People*. He talks about the water rat and the powers it uses to get food. The story goes that the water rat can blow out terrific heat and is able to open the shell of the freshwater mussel without difficulty.

Algabonyah, a word that was often used by Yorta Yorta people to mean 'good-looking' or 'handsome', referred to the green-grassed plain on the riverbank about 3 kilometres down from Moira Lake.[13]

It was a traditional meeting place for local and surrounding tribal groups, who gathered annually to celebrate and to conduct tribal business, including arranging marriages between Traditional Owner groups. It is recorded that up to 500 people gathered near Moira Lake in autumn to partake in ceremonies that included dancing and sporting activities.[14] Remember that these observations were made after a significant depopulation had taken place due to the impact of colonisation and introduced diseases like smallpox. No Western time factors apply to such gatherings. Indeed, they were unique and came from time immemorial cultural knowledge and practices. Large gatherings were mostly connected with celebrating the arrival of a particular food source to support the mob. Under tribal law this required reciprocal totemic and ritual obligations to ensure the continuity of local food sources. Being part of a forest wetland system, Algabonyah was rich in fish and food plants that would have supported large gatherings of this nature.

The arrival of seasonal foods on the lakes and surrounding habitats was like a smorgasbord. Plenty of wild duck, swans and the nutritiously rich swan eggs, turtle and a variety of shellfish and tuba (*Derris*) plants supported larger ceremonial gatherings. The oral record suggests these gatherings usually lasted for a week or more. Translated into what we call Koori time in the Aboriginal world, there were no time restrictions or clocks to regulate human endeavour: it flowed with the seasons and what the land and waters were capable of producing. The well-honed tools of food production and firestick farming helped it along the way.

The first item on the agenda at the gathering would have been the tribal business that needed to be dealt with to maintain harmony and kinship relations between tribal groups. After the tribal business was done, leisure time began, with dance, music, stories and sporting activities. A game played at these gatherings is believed to be the source of Marngrook and those clever skills that seem to give Aboriginal players a vital edge in Australian Rules football. Many historians and Indigenous people would agree that Aboriginal people are very well suited to that sport. In tracing its roots to the traditional Aboriginal game called Marngrook, there is sufficient support for this view.[15] Marngrook was a traditional teamlike game that involved lots of players and was played over a large area. It was played by river people of the upper and lower Dungula. The game was usually held on ceremonial grounds like the Algabonyah Plain. Individual players were commended for consistently exhibiting outstanding skills such as leaping high over others to mark the possum-skin ball and evading opponents who were trying to take the ball from your possession. Indeed, Marngrook can be likened to the game of keepings off, a contest to keep the ball in your possession for as long as your opponents allow. It was a highly competitive game played within the rules of the totemic moieties of eaglehawk and crow—the two moiety divisions of the Yorta Yorta Nation. Your alliance and loyalty came from the totemic ancestor that you inherited from your birth.

High marking, long kicking and handpassing characterised the game. It is thought that the sharp reflexes and hand-eye coordination developed through centuries of hunting and living off the land were sharpened by Marngrook.[16] These are the superb skills that characterise Indigenous sportspeople across Australia and particularly in Australian Rules footy. Other aspects of Aboriginal culture manifest in the world of football explain why Indigenous people have been so successful in this original game.

~

Fire was another important tool our ancestors used for land management and food production. They used fire, or firestick farming, for hunting and regeneration, for clearing tracks through reed beds, and as a way of dissuading Europeans from invading Traditional Owners' land.

Bill Gammage's book *The Biggest Estate on Earth* shows how Indigenous land philosophy and management prepared the land for its newcomers. Gammage argues that the settlers should acknowledge they were privileged to take possession of land that was so well cared for. There should be recognition of the traditional management and care of the land and waters for millennia by our ancestors. He sees fire as the 'closest ally' to our people's land management philosophy.[17] What an ally to have when it is needed most in land management practices. Gammage equates it with the totemic system. Because fire helps regeneration and the fertility of all living organisms in Indigenous land lore, it became embedded in the totemic system and played an integral part in the life and wellbeing of all living entities.

The origins and use of fire in Indigenous Australia are now being explained through a combination of scientific evidence and Indigenous knowledge. As a result of the study of ash sediment in pollen analysis studies at Lake George near Canberra, we know that fire has been used since 120,000 BP.[18] Cultural burning is being acknowledged for its value in land management, and scientists and Indigenous people are working together to see how it can be reintroduced.[19] Around Australia, traditional burning is being used in Kakadu National Park, Gariwerd, Beechworth Historic Park and the Dja Dja Wurrung land management program. The reintroduction of bitja and cultural burning as a land management strategy is used by the Yorta Yorta Nation Aboriginal Corporation in its management plan for Barmah National Park.[20]

~

Yorta Yorta people witnessed many changes to Dungula over the millennia, but it has withstood the test of time. In particular, our ancestors saw the Cadell Fault and Great Flood cause significant changes to the land and river systems. Thirty thousand years ago, a rift of land pushed up between Deniliquin and Itchica, creating a significant flood. That rift, now called the Cadell Fault, was in front of the river as it flowed westward. The existing river system had to divert and flow north towards Deniliquin before turning west again near the end of the 12-metre-high escarpment.

The rift of land also caused the Kaiela River to dam itself into a large lake system. This formed Lake Kanyapella, stretching from Itchica to the Barmah sandhills in the east. The sandhills were formed by the prevailing westerly winds; this is very common when lakes and sandhills form. The lake was there until about 8000 years ago, and then a channel cut into its southern end, letting it flow into the ancient Kaiela. The sand ridge today is the most visible remnant of the fault. The best place to see the Cadell escarpment is from Picnic Point Road near Mathoura in New South Wales. The site is an important part of the Yorta Yorta storyline.

Yorta Yorta elders speak of a great flood that happened in the distant past. The power of the flood caused water to back up until it nearly covered the tops of the old gum trees in the Barmah–Millewa Forest. The storyline shares the alarm our ancestors felt as rising water forced them to move to higher ground on the sand ridge on the edge of the forest. As the water kept rising, the elders gathered. They could see their prized hunting and fishing grounds being taken out of reach. This forced them to act, and they used their digging sticks to release the water by digging a drain through the sandhill. The pressure was released and the water cut its way through the sand ridge to create its new course.

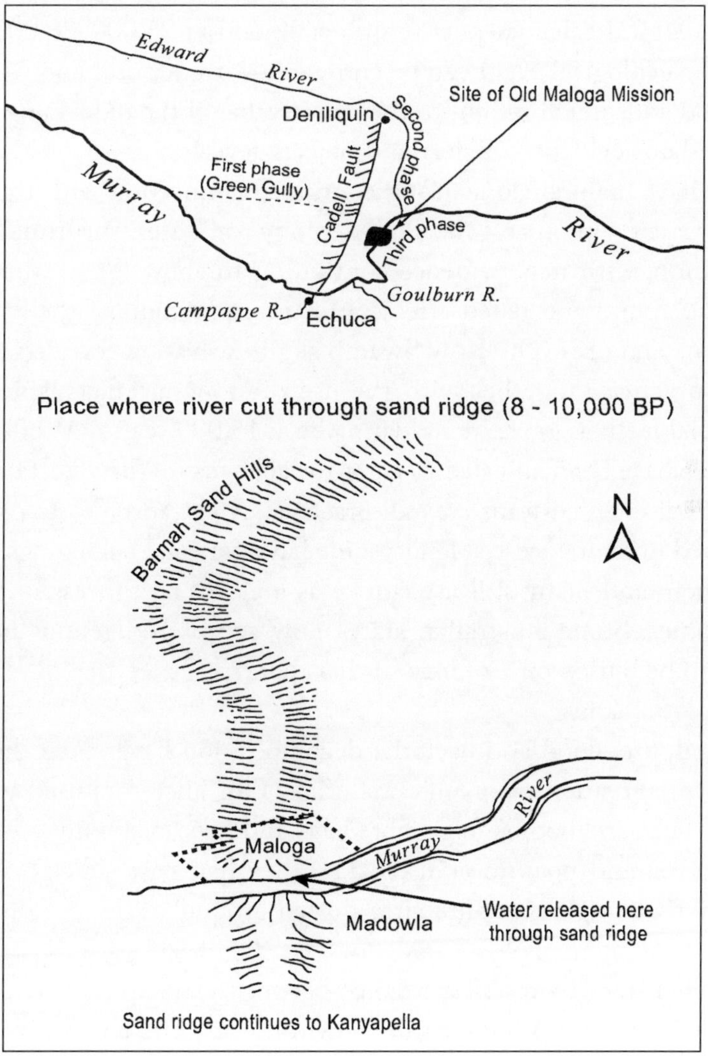

Ancestral phases of the Murray River that affected Yorta Yorta occupation. *Courtesy the author.*

Yorta Yorta elders developed skills to release the water and return to an equilibrium with the land. We can see that life wasn't totally free of natural changes to the land and environment. The Great Flood wasn't catastrophic: it was dealt with and adjusted to in due course. Time was slow and survival remedies were abundant within the hunting and fishing way of life.

It is no coincidence that the site of this iconic change in the river course became the home of the Maloga Mission Station in the 1800s. The geological calendar puts the Great Flood at 25,000–30,000 BP.[21] That the geological event can be correlated with our oral knowledge of the flood adds much weight to the iconic value of the old Maloga site.

The hard evidence of sites and objects reveals that the Yorta Yorta people have maintained a strong continued connection with the woka and wala of our ancestors. Archaeology validates the timeline of occupation, with new evidence continuing to show longer timelines. We have found and dated artefacts for interpretation of their various functions and uses. The Kow Swamp skull excavation revealed various burial practices, together with the use of stone artefacts, shells and marsupial teeth as grave items, dating back 15,000 years.[22] While burial practices have been adjusted to cater for changes in Yorta Yorta society, some traditional customs are still practised. Most Yorta Yorta prefer to be buried in their ancestral lands; some have personal belongings buried with them and many still use smoke as a cleansing process in funeral ceremonies. Some Australian states now accept Indigenous people's rights to be buried on Country so that their spirits are free to return to the ancestral lands.

Wind, fire, flood and bacterial decomposition have taken their toll on the preservation of organic materials. Our ancestors used wooden spears, clubs and boomerangs; fibre bags and nets; shell knives, scrapers and hooks; and possum-skin cloaks. They had bark and grass huts. The myriad single-campfire sites dotted around water margins need proper care.

Scarred trees represent a balance between extracting resources and living in harmony with the natural environment. The term 'scarred tree' has become common usage in cultural resource management to describe the way bark was removed from trees and used for a variety of purposes;

over time this practice left a scar in the tree. Canoe trees are those from which canoes have been cut; they have larger scars. Scars also resulted from bark cut and used for coolamons to carry things, temporary shelter where a strip of bark was leaned against a tree for shelter, and bark paintings. Hardwood was used for artefact production and ceremonial and hunting tools.

A yama muttar cut from a river red gum with a ground-stone axe head is a traditional artefact of profound cultural significance. My ancestors could make a yama muttar with timing, speed and precision that shows quality control at the traditional level. They had millennia of cultural practice and refinement to reach a high level of dexterity.

Many scarred trees were cut down due to short-sighted forestry management practices. Those that have survived are an important part of learning from traditional cultural practices. The age-old craft of extracting bark for various uses continues as a cultural practice today. We have cultural activities like these as part of the Yorta Yorta Cultural Heritage Management program.[23] Local cultural workers demonstrate the delicate procedure of taking bark off a tree. It is best to do this at the time of year when the sap is flowing so the bark can be removed without damaging the tree. While the sap is fresh, the canoe bow and stern can be shaped over a small fire.

The bark canoe is an exceptional invention in watercraft technology. On the rivers of remote Victoria, nineteenth-century European settlers depended on Aboriginal navigators and canoe builders to transport goods, stock and people. The larger canoes could have been used to mount attacks on stations around the Moira wetlands during the resistance campaign. The canoes also contributed to the pastoral economy. A local farmer relied on a bark canoe to carry a ton of flour from Ulupna upstream to Deniliquin via the Dungula and Kolety rivers, a journey of over 100 river miles.[24]

~

After painting a picture of the niceties of Aboriginal life, culture and philosophy and the beauty of the eternal Dreaming in my Oncountry Learning courses, it was time for goopna ngarwu (deep listening). When

I talked about the timeline of the cultural mounds, the students and I tried to imagine the old ways: the clan groups, the gatherings around the water resources, and the huge cook-ups that created the extensive mound culture of the river people. The moderate amount of energy invested in the food quest allowed quality time for cultural development, the maintenance of family kinship and the law, which ensured peace, harmony and survival and allowed much time for caring for Country. These are values that I like to teach in Indigenous Studies courses.

Features in the Yorta Yorta landscape are monuments to the activities of ancestral beings. Like other religious monuments, they are sacred sites. Aboriginal people did not seek to alter these features, as to do so would bring disaster. Our ancestors were responsible for caring for the land and its sacred sites, including spirit centres. Animals were linked to our people through totemic relationships. There were ceremonies to make sure there was enough food, and there were restrictions on eating totem animals. Our ancestors did not exploit the land or herd animals. Instead, they kept things going, caring for the land as taught through Dreamtime laws.

In living and practising this worldview, there was no rigid distinction between people and other living beings—they were all part of the one system. Property rights were community-based, requiring the community to care for Country and to pass them on to future generations. Indigenous land relations contrast sharply with the Western notion of land as a commodity. First Nations Peoples are owners of the land in the fullest possible sense. It is a complementary, holistic process—people, land and all things in nature are intimately interconnected. Our ancestors taught us to nurture and sustain life. The term 'mother' appropriately describes our relationship with Country.

When I'm on Country, I visualise the huge gatherings at the Algabonyah ceremonial ground in the forest. As I contemplate this story, I ask myself, *What the fuck happened here?* They are words I seek licence to use only in this context, to measure the extent of the remorseless blow my people suffered. They convey the reality of the shock wave that hits home at this part of the goopna ngarwu learning. What happened to the mobs of clanspeople who lived here in peace and plenty? Why is the forest now silent of the families' and children's voices? What could our world have been had Yorta Yorta people been left to develop in their own time and at their own pace?

These are questions I continue to ask myself each time I drive from Melbourne to Yorta Yorta Country, a journey of about 250 kilometres. On the way, I travel through at least six major towns—Wandong, Whittlesea, Kilmore, Heathcote, Elmore and Rochester—that have no visible Aboriginal community presence. The same reality hits home to me: *What the fuck happened to the tribal groups who had lived here since creation?* They were wiped out and any survivors were rounded up and put on reserves, is the answer. That this was allowed to happen in such a short period of time is a huge wake-up call for the truth justice process.

2
An Undeclared War

In my family, our great-grandmother Granny Kitty and great-great-grandmother Maria are our apical ancestors. We often think about the life Granny Kitty and her mother, Maria lived before and after the colonial invasion.

The role and responsibility of mothers to raise their children against the exploitation of the pastoral industry created a powerful line of dhama winyarrn leaders. In traditional cultural practices of childcare, children stayed with their mothers and were bought up as Yorta Yorta and Dja Dja Wurrung people. The women stood strong in their identity and the care of their children.

Kitty was one of the first generation of Yorta Yorta women to have children to a white man. Just who were these mysterious white men of no accountability? What was Kitty's life like at the time? How did she protect her children in those grim days? How did she raise them to be important leaders in Yorta Yorta history? These are questions often shared within family history and kinship discussions.

Kitty's mother, Old Maria, was born in the bush in the early 1800s and bore Kitty in about 1834. In Kitty's childhood the clan groups of the Yorta Yorta Nation lived peacefully in their Country of rivers, lakes and forests. They enjoyed an abundance of fish, mussels, turtle, possum, kangaroo and emu as well as the variety of vegetables and traditional fruits growing around them. Granny Kitty's elders were grounded in Yorta Yorta culture, law and custom, living off the land as they had done since creation. She learned the stories of times past round the campfire at night. The old people were both strict and loving.

Tragically, the effects of colonisation were felt by the Yorta Yorta long before they met any white people. They were ravaged by the devastating impact of the smallpox epidemic of 1789, which killed 50–60 per cent of the Aboriginal population.[1] Aboriginal communities had not had time to build up immunities against foreign diseases, so they were acutely vulnerable. Smallpox travelled along the river systems from tribe to tribe. Charles Sturt saw the ravages of smallpox scars on Aboriginal people when he travelled down Dungula in 1830.[2] Kitty, born in 1834 just after the second smallpox outbreak of 1829–31, would have been a very precious surviving child to Maria.

The next invasion was neither invisible nor fleeting. By 1840 squatters had begun to push the Yorta Yorta off their Country, taking up the prime land along the Dungula, Kaiela and Yakoa river flats for their herds of sheep. Yorta Yorta people were forced to defend their traditional rights to land—indeed, their very survival. They developed an effective defence of their Country, mounting attacks on homesteads, dispersing and killing stock, using fire to burn huts and push back intruders, and forcing many pastoralists off their stations.

We found records of squatters with a familiar story that spoke to us in new ways. We realised the Yorta Yorta men described in these written records would be related to Kitty and Maria's family clan. An example is the observations of Edward Curr, one of the first white squatters to invade Yorta Yorta Country, in 1841.[3] He arrived at his land lease on the Kaiela near its junction with the Dungula, bringing with him a group of station hands and herds of sheep to run in traditional Yorta Yorta territory. This was the time when conflict was most intense between invaders and Traditional Owners in the northern reaches of Victoria. Curr was an enterprising young man of twenty-one who had come across Bass Strait from his family home in Tasmania to manage various stations for his father, Edward Curr Senior, head of the Van Diemen's Land Company. That company was responsible for the dispossession and murder of many Aboriginal people during the killing times in Tasmania.[4] For his part in this violent colonising process,

Curr Senior was granted huge stretches of traditional palawa lands in north-west Tasmania.[5]

On arriving in Yorta Yorta Country, Curr Junior and his men were making a yard for his sheep when they heard a cooee from across the river. Three fine-looking Aboriginal men (Traditional Owners) stood on the opposite side, and when asked what they wanted, 'they replied in broken English that they had come to see us and would cross the river if we liked'.[6] On learning they would be welcome, the Aboriginal men examined the trees around them and set to work to cut a canoe out of a gum tree. In about half an hour they were approaching the campfire. This was clearly an act of friendship to accommodate Curr as a newcomer to Yorta Yorta land and waters.

The story of the men's skill and speed in crafting a canoe using traditional stone-axe technology was firmly planted in Curr's mind. Under traditional law they carried their portable toolkit with them:

> They were all muscular, active men, two out of three being about five feet nine inches [175 centimetres] in height. Their dress consisted of an opossum skin cloak, which was fastened at the chest. The fur was worn next to the person, and the skin, outside, was painted in various carpet-like patterns with a sort of red clay which the Blacks burn and use for this and other purposes of ornamentation.[7]

This is a graphic description of the fine physical condition, stamina and wellbeing of the Traditional Owners before the full brunt of colonisation hit them. Curr continues:

> In a sort of rude kangaroo-skin bag carried on the left shoulder, which opened out … for sitting or sleeping on, were conveyed their tomahawks, shields, wadies, and other utensils; their spears and throwing sticks being carried in the hand. Their hair, which was straight and black, was confined round the forehead by a narrow net, through which were thrust the barbed switches with which they extracted the edible grubs from the trees.[8]

Note the privilege of Curr arriving in Yorta Yorta Country and watching such a remarkable cultural performance—that is, before he rises to his ordained power position and makes clear his intentions to usurp the people's land and labour for a stick of tobacco.[9] As a newcomer arriving in Yorta Yorta Country without permission, he flagrantly breached traditional protocols on rights of passage and reciprocal obligations to the Traditional Owners.

The men were invited to join Curr at the fire, and they sat with him. He was aware that they had had little previous communication with white people and had only picked up a smattering of English. After explaining what he was doing there, he stamped his authority. He was quick to warn the men about sheep stealing and then offered djitiga, yalca and dhangan, which he said:

> They ate unhurriedly as they continued the conversation … In fact, their manners generally were easy and pleasing, and there was a sort of propriety about their ways … a certain politeness, which made them, for instance, prepare a firestick [bitjau] when they saw me cutting up tobacco, and offer other little attentions.[10]

Curr took no time in getting local clans to work for him, and soon discovered how skilled they were. They agreed to make him a canoe to transport his sheep across the river. The canoe they made was about 18 feet (5.4 metres) long and 2 feet 6 inches (76 centimetres) wide and would carry five people.[11]

When I was reading Curr's account I felt emotionally connected to these Traditional Owners as my ancestors. Furthermore, Cathy could see something of me in them that brought them right into our experience of the world. Indeed, to me they are like eternal kinsfolk whose stories and images are firmly imprinted in the blood and spirit of our land. I was proud that they were such highly skilled and cultured Yorta Yorta people. They belonged to a sovereign territorial and linguistic Nation and lived independent lifestyles under their own laws. Everything they needed was provided by their country's rich resources and materials. They laughed at the white men who seemed so helpless in the forest wetlands.

~

Yorta Yorta Nation may not have realised it in 1841, but they were on the frontier of an undeclared war that required resistance and defence of our sovereign territorial rights and our community. The opponents were the invading pastoral colonists from a faraway land. They were the leaseholders in their homesteads employing shepherds who were dispersed around the property minding flocks of sheep and cattle de-pastured in Yorta Yorta woka.

The pastoralists were backed by a paramilitary force, the Border Police, and the treacherous Native Police force. In these encounters there was loss of life on both sides. The killing of white people in this war was very carefully documented, but the number of Aboriginal people killed was covered up by the perpetrators. The tragic stories have only recently become a matter of more in-depth analysis: they are recorded in the University of Newcastle's project *Colonial Frontier Massacres in Australia, 1788–1930.*

Before invasion and colonisation, the Yorta Yorta population is estimated to have been 5000–6000.[12] Colonisation and frontier violence had a major impact on river-based Indigenous populations, and by the end of the first generation of contact (1835–63), there had been a shocking decline of 85 per cent of the total Yorta Yorta population.[13] Introduced diseases, including the smallpox epidemics of 1789 and 1830 that spread along the river systems, were the main killer. It didn't stop there, however, and mass deaths continued through Aboriginal resistance and frontier violence. The Victorian Aborigines Protection Board estimated that in 1863 there were only 365 Yorta Yorta survivors.[14] If that trend had continued, the Yorta Yorta certainly would have been staring extinction in the eyes.

Victoria as a whole experienced the same decline. By 1863 there were only 1920 Kooris remaining out of an estimated pre-colonisation population of 15,000–20,000.[15] Introduced diseases, settlers' guns, poison, and conflict over the ownership of land and resources were the main causes of the catastrophic population decline.

Yorta Yorta resistance was strong in the heartland around the Moira area, where large numbers attacked Moira Station in 1843 with firebrands of spears, using bark canoes to retreat into the thick reed beds.[16] Employing traditional knowledge and skills to defend Country from white occupation was an effective strategy. Indeed, the evidence suggests that at the height of resistance (1843–50), the Yorta Yorta were gaining the upper hand.[17] Moira Station became a refuge for local squatters. Its owner, Henry Lewes, reported:

> Mr John Clarke's people driven out by natives from their station down the Murray; A part of Messrs Gwynne's herd came here from the Edwards River driven out by natives; All Mr Green's men came here having been driven out of his station down the Murray; Messrs Gwynne's again driven from station; Mr Will's people came here for aid.[18]

This was a clash of two opposing cultures and law systems, a head-on battle over the ownership and control of land and resources. The clash between pre-existing and imposed laws inflamed the conflict, and the invasion of imported stock into the delicate balance of the traditional lands and waters further intensified hostilities. The other cause of conflict arose from the violation of Aboriginal women, which led to attacks on the perpetrators for breaking tribal law.

We know that massacres happened. Much research work has been done on the impact of colonisation by the *Colonial Frontier Massacres* project, which grew out of the so-called Aboriginal history wars of the late 1990s. The key questions for the project were: What is a frontier massacre? Where is the evidence? Where did they take place? Were they widespread? Who were the perpetrators?[19]

The *Colonial Frontier Massacres* project defines a massacre as the killing of six or more people.[20] In the hearings on massacres in Victoria, the Yoorrook Justice Commission has heard evidence from University of Newcastle researcher Dr Bill Pascoe of the massacres project. He said there were forty-nine known massacres in Victoria.[21]

One of the large-scale killings we know about in Yorta Yorta Country is the Moira Swamp massacre of 1843. Kitty was a young girl of about nine at the time, and Maria was in her late thirties. Both would have known something about the massacre and may have been directly affected. Those killed were Moira people of the Yorta Yorta language group. The Moira Forest wetlands and reed beds was the rich heartland of Yorta Yorta territory, and became a stronghold for Yorta Yorta survival and for defence of their sovereign territorial rights. The *Colonial Frontier Massacres* project carefully re-examined the evidence for what happened on that day, and the following account is based on information available from the project as well as from Edmund Curr's and Daniel Matthews' writings of the time.

On 15 December 1843, a violent encounter took place in the Moira Swamp between a pre-organised force of armed men and a group of Yorta Yorta Traditional Owner families. This was a premeditated and planned attack on Yorta Yorta lives. Moreover, it was like a military operation in what was an undeclared war, sanctioned by the colonial law enforcement agencies. Charles La Trobe, superintendent of the Port Phillip District, ordered a reprisal expedition after squatters suffered the killing of two employees at Calimo (Tumudgery) Station on the Edwards River, and the loss of imported stock at other stations along Dungula wala. There was no evidence presented on the underlying causes of the attack on the two employees as Aboriginal people's evidence was not considered in the Anglo court system of the time. The armed men were led by Henry Dana, commander of the Native Police Corps, and Henry Smythe, in charge of the Murray District Border Police. Each took a detachment of mounted men to the Barmah and Moira lakes. They were joined by a detachment of Henry Bingham's Murrumbidgee District Border Police. The invading party was accompanied by Henry Lewes, owner of Moira Station, his overseer, John Oldbury Atkinson, and Edward Hogg. Mention is made of John Oldbury Atkinson seeing bodies of natives shot.[22]

Yorta Yorta families camping in the Moira, as they had done for millennia, were confronted by the invasion of about twenty mounted men armed with carbines and swords, presumably led by the Native Police. The evidence about what happened was deliberately suppressed, and the details given here rely on information from *Colonial Frontier Massacres*. Whether the Native Police played a part in the attack is unclear. They were certainly renowned for their traditional tracking skills and proved to be a 'brutally destructive instrument in the dispossession of Indigenous Australians. Armed with rifles, carbines and swords, they were also deployed to escort surveying groups, gold convoys and groups of pastoralists and prospectors.'[23]

The leader of the punitory party, Dana, was quick to minimise any wrongdoing. He initially sent a brief report to his friend Superintendent La Trobe saying he had joined Smythe's party on the Murray and his men had 'behaved exceedingly well and were of the greatest use in the expedition'.[24] However, Assistant Protector William Thomas had already heard that several Aboriginal people had been killed, and he confronted Dana about it. In response, Dana 'abused him … in a violent manner, damned and threatened to kick him'.[25] Protectors were vested with the powers of magistrates to report crimes and enforce the law in the colony, and the *Geelong Advertiser* reported on 8 January 1844 that Thomas had charged Dana with 'the murder of several natives' and an investigation was underway.

Further evidence was presented to George Augustus Robinson, Chief Protector of Aborigines:

> On 4 January 1844, Dr James Allen, Robinson's son-in-law, and medical officer at Narre Warren Aboriginal station, met Robinson. Allen told Robinson that 'the blacks had told him that a number of men also women were shot by Dana's party at the Murry [*sic*] and the children were knocked on the head with carrabines. They first sent a party to look for the natives and then went and planted themselves in a scrub and sent two or three troopers to round or drive them up like sheep to be large party carrelled; they then commenced firing and shot some of them in the river etc.[26]

Dana told Robinson that 'he had had a brush with the natives. He went to the Murray by the Campaspe [Yakoa River] and returned said twenty men, one woman, five children were shot.'[27]

The inquiry was a cover-up. It exonerated Dana and did not record the number of people killed.[28] However, on 17 April 1844 former sergeant Edward Broderick of Smythe's mounted border police wrote to La Trobe complaining of his recent dismissal from the force; he said he had kept quiet about the illegal shooting of Aboriginal people at the Murray River on 15 December 1843. Smythe and his men had attacked an Aboriginal camp and shot men, women and children 'indiscriminately', Broderick said, and his evidence could be supported by the three settlers and Sergeant James.[29] La Trobe demanded an explanation from Smythe and the three settlers, who all said that they had fired in self-defence and there was no indiscriminate firing. Smythe said two Aboriginal men were killed and one woman was wounded in the wrist. Hogg said that Broderick had done most of the firing.[30]

The inquiry came to an end in August 1844 when the colonial secretary in Sydney said that NSW governor George Gipps could see 'no reason to suppose that Mr Smythe encouraged or sanctioned the exercise of any unnecessary severity towards the Natives, on the unfortunate occasion of his collision with them in the Swamp called "Moira"'.[31] This incident is one of very few that led to two formal inquiries. In each case the ringleaders, Dana and Smythe, were exonerated. The conclusion reached by the massacres project is that twenty-six Aboriginal victims were killed and no attackers were found guilty of murder.

The criminal intent of this incident illustrates 'the profound misalignment between law and life' that historian Henry Reynolds describes in his book *Truth-Telling*.[32] Governor Gipps in May 1839 had issued a proclamation that the Aboriginal peoples were subjects of the Queen and had an 'equal right with people of European origins to the protection and assistance of the Law of England'.[33] Yet the colonial governors themselves ordered 'punitive expeditions to strike terror among insurgent bands. Enquiries were held, but no one was held accountable for Aboriginal murders. This failure of the law supported a community consensus that killing Aborigines was justified.'[34]

Further to this violent attack, Curr recorded another incident in which he was involved. He describes how 'the Blacks, who were to be taught manners' to punish them for feasting on a large number of sheep, were decoyed away from the river so they couldn't escape into the reed beds, and then the troopers charged. Curr was one of the party and was armed with sword and pistols, but he dodged making any comment on what happened. He admitted that he didn't completely agree with the report prepared by the officer but was told that 'civilians from first to last are ill fitted to describe collisions of the sort, being apt to blurt out statements more properly held in reserve'.[35] No deaths or injuries were reported. According to Curr, most of the Yorta Yorta escaped into the river. He further comments that 'those [Blacks] who firmly believed that unnumbered police troopers and officers in shell-jackets would be sent to the Moira to punish any undue indulgence in mutton on their part, became thenceforth quite reclaimed characters'.[36]

This murderous stage of colonial expansion was euphemistically called 'pacification by force'.[37] Along Dungula the Yorta Yorta used their superior bushcraft to wage prolonged and effective guerrilla campaigns until they were finally overwhelmed by force of arms. In his published recollections Curr avoided any reference to the massacre that occurred in his neighbourhood but rather told amusing stories that minimise the seriousness of the conflict he is describing.[38] In his opinion, 'the native is a child' and should be treated as such.[39] Curr's paternalistic approach is deeply offensive to the living descendants of the Moira Swamp massacre. One can only imagine how the massacre would have reverberated throughout Yorta Yorta minds and Country. Attempts to accommodate the newcomers on their land were shattered. Now those white men whom they had thought were friendly, like Curr, had proved capable of extreme violence at the end of gun and sword.

The survivors would have been deeply impacted by the loss of twenty of their men as well as women and children. Women lost their husbands, their sons, their fathers. These men were not only a loss to their families but keepers of the law, knowledge and cultural traditions. These are the fine men that Curr first met and described in such glowing terms. He admired their physical mastery of canoe-making that led to their crossing the river and joining him at his campfire.

These same people are our ancestors who suffered the full brunt of colonisation, invasion and crimes against humanity, impacts that are yet to be fully repaired. This goes directly to the question of how historical systemic injustice can be effectively and fairly acknowledged and redressed in a culturally appropriate way. These are matters for investigation within the jurisdiction of the Yoorrook Justice Commission inquiry (2021–25). Evidence already heard on these matters at truth justice hearings is alarming. For example, Dr Bill Pascoe said, 'Some of the things I've encountered in this research are the worst things I've ever heard of anyone ever doing to anyone in human history.'[40]

Twenty years after the Moira massacre, Matthews was talking with old men at their camp on the Moira Lake. He wrote in his diary of an incident they shared with him: 'At Maloga—early days (1840)—shepherd's tent—shepherd's gun—theft of flour etc.—vengeance—police—ran into the Lakes, shot down.'[41]

We will never know how many deadly encounters took place in Yorta Yorta Country in the 1830s and 1840s. The repression of the truth is part of the fabric of forgetting that has characterised the colonists' way of coping with their shameful past. But the Yorta Yorta have not forgotten this traumatic period. This was only their first experience of brutality being used to control them. They may not have burdened their children with the details, they may have made fun of the white man and his sheep and guns in their stories and dances, but the scars remain. A distrust of the police and other white protagonists has never gone away. As for British law, there was no evidence it would protect them or regard them as equal to the white man. Aboriginal law was based on clear justice principles, but where was justice when British law was enforced with such corrupt and double standards?

Granny Kitty was one of the survivors. After the massacres, women were abducted, children worked as domestics on farms and people were sent to missions. Understanding this history makes it even more remarkable that Kitty's children, including William Cooper, Ada Cooper and Pastor Eddie Atkinson, provided such strong and principled leadership. They took the best of the colonisers' values and forged them into tools of resistance.

~

Historians have in recent years re-examined the extent of frontier violence. Indigenous scholar Michael Christie argues that between 15 per cent and 25 per cent of the Victorian Aborigines died by the rifle alone, while Reynolds claims that the number of Aboriginal people killed by rifle in northern Australia was higher than that of Australian lives lost in all the overseas wars.[42]

The extent of violence over land is a tragic reflection of colonial race relations in Yorta Yorta Country. The current Yorta Yorta population is between 5000 and 6000. The population recovery rate from near-extinction is an extraordinary human achievement, a heroic example of human survival against the odds. Nonetheless, it is a sad reflection on the brutality of colonisation, not to mention the underlying human-rights value of justice and equality before the law.

The award-winning documentary series *Australian Wars* by Rachel Perkins is a chilling account of the injustices and crimes against humanity in colonial Australia. On receiving the Australian Academy of Cinema and Television Arts (AACTA) award for Best Documentary in 2024, Rachel said she hoped the series would change generations of Australians who are now coming through schools. From the documentary, she said, they 'will learn a different history of their country'.[43]

Research, analysis and First Peoples voices are all helpful for the emerging truth justice process in Victoria and Australia. The winds of change are blowing, and the tide of history has turned for this violent part of Australia's colonial history. These tragic events underpin our land struggle and remain indelibly embedded in the consciousness of Yorta Yorta people.

3

Moira Station and Maloga Mission

Pastoral stations were at the forefront of the violent dispossession and exploitation of Aboriginal people. Once the word got out about the rich alluvial pasture lands and forestry resources of the Murray region, the invasion of Yorta Yorta Country intensified. The sacred lands and waters that had been nurtured and cared for under traditional management practices were taken for granted. The lack of acknowledgement of the rich estate that squatters acquired remains a legacy of the land rights story. They were privileged to be granted our land free of any obligation to the Traditional Owners and without their consent. Over time, however, the Yorta Yorta learned to coexist with the pastoralists. In doing so, they made a significant contribution to the development of the pastoral industry.

The story of Moira Station describes this process of adaptation. Survival went hand in hand with the pastoral economy, and this especially affected the women, who suffered extreme sexual exploitation in the process. Missionaries offered the Indigenous people an alternative to camping on stations, and many found refuge at missions. One such place of refuge and protection from sexual harassment was Maloga Mission (1874–88). As we will see, this created a clash between Moira Station and the mission.

These times were in the living memory of my elders. My grandfather Puppa Henry was a boy when his parents brought him to Maloga, and as a man living at Cummeragunja he worked at Moira Station. He told me stories of these times when I lived with him in Itchica.

With the devastating impact of colonisation, many Yorta Yorta people gravitated to pastoral stations. The right to continue to use the land as their forebears had was an inherent right that was drafted into the pastoral leases Australia-wide. The coexisting nature of such rights was brought home in the famous Wik case in 1996,[1] when the High Court held that native title rights could coexist on land held by pastoral leaseholders. When there was conflict of interest between the exercise of rights, however, the pastoral leases overrode Indigenous rights.

Moira Station was a pastoral lease on the northern side of Dungula, upstream of Itchica. Henry Lewes, a local magistrate, and Charles Throsby of Sutton Forest, near Moss Vale in south-eastern New South Wales, were the first leaseholders of the station in 1842. The original lease of 100,000 acres (405 square kilometres) overlapped traditional base camps of Yorta Yorta on both sides of Dungula. Our people had to find ways to replace the food sources they lost to the pastoral stations and their huge flocks of sheep and cattle.

The commissioner of Crown lands for New South Wales commented on the 'mutual arrangement' that developed between Moira Station and the Indigenous residents,[2] which allowed for the Yorta Yorta people to continue their traditional food subsistence practices. The main beneficiaries of the relationship, however, were the pastoralists, who gained significantly from the availability of Aboriginal labour, including women as domestic servants. History shows without any doubt that this advantage underwrote the success of the burgeoning pastoral economy—a debt still to be properly acknowledged in the local history narrative.

The Yorta Yorta men quickly adapted to farming work, for which they were paid in food and tobacco. They stripped bark for roofs, helped in the woolshed collecting and packing fleeces, and proved to be superior stockmen and shearers. During these tumultuous times, the women were trying to feed and protect their children. Their options were narrow. They could live on the edges of town where they could beg for food but would be subjected to the harassment of hundreds of white men and the negative impacts of alcohol. Alternatively, they could live on the pastoral stations where they could work as domestics while the men worked as labourers and station hands. At least here they could maintain their connections with their traditional camps, which gave them some independence from the pastoral station but did not protect them from exploitation by the station hands and forest workers. In either case, our people were continuing to rely on the dwindling resources of bush tucker and the river.

In 1862 Moira Station changed hands: the lease was taken over by Sir John O'Shanassy. An immensely powerful man, he was premier of Victoria three times, the last from 1861 to 1863, and continued as a politician through to 1877. He was Irish and a leader in the Catholic world in Melbourne. O'Shanassy took over the running of Moira Station and the labour pool he inherited from Lewes and Throsby. Despite the fact that the lease was on traditional Yorta Yorta Country, he was 'against the granting of any reserve land to the Aborigines'.[3] Unlike his Irish counterpart in parliament Sir Charles Gavan Duffy, who granted land in the Acheron valley to the Taungurung and Wurundjeri in 1859, O'Shanassy was dead against such a move and visited Sydney to use his influence against the granting of any reserve land to the Aboriginal people in what was Moira and Yorta Yorta woka.[4] Even though there were provisions in the pastoral leases designed to protect Aboriginal rights, O'Shanassy did not put a stop to the immoral exploitation of women.

~

In 1864 the Yorta Yorta noticed that a new white man was coming to visit the camps. Daniel Matthews did not come looking for workers or women, but to sit down with the people and listen to their stories. He fished and hunted with the men and became trusted as a friend. Matthews was an Echuca merchant who gained respect from the local Yorta Yorta clans. He started the mission at Maloga after visiting Coranderrk, a successful self-sufficient Aboriginal reserve near Healesville, Victoria, in 1863. He hoped his mission would provide protection from the violent impacts of colonisation and give Aboriginal people a better standard of living.

Matthews saw the state of the children, half-starved and begging for food, dressed in rags or covered in a blanket, but so eager to learn from him. He saw how introduced alcohol was affecting their parents. Why not start a school for them? Matthews was one of the few men of his time who felt a moral responsibility towards Aboriginal people. He counted the Aboriginal children in the district and estimated how many would be willing or allowed to come to school. Ten years later, in 1874, he fulfilled his dream and opened a mission school at Maloga on the northern side of Dungula opposite Madowla Station.

Although Dungula was the political boundary between Victoria and New South Wales, it was never a political boundary for Aboriginal people. The majority of them were from the local Yorta Yorta, who occupied both sides of the river. Others came from neighbouring tribes from the upper and lower reaches of Dungula. Between 1874 and 1888 Maloga was intermittently occupied by the Yorta Yorta, many of whom continued also to camp at traditional places in the bush, along the rivers and at pastoral stations.

The diary Matthews kept is a detailed record of his work and of the Aboriginal people who joined him and his wife, Janet, at the mission. Granny Kitty's name is recorded in Matthews' diary in 1874. While Daniel and Janet's aim was religious conversion, they provided some protection for Yorta Yorta people from the evils of the station camps, as well as education for the children, building skills for the men and dressmaking work for the women. However, conflict often occurred with elders over cultural practices, including marriage customs and tribal law business.[5]

With the first two girls at Maloga, who were each about fourteen years old and had an infant, Janet started her school. As Daniel noted, 'every girl who entered the Mission had been victimised by white men'. One of them was Kitty's daughter Lizzie Barber (Atkinson) from the Moira Station camp. Daniel had managed to persuade Kitty and the mother of Sarah Walker that the girls would be better off at the school. At the Moira camp they were being used by white men and were in 'moral and physical danger'.[6]

At the time of O'Shanassy's leasehold of Moira Station, there were many Yorta Yorta people living and working there as farmhands and domestic servants. O'Shanassy fought tooth and nail with Daniel Matthews to ensure that the labour force gained with his lease could be kept for work and service under his control. The bitter dispute between the two over the exploitation of Aboriginal labour and women came to a head in 1874 when Matthews approached O'Shanassy about the matter. O'Shanassy was very hostile because the Maloga property had been selected on Crown lands that were under lease to him, and he thereby lost a valuable section of river frontage. Matthews recorded an altercation with him in his diary on 7 September 1874:

> Crossed the sandhill to O'Shanassy's station. Rode across to the woolshed [5 kilometres]. Saw Aaron branding some sheep. While we were talking Mr O'S dashed up on his horse and dismounted. I approached and said, 'You received my note, Mr. O'Shannasy?' He said yes and then approached me and said, 'I'll knock your damned eyes out.'
>
> He then referred to the Blacks I had taken away and spoke in language more suited to a Public House loafer—alluding to the girls Lizzie and Sarah he said, 'You have got two nice Gins for yourself' … He had been drinking and was pale with rage … I replied, 'We intend protecting these poor girls from such men as they meet at the Stations.'[7]

This gives a glaring insight into white men's attitude of entitlement to sexual relations with Aboriginal girls. The police were unwilling to act against this exploitation.

When an Aboriginal woman was killed in 1884, Matthews recorded the result of the inquest into her death. She and her husband had been camped near a group of drunk timber workers on the edge of the Barmah Forest. The workers knocked the man unconscious, raped the woman, then kicked her and burned her with a piece of hot iron. She died of her injuries before police arrived. Three white men were arrested, but the coroner decided they did not have a case to answer as the woman 'had died of natural causes, accelerated by illness and drink'.[8] 'A very strange verdict!' commented Matthews. He added that Aboriginal witnesses were easily intimidated. He wrote: 'Many at Maloga would have died in the same way after leading a wandering life … Every girl who entered the Mission had been victimised … by white men and reached us as mothers of illegitimate offspring or soon became so … girls of tender age.'[9]

Maloga Mission grew in number as people gained confidence in Matthews. He gathered people from along Dungula, including Ulupna Station some 50 kilometres upstream. In her memoir Theresa Clements, a dhama winyarr from Ulupna, recorded:

> I can remember what happened when I was three. Oh, I remember as if it was yesterday. Mr Matthews came. My brother and sister and I ran and hid near the bank of the river. 'White man going to take us away,' people said. We were terrified. Mr Matthews had a big dray with four horses. He was collecting all the Aborigines along the river from Swan Hill to Tocumwal. Some objected. I don't know what happened to them. We didn't want to go, but soon we found that our mother and grandmother were coming. We were promised housing, food, and clothing if we went. Off we went. That dray was the first vehicle I ever rode in. Mr Matthews took us to the Maloga Mission, about three miles [5 kilometres] from Cummeragunja.[10]

Lizzie was soon asking for her mother to come over from O'Shannassy's. Granny Kitty agreed to leave Moira Station to camp near the school together with her younger Cooper children, Jack, seven, and Ada, five. Billy (William), twelve or thirteen, and Bobby, eleven, followed on horseback. Her older Atkinson sons, Johnny, Aaron and Edgar, were in their twenties and doing station work when they also came to reside at Maloga in 1877.

Granny Kitty and her children had remained on Country before coming to Maloga, living with Kitty's mother, Maria, and other clan members in their traditional camps. Their first language was Yorta Yorta and they were living on their own land. At Maloga Kitty continued to live in a traditional shelter, a mar-noo, down by the river while the girls slept in the schoolhouse. She used to join them in the schoolroom when the children took their lessons, and she learned the alphabet. From time to time she became restless with mission life, rolled her blankets up and left, taking her younger children back to Moira Station.

Sadly, at the end of 1885 Granny Kitty died of tuberculosis at the age of fifty-nine. Her eight Atkinson/Cooper children would have many families between them. As noted earlier, Granny Kitty and Maria are honoured as the apical ancestors of our Atkinson/Cooper clan. Several of Granny Kitty's children became important leaders in the struggle for

Aboriginal rights. She is an outstanding person in our family history. Her grace, her ability to make the best of horrendous times, and that she raised such a strong group of men and women are her powerful legacy.

Research into family connections has produced information about who the fathers of Granny Kitty's Atkinson and Cooper children may have been. They include John Oldbury Atkinson and James Cooper.

John Oldbury was the overseer at Moira Station from 1843 to 1859. He came from the Sutton Forest district in New South Wales, following Charles Throsby to Moira Station in 1843. His overseer job put him in close contact with Granny Kitty's people of the Moira Country. I traced his birthplace to Sutton Forest, near Moss Vale. His English connections go back to Oldbury, a former marketplace in the West Midlands of England. It is no surprise that my father's middle name is Auldenby, which has a similar ring to Oldbury. To be given a foreign name like Auldenby, however, is out of character with the cultural context of middle-name inheritance in our family. Whether my father's middle name was corrupted on the way down and should have remained as Oldbury is part of the jigsaw puzzle.

A letter I received from a descendant of John Oldbury in Melbourne helped to throw more light on the subject. Her name is Joyce Atkinson, and her letter of 1996 is revealing. She says, 'We were always given to understand that the tribe at Moira took the name [Atkinson] out of respect for John Oldbury Atkinson.' I assumed that this could be interpreted to include the four children Kitty had in the Moira camps as indicated in Matthews' diaries. These were Johnny (born 1848), Aaron (1851), Elizabeth (Lizzie; 1853) and Edgar (1855). It is no coincidence that the four Atkinson children to Granny Kitty were all born within Oldbury's time as overseer of the station. His contact with the Moira camp labour pool, including the women who gravitated to and from Moira Station, supports this proposition. For the oldest son of Kitty to be named John adds further weight to the Oldbury connection.

Evidence of this is further supported on the *WikiTree* genealogy website, which shows the two white fathers of her eight children as James John Oldbury Atkinson and James Cooper. It shows Aaron's father as John Oldbury Atkinson and his mother as Kitty of the Yorta Yorta people. The marriage certificate of Aaron and Louise in 1873, indicating the father of Aaron to be John O Atkinson, confirms him as father of Aaron. It was witnessed by John O'Shannassy.[11]

Kitty's four children of the Cooper line—William (Billy), Jack, Robert (Bobby) and Ada—are listed as children of James Cooper. The identity of the white man Cooper is uncertain, as the names James and William are both listed as William Cooper's father on his marriage and death certificates.[12]

The story of Louisa Atkinson (1854–93) takes us on a similar trajectory regarding the father of her children before she took the Atkinson name after her marriage to Aaron Atkinson. Her birth name is recorded as Louisa Frost, born in Mathoura, New South Wales, circa 1855, parents Thomas Frost and Topsy. When she married Aaron she already had three children, William, Henry and Minnie. There is speculation in the oral record that their biological father was a white man from Mathoura, where Puppa Henry spent much time when he was working on the adjoining Moira Station. Identifying his father is still a work in progress.

We can deduce that at the time of the O'Shanassy family's hold on Moira Station, Louisa would have been one of the young girls living there as a domestic servant. Matthews recorded her coming to Maloga from the Moira tribe. She spent time at Maloga making clothes for her second son, Puppa Henry. William was the oldest and Minnie the youngest of the three children she had before she married Aaron at the Junction Hotel in Moama in 1873.[13]

That is where research has taken us on the origins of the Atkinson/Cooper families, from whom I am a direct descendant on my father's and mother's side. There is a void in the historic records for this period except for the diaries of Daniel Matthews and what has come to light in the genealogical database. We were able to use much of this history in the 12,000-page transcript of mostly oral evidence presented in the Yorta Yorta native title case between 1984 and 2001 (see Chapter 16).

When looking into the sexual activity that happened on the pastoral stations, it is difficult to distinguish between abuse and seduction. We know, however, that the power relations with young Aboriginal women sprang from the imposed rights of ownership and compliance. This was further reinforced by the threat of violence, as indicated in O'Shannassy's clashes with the benevolent Matthews. According to

Matthews' diaries, 'Each station had its Blacks' camp, with its quota of young girls for the use of the station hands, and sometimes the squatter's sons.' In the first years at Maloga, 'every young woman admitted to the mission was carrying a child to white fathers, though many were thirteen and fourteen years old'.[14]

It is clear that Granny Kitty and other women of that tragic era cared for their children and kept them safe. Granny Kitty stayed strong in her Aboriginal world, camping with Maria and other clan members in the traditional lands. With no accountability for their actions, the fathers faded into obscurity while the women stayed strong. The children grew up hearing the old people tell stories of times before—of Biami, of the bunyip in the deep waterholes, of the Great Flood, of the min-min lights and the scary hairy becker in the forest at night by Dungula. These same stories were passed on to me, including the location of the corroboree and ceremonial site Algabonyah, and the importance of the Maloga Mission site. Old man weed, or gukwonderuk (*Centipeda cunninghamii*), growing along the waterways is still a valued medicine. These are storylines of our survival and continued connections that are still passed on by the Yorta Yorta Nation.

~

As a lot of Aboriginal people were coming to Maloga from Victoria, Matthews asked the Victorian authorities for assistance. He was supported in his requests by two settlers on the Victorian side of the river, James Rutherford at Ulupna and Hugh McKenzie of Wyuna. In 1874 Rutherford and McKenzie were still receiving supplies and rations from the Victorian Aborigines Protection Board for the people at their stations, but the Board was not forthcoming with assistance for Matthews because his station was in New South Wales, arguing that it was the NSW Government's responsibility to provide assistance. The Victorian border was a thorn in Matthews' side for many years. Even though Maloga was closer to Melbourne than Sydney, neither government would take responsibility or offer any assistance for Maloga Station.

Towards the end of the 1870s Matthews turned his attention to Sydney, where he made 'several important journeys between 1878–81'.

With the assistance of the Reverend John Gribble of Jerilderie he formed the first Aborigines Protection Association in New South Wales 'for the purpose of ameliorating the present deplorable condition of the remnants of the Aborigine tribes of this colony'.[15] From 26 February 1883, the NSW Government prioritised subsidising Maloga Station.

By the 1880s the population of Maloga had risen to 250, consisting of the original Yorta Yorta people and those who had come from Coranderrk to be with their kinsfolk, and people Matthews had brought from Sydney and Gosford. The Victorian *Aboriginies Protection Act 1886* (popularly known as the Absorption Act) made 'part-Aborigines' under the age of thirty-five leave the reserves. This forced many people of cross-cultural parentage from Coranderrk to seek protection from the Act at Maloga and Cummeragunja, not knowing that similar laws would be introduced in New South Wales in 1909.

The amalgamation of Aboriginal people from Nations around Sydney and from outside the Moira caused internal conflict that had to be dealt with. Matthews had brought people in without understanding established kinship ties along traditional lines and traditional customs and laws. It took a long time for the newcomers to be accepted.

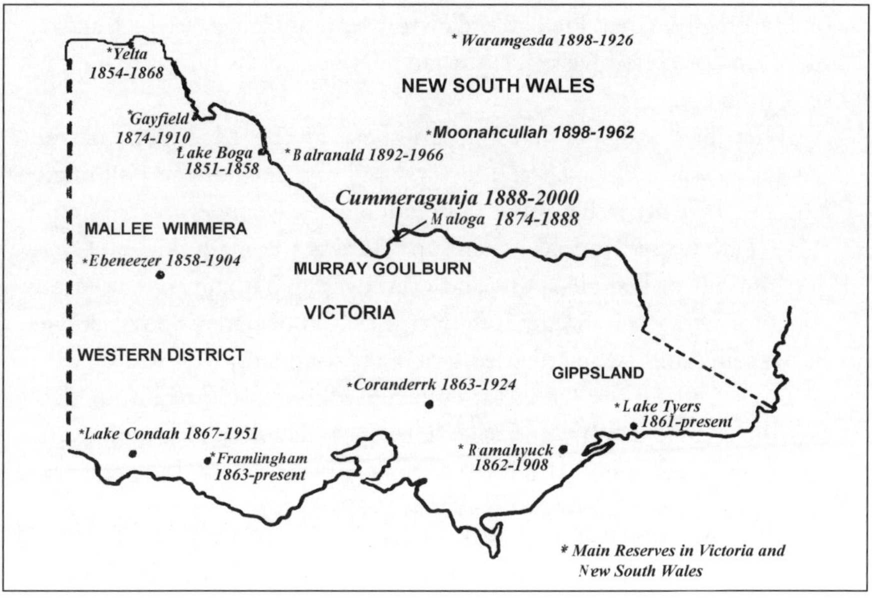

Locations of Cummeragunja Reserve and Maloga Mission. *Courtesy the author.*

Two important events of the 1880s remain vivid recollections for present-day Aboriginal people. Firstly, in 1881 Thomas Shadrach James met Daniel Matthews and volunteered to teach at the Maloga school. His parents were Indian and he had arrived in Australia from Mauritius as James Peersahib. The same year, the Maloga school was recognised as a government school and a salary was provided for the teacher.

In 1885 James married Granny Kitty's daughter Ada; he is my great-grandfather Granpa James. His marriage into the people and his dark skin made him one of us, and his skills as a community teacher, doctor, dentist and medical dispenser made him an outstanding leader of the community. Later he became headmaster of the Cummeragunja school. People today still have the utmost respect for him. Because of his Indian background he is sometimes referred to as the Gandhi of the Cummeragunja people. His dedication to Yorta Yorta people's education and wellbeing left a remarkable legacy. His daughter Priscilla, my grandmother, spoke of his medical work and leadership at Cummera:

> My father was their main doctor there on Cummera, and when the doctor used to be busy, in Echuca, he'd say 'you've got a doctor there—go to him. Go to Mr James. He'll do as good as I can for you.' Yes, and my father used to extract teeth. He used to lance their sores or anything like that. He had the instruments and all, cause he trained for a doctor. They were lucky that he was there—he saved many on Cummera.
>
> They had a dispensary put up there at the Manager's place. My father was the dispenser. Doctors used to come out and visit once a month, take my father round different ones, leave their prescriptions there. Father used to make them up. He was the main doctor. They got him out of bed all hours, and even over at Barmah they used to come for my father and get him out. He saved Maloney's boy Lennie [a Barmah family who attended school at Cummera] who was very ill with pneumonia. My father sat with him all night. Next morning he saw the change coming and said, 'He's met the crisis. Now you keep on with my treatment with him.' Lennie got better.[16]

My lifelong journey of learning has been strongly influenced by Granpa James. In places like the Scholars' Hut at old Maloga and Cummeragunja, he mentored and taught a generation of outstanding

Yorta Yorta leaders. My great-uncle William Cooper's generation were students of Granpa James. Together with Doug Nicholls, Jack Patten, Theresa Clements, Marge Tucker and Shadrach James Junior, he was a key activist in Victoria and New South Wales in the early 1930s. They established the Australian Aborigines' League in Melbourne in 1933, the first political organisation in Victoria that fought for Aboriginal rights and education equality, and they taught us about the power of the voice, the spear of the pen and collective organisation.

The second major event was the petition for land by the Maloga people in 1881. This could be seen as the first land rights petition in New South Wales by descendants of Traditional Owners. Victorian Aboriginal people had made a similar attempt in 1859 when members of the Kulin tribes made a deputation to Guardian William Thomas, the chief government adviser on Aboriginal affairs.

It seems ironic that when the 1881 Maloga petition was organised, there were Coranderrk people at Maloga. They had been instrumental in the 1859 claim for land shared by Wurundjeri and Taungurung people of the Kulin Nation. That land was located in eastern Victoria on the Acheron and Little rivers overlooking the sacred Cathedral Mountain. One of the tribal leaders of the 1859 land rights deputation to Guardian Thomas was William Barak, headman of the Wurundjeri Woiwurrung Nation. At the time of the Maloga petition he was visiting with his only son, David, who was very ill and dying. Sadly, Barak's direct lineage died with David, as did his status as Ngurungaeta, holder of the tribal word. There were twenty other Coranderrk people either visiting or settled in 1881. This was a long-established relationship between the two reserves before and after the invasion. Much of this story is recorded in my oral history manuscript *A Picture from the Other Side*.

Forty-two Maloga residents signed the 1881 petition to the NSW governor, one of the many claims made by our people for land justice. The petitioners requested a sufficient area of land to cultivate and raise stock 'that we may form homes for our families and in a few years, support ourselves by our own industry'. They asked this as compensation 'because all the land within our tribal boundaries has been taken possession of by the government and white settlers'.[17]

4

Cummeragunja: Courage and Defiance

On 9 April 1883, the NSW Government responded to the 1881 petition by reserving 1800 acres (7 square kilometres) of land for Yorta Yorta use some 5 kilometres upstream from the Maloga Mission. The land was selected in consultation with Yorta Yorta elders, who chose the site and called it Cummeragunja. It means 'our home' in the Yorta Yorta language, a place that was believed to be for eternity. This action followed an official inquiry into the administration of Maloga and other reserves after the Aborigines Protection Association in Sydney put pressure on the government.

On 19 July 1887 Jack Cooper, son of Granny Kitty and brother of Bob, William and Ada, read an address of welcome to visiting governor Lord Carrington at the Moama railway station. Like his famous brother William, Jack acted as a voice for our people. The group from Maloga presented another petition, asking that 100 acres (40 hectares) be granted to 'such Aboriginal men who wished to farm for himself, to support them and their families'.[1]

Combining the two petitions (1881 and 1887) was a clever strategy to put further pressure on the governor and the NSW Government for Yorta Yorta land rights. No doubt the knowledge of the power of the pen and the skills of petition writing came from the quality teachings of Granpa James at Maloga. One can see the power of his teaching coming through in the short period of his important work at Maloga, which continued over the next four decades of his life at Cummeragunja and beyond.

The Aborigines Protection Association rejected this petition and withheld further funds to Maloga Mission until all the buildings were moved to the new government-administered reserve at Cummeragunja. It warned that those who remained at Maloga would lose their cottages and the chance to farm a block of their own, while those who had already moved to the new site would have their rations taken away if they visited anyone remaining at Maloga.

The Maloga community was fully relocated to the new reserve in 1888–89. The reasons given for the forced removal included concerns about undue influence of the missionaries and the administration of the mission. But the underlying reason was that the land on which Maloga was established was Daniel Matthews' private land. The government assumed responsibility for Aboriginal people in New South Wales under the *Protection of Aborigines Act 1883*, which emulated the Victorian protection regime in forbidding financing of privately run ventures. Matthews' authority was taken from him. George Bellinger became manager of the new site and was instructed to pull down the existing houses at Maloga and move them to the new site of Cummeragunja. Matthews 'was told he was not wanted in any capacity'.[2] Sadly, it was the death knell for his mission venture, and he and Janet resigned in 1888. This was a heartbreaking blow to the Matthews family.

Over the next few years, the Aboriginal community moved their houses and rebuilt the school and church at Cummeragunja. The reserve was on a bend of Dungula on the NSW side of the river opposite the Victorian township of Barmah. It was an emotional move, but they welcomed it in good faith as an opportunity to settle down and farm their own land. They chose the name Cummeragunja, and the reserve became known affectionately as Cummera. For the next fifty years the Cummera people lived there under the control of the Aborigines Protection Board.

Granpa James moved with them and continued to provide health care and quality education in the school. He also ran the adult education centre, known as the Scholars' Hut, where literacy skills and civil rights were taught. Granpa's life in Mauritius had taught him about British colonisation and racism. He knew that Mauritian Indians were excluded from equal participation: they were not allowed to vote until Mahatma Gandhi's influence was felt in the 1900s. It was through the interpreter work of his father that Granpa James had learned the importance of giving Indians their civil rights and representation in the justice system.

Cummera was a community that valued caring and sharing. Strong bonds, built on traditional values and the necessities of poverty, ensured that the numerous barriers the people faced were dealt with collectively.

Aunty Sophie Briggs reflected on life at Cummera:

> The good old days are gone now. See that picture on the wall there? That's all the old people of Cummera which was taken in front of my husband's mother's place. Alick and Minnie Briggs.
>
> Houses were everywhere in those days, and we had good times then. Granpa James was teaching in the school. We used to have sports, processions, concerts. Then the reserve started to go down when the people went away to work, and their houses were pulled down! They had nowhere to live then! I never left my house, and my family stayed with me until they were married and went away. Evelyn Briggs and I were in hospital together having our children at the time those houses were pulled down. Then they pulled the church down also. That was terrible! They shouldn't have pulled them down! The people were very shocked when they found out.
>
> My house was one of the original Maloga homes that was shifted up on wooden sledges to Cummera, pulled by horses. Jessi Cooper's is the other one around the corner. They are the only two old Maloga homes now. The manager who was here then made them pull the houses down.[3]

~

The Cummera reserve of 1800 acres was inadequate for pastoral and agricultural development. Only 400 acres was suitable for farming; the remainder had a lot of trees and was subject to regular flooding. The Board applied for extra land, but pressure from local settlers defeated its applications in 1885 and 1887. However, soon after 1900 the NSW Government granted additional land, making a total of 2965 acres (12 square kilometres) for the original Cummera reserve. This amounted to 0.6 per cent of our traditional Yorta Yorta lands, which are estimated to be 20,000 square kilometres, or approximately 5 million acres. Through to the early 1900s there was pressure to lease the Cummera land to surrounding farmers, culminating in the lease of most of the reserve lands to a white farmer in 1934. Further leases of almost the entire reserve to whites continued through the 1940s and 1950s.

When Cummera began, 500 acres (2 square kilometres) per family was the minimum holding for mixed farming in the region by white settlers. How could 2965 acres be justified for a population at the time of approximately 400 Aboriginal residents? The land was also only a temporary grant of permissive occupancy—there was no security of title. The Board had total control of land development and Aboriginal residents were merely tenants at will (that is, they could be evicted without notice).[4]

Cummera people had a strong desire for their own land to farm. This was fulfilled to some extent when 40-acre blocks were allocated to some of the men between 1896 and 1907. Eventually eighteen men, including my grandfather Puppa Henry, were allocated farm blocks. Believing they owned the blocks, they worked hard and shared equipment to make them productive.

Twelve years later their farming efforts were dealt a severe blow when the Board took the blocks back. Memories of the bitter injustice of the farm blocks being given and then taken back are etched into the oral history memory bank. Puppa Henry and my father told me stories of the way the land was given and taken back with no consultation. My grandmother Priscilla McCrae told me about the disappointment of the block holders:

> Oh yes, to this day we think about that! The way they treated them very badly and took their farm blocks back without telling them why … They used to get real good crops and that's one thing I've never forgot how they took them like that. They lost trust with the Board then, but they couldn't do anything about it. They just had to abide by what the Board said or if they spoke out, they were told to leave the reserve. Granpa James was very put out about the Board's decision, and he used to write on behalf of the block holders to the Board, but they never responded to his letters … I was only a young girl then and I used to take food down to Uncle Johnny [Atkinson] and them [Granny Kitty's sons] while they were working.[5]

Dan Atkinson told me about the inadequate machinery the block holders had to share:

> they never had much machinery between them, so they used to work their blocks with one single furrow plough and a horse ... They used to help each other work their blocks, and then after a while they came and took them off the people for what reason I don't know.[6]

Looking back, it's clear that the blocks were hopelessly inadequate to support a family, being only 40 acres. This was a stark contrast to the 320 acres that could be accessed under the NSW *Crown Lands Act 1861* as a sufficient starting point for white farmers and their families. In addition, the men had cleared 1400 acres of the reserve, some of which was heavily timbered, for a government farm and had more than 400 acres fenced and under cultivation. While the men were paid in rations for this work, the surplus produce was sold and returned to the Aborigines Protection Board.

Why then did the government take back the land? The Board claimed the block holders were not using them properly and said it would benefit everybody if all the Cummera land was again put under the care of the white manager. Aware of the unfairness of this treatment, several of the men stood up to the Board and engaged a local lawyer to represent their interests. While the Board listened to the men and their case, it was like another dead letter: they turned around and rejected the case for the return of the blocks and denied compensation to the men for the work they had done on them. So, while Cummera gained a reputation for being one of the most successful of the Aboriginal stations, the reality was that the people had little say in their affairs. All the power was held by the manager, backed by the Aborigines Protection Board and the police. This is an example of the structural racism that our people were forced to live under.

One of Granpa James's sermons in 1909 was interpreted by the manager's wife as inciting unrest about the Board taking back the farm blocks. The Board and the manager began speaking openly about their fears that Granpa was empowering people, enabling them to write petitions and articulate their human rights. They tried to sack him twice, but this was not so easy as he led a very successful teaching team and the marks of the children, both black and white, and the quality of his teaching were outstanding for the state.

The Aborigines Protection Board was no more than a front for the colonial project. The system under which the residents were forced to live conjures up an image of an institution aimed at social control. It was one of the systemic structures that prevented our people living normal and equal lives to other citizens in a civil society. Indeed, my generation is still fighting to change these structures today in our struggle for treaty, sovereignty and self-determination.

The Board's reasons for revoking the farm blocks were not spelled out. The laws about protection were in fact race laws: the reserves were to be training institutions preparing the people for absorption into the general community. They were trying to breed out our culture along with our race—a form of cultural genocide was in place. Our people were to be educated only to Grade 3 to be part of the working class. Granpa James's ability to teach above the prescribed level of education and give his students a quality education was a remarkable achievement.

~

To understand the background to our struggle for Aboriginal rights, one needs to understand something of the way the governments of New South Wales and Victoria set up 'protection Boards' to control Aboriginal people. What were they to be protected from? They had already suffered from colonial violence, sexual predation and economic exploitation and had been hounded off their land. But the governments were more worried about the growing population of people of mixed descent, those Aboriginal people with white ancestors. In reality, protection was a policy of segregation and control.

Governments responded to the growth of Aboriginal society by segregating Aboriginal people in institutions, reserves or missions where they were to be disciplined to live the white man's way. They would be normalised into a Christian working class, with the girls trained to work as domestics and the boys as labourers. Their status, however, was increasingly one of an underclass, perpetuated by discrimination, injustice and poverty. This status was the result of mission and government action rather than an outcome of Aboriginal culture. To blame Aboriginal shortcomings on Aboriginal people is to blame the victim.

Governments used their protection Acts as an instrument of control. There was no escape. The NSW *Aborigines Protection Act 1909* had powers to control who lived in or visited the reserves; to expel people for 'misconduct' or for being 'of mixed blood'; to define terms of any work contract between Aborigines and whites; to take charge of Aboriginal children; to control all machinery and livestock; to inspect people's homes at any time; and to use police to enforce all this. These powers were used and abused by the managers of the reserves and institutions.

Missions like Cummeragunja, Coranderrk and others were turned into concentration camps under the control of the state governments. The laws were commonly called 'Half-Caste Acts', which is a deeply offensive term. They effectively created a new racial category of people under separate laws. The laws were used to divide and rule people on the basis of their skin colour, which in effect institutionalised racism and inequality.

It is said that Aboriginal people were treated like children under such a paternalistic regime. When you look at the reserve system, it is more enlightening to compare it to the way criminals and people with mental disorders were treated: they were locked away and made to work for their keep until they could be returned to society. Aboriginal resistance was redefined as criminality.

The NSW *Aborigines Protection Act 1909* mimicked Victoria's *Aborigines Protection Act 1886*. It was about cultural absorption, giving reserve managers the power to expel people of mixed parentage. Many Cummeragunja families were forced off and ended up camping on the Victorian side of the river with no access to housing. One of those expelled—for standing up for the rights of his community—was Granpa James' son Shadrach James. Uncle Shady camped on the Victorian side opposite Cummera and lived there before he moved to Mooroopna.

Within ten years this policy had halved the Cummeragunja population, which had reached its peak of around 400 in 1908. Rations were not allowed to be issued to any of the men, and they had to find work outside the reserve to support their families. Farming on Cummera was disrupted by the lack of labour and 150 people were made homeless.[7]

The dream of a secure, self-supporting community was dealt another severe blow.

By 1933, during the Great Depression, there was a large camp of around 200 Aboriginal people just outside Cummeragunja. They were refused the dole because they were said to be 'too black', but at Cummeragunja they were too white to receive rations because they were not considered 'predominantly of Aboriginal blood'.[8] Expulsion from the reserves did not come with full citizen rights.

Another issue that came up on Cummera was the Board policy of stealing the girls to send them away to the training institution for domestics in Cootamundra, 400 kilometres away. The story is told of how Granpa James held up the welfare officers out in the schoolyard while telling the girls to run and hide: he did his best to protect them from the pernicious policy of tearing children from their families and confining them to institutions designed to mould them to white ways. At the Cootamundra Domestic Training Home for Aboriginal Girls (also known as 'Bimbadeen' and Cootamundra Girls' Home), they experienced systematic racial discrimination to obliterate their Aboriginal identity and alienate them from their families. The girls were between fifteen and eighteen when they were sent out as servants to white households and subjected to harsh conditions, with their wages paid to Board trust accounts.

Sir Douglas Nicholls' sister Hilda was taken under this policy, as was my aunty Margaret Nelson, the sixteen-year-old daughter of my grandparents Henry and Margaret Nelson. In a tragic turn of events, the family was eventually told that Margaret was returning home from Cootamundra on the train but when they went to meet her, they were greeted by her bags on the platform of Itchica station and no Margaret. Unbeknown to them, she had died in Bimbadeen with no notice of her death given to the family. What a shock. They never forgot the callousness of the Board or the sad loss of their daughter, a loved aunty of our family. As I found in my oral history interviews in the 1980s, nearly every family was affected by the Stolen Generations violations. They are still uppermost in people's minds as if they only happened yesterday.

~

The constant frustration of Aboriginal initiative and continued interference by the Board pushed the Cummera residents to the point of rebellion. The unrest created by the Board's shady land dealings, together with the oppression of being continually controlled, led to Cummera people deciding to take direct political action. They wanted to break free from the shackles of oppression and enjoy the same citizenship rights as white people. Meanwhile, under the leadership of Uncle William Cooper and the freedom fighters of the time, the Australian Aborigines League in Melbourne took these grievances to the federal level.

Uncle William's role as a political leader developed from his education under the brilliant teaching of Granpa James. It was grounded in his experience of work in the pastoral industry in New South Wales and Victoria—work that put him in contact with Aboriginal people from other reserves. As noted earlier, with other Cummera people he founded the Australian Aborigines' League in 1933. Uncle William and AAL secretary Uncle Shadrack James sent many letters to Federal parliamentarians raising the issue of the immorality of dispossession and land injustice. They called for full Aboriginal citizenship rights and demanded a more coordinated approach to the administration of Aboriginal affairs in each state, underpinned by Aboriginal representation in Parliament. When these pleas fell on deaf ears, Uncle William decided to appeal to the King himself. In 1935 he drafted a petition to the King, asking him to intervene and he gained the signatures of some 2000 Aboriginal people from Victoria, New South Wales and other parts of Australia. The petition was sent to Prime Minister Lyons in 1937 to be forwarded to the King.

The sad irony is that the King never received the petition. The federal government overruled the petition with the excuse that, as the appointment of an Aborigine to parliament was currently a constitutional impossibility, it was useless to forward it to the King. Once again, no action was taken. As Uncle William's daughter Sally Russell told me, when he found out that the petition never left Australia he was a very disappointed man. This setback didn't deter the fighting spirit of Uncle William. On 26 January 1938, he and other activists held the nation's first Day of Mourning in Sydney. This developed into the Survival and Invasion Day protests of today. Almost eighty years later, their calls for representative democracy were revived in the 2023 Voice to Parliament referendum and inspired the Treaty and Truth Justice Process in Victoria (2016–2025).

The struggle continued, and in 1938 Cummera people led the first Aboriginal deputation to Canberra to advise the prime minister on the need for Commonwealth intervention in the policy and administration of Aboriginal affairs. Meanwhile, growing unrest at Cummera over land and the management of the reserve by AJ McQuiggan came to a head in 1939.[9] Managers had full control of Aboriginal reserves, and many, including McQuiggan, ruled with an iron fist. They had wide powers to regulate the lives and movements of residents and all other matters relating to Aboriginal reserves. They also had power over Aboriginal people who moved off the reserves and the powers of the racist Aborigines Protection Acts of Victoria and New South Wales.

Aunty Geraldine Briggs reflected on her experience of reserve life under the McQuiggan regime and her resolve to stay strong:

> I learnt a lot when I was outside the Mission in other places in NSW and Melbourne, which made me more aware of things, and I grew to dislike the superior ways of managers and matrons towards Aborigines. I wasn't prepared to give in to anyone who held that sort of attitude.
>
> When people moved away from the reserve the manager McQuiggan moved things out of people's houses. He went about it in a very cunning way, too! He formed a committee after a few people had gone back there [which] consisted of a bailiff, sheriff, etc. who were then delegated with the authority to go into the houses and get the contents out. The reason he did this was because he wasn't game to do it himself, so he had to get someone else to do it. When people found out about this, they were very annoyed, but they couldn't do much about it because McQuiggan had the power to call the police in if anyone caused a disturbance on the reserve. The movement created a lot of divisions and unrest amongst the people and McQuiggan used this to try and divide the people and blame them for the movement away instead of his own bad management and the inadequate conditions of the reserve.[10]

Uncle Bevan Nicholls shared his story of living on the reserve under a manager. He told me:

> The only person we had dealings with was the manager who was nearly always an Englishman, who usually wasn't long out here from the old country. And the reserve would be worked something like these

> other British colonies. This was their way of thinking ... they imposed their own ways of living onto us as they did in the other colonies.[11]

The key event that inspired the Cummera people's courageous decision to walk off the reserve was a visit from Jack Patten in 1938. Jack was a freedom fighter and a member of the Melbourne- and Sydney-based political organisations that were campaigning for justice and change. An alliance had been formed between the Australian Aborigines' League in Victoria and the Australian Aboriginal Progressive Association in New South Wales; the latter had been created to pressure the government into abolishing the infamous Aborigines Protection Board.

Jack's visit to Cummera is an iconic event in Aboriginal activism in Australia. He stood on the verandah of the old Cummera school and spoke to residents about the discriminatory nature and conditions of Aboriginal reserves. As well as being a very skilful public speaker, he was editor of the Australian Aboriginal newspaper, published monthly from April to September 1938. From accounts of the strike, it is clear that he had a big impact on the decision of the people to move across the river. Exactly what he said is not recorded, but going by the philosophy he expressed in the newspaper, he was trying to get people to unite against the oppressive laws and restrictions they were forced to live under. In his editorial in the May edition, he said, 'Look at our Reserves! What is it that greets us on investigation? Starvation, poor housing and education, and general oppression.' He then attacked the Protection Board for appointing men like the manager McQuiggan:

> to torture us mentally with bullying tactics. This, with the wrecking of our physical condition through inadequate food supply has only one object—Extermination. What have we to lose if this so-called 'protection' Board is abolished?
>
> So, all Aborigines in Australia who want the privileges and benefits of civilization for the welfare of their wives and children should get behind this movement. Say goodbye to the damper and ashes, and to compounds. We want to survive in the land of our forefathers, on equal terms.[12]

Uncle Hilton Walsh recalls the 'fantastic effect' Patten's speech had on people: 'It was as though he opened the bloody gates and let us out and we had the outside world to look at.'[13] Jack was reportedly one of those fiery speakers who could make the hair stand up on your neck. He didn't pull any punches and was able to articulate issues clearly. Unfortunately, there was a clause in the protection laws that made incitement of Aboriginal people on reserves illegal, and Jack was arrested.

After his visit and with all diplomatic avenues exhausted, the people of Cummera retreated to base-camp politics. Their long-term plans had been continually undermined by the Aborigines Protection Board. The tyrannical control of McQuiggan and the leasing of most of their land to a white farmer was the straw that broke the camel's back.

The date 3 February 1939 is both a heroic and an iconic one in the Yorta Yorta calendar. It is the day when most of the Cummera residents decided to rise and to leave the reserve. Courageously, 200 men, women and children packed up and went on strike for freedom, liberty and better conditions. This was an organised political protest against the oppressive conditions they had been forced to live under for so long. The community rose up and crossed the river into Victoria, where they camped as political refugees.

The Cummera walk-off is a defining moment of our history, a story of courage and defiance. It is remembered in our oral history as a profound people's struggle to break the shackles of segregation and control. The Cummera people were rejecting the tyrannical powers of McQuiggan, and the leasing of most of their land to white farmers.

~

This walk-off was not a one-off occurrence. It came from a long history of protest by Yorta Yorta people. Cummeragunja Reserve was the outcome of continuous efforts by Traditional Owners of the Murray-Goulburn region to reclaim their traditional land and to live self-sufficiently. Records dating back to as early as 1861 show that Yorta Yorta people sought compensation for the effects of the European invasion and forced dispossession.

Just how difficult was it for Yorta Yorta people to leave the place they loved and had believed would be their home forever? To understand the significance of Cummeragunja to its people, we first need to locate the 1939 walk-off in its historic context. Before the walk-off, Cummera had come to symbolise the survival of a flourishing Aboriginal community in the face of dispossession. It had defied the widely held narrative of the late nineteenth and early twentieth centuries that the fate of Aboriginal people was hopeless and that these poor wretched people and their culture would eventually die out. Cummera was a place that represented resistance to government control over Aboriginal affairs and the defiant continuation of culture and identity.

At the same time, those who lived on Cummera were constantly answerable to the Aborigines Protection Board, which had the power to take away not only their land but also their children. It was a place of family and recreation, yet Aboriginal people's opportunities—from access to employment and land, to welfare and equal wages—were invariably restricted by the prejudice and ignorance of the wider community. Cummera is remembered bitterly and sweetly with pride and sadness, but it connects generations of Yorta Yorta people and is tied up in all our success stories and achievements under extremely oppressive circumstances.

I was born just after the walk-off and learned of the cultural and emotional attachment of people to Cummera. My parents and relatives told me stories. I would often visit with them for family gatherings and burials, and to fish at the special places for the favourite gangupka (yellowbelly) and burnanga (Murray cod). My parents and grandparents would always talk about Cummera in affectionate terms, saying things like 'poor old Cummera' or 'dear old Cummera'. My mother would yearn to visit and relive the old days and would embrace those whom she visited, shedding a tear for the place they loved. This emotional experience brought home to me that Cummera was a special place in our history as proud Yorta Yorta people and is the key factor that motivated me later to learn more through the oral history project, and to use this knowledge in our native title claim.

Fortunately, connections with Cummera continued and it was never disbanded. Some families stayed, and many returned to eventually regain control. The NSW *Aboriginal Land Rights Act 1983* returned some land for social and economic development, and Cummera is now managed by the Cummeragunja Local Aboriginal Land Council.

The testimonies of people who grew up on Cummeragunja create a picture of one very big extended family. As Merle Jackomos explained,

'We were all related on Cummera, we more or less had the one common great-grandmother.'[14] Similarly, Melva Johnson remarked that 'everyone was Auntie, everyone was Uncle, and there was a deep respect for everyone'.[15] Uncle Hilton Walsh, who grew up on Cummera during the Depression years, recalled that 'our people always had extended family, where you could be billeted out anywhere as soon as you got into your teens, to make room for the younger children'.[16] This sense of community at Cummera grew out of our traditional values and the necessity for survival and it remained after the walk-off, when people moved to the riverbank at Mooroopna and to nearby towns.

Living on Dungula at Cummera, Yorta Yorta could fish and cook the way their elders had in the old days. Aunty Ellen said, 'We used to cook turtle, fish, swan or ducks on ashes. We used swan and emu eggs (they're rich!) for cakes, birthday cakes. We used to have wonderful meals.'[17] Although people adapted to a sedentary life and were eager to learn European modes of production, there was a continuity of traditional practices.

The sense of community was further strengthened by our unique language. The Cummera dialect is a secret language used within our families and at community gatherings. Cummera people learned English, but not without adding their own pronunciation and vocabulary and grammatical structures. This dialect is one of the many that were created by the segregated communities on reserves and missions, a process that is clarified in the book *Bina: First Nations Languages, Old and New*, which refers extensively to Aboriginal Englishes as being distinct from traditional languages.[18]

Some Cummera dialect words are derived from English and are well known, such as tiddas for 'sisters'. Then there is the word deadly, which means 'excellent' or 'very good' in Aboriginal English, and gammin, which means 'rubbish' or 'not fair dinkum'. There is the particular use of the word shame, where 'shame job' means 'embarrassing'. Shaming is a system of social control used to change someone's behaviour into more acceptable ways. Elders use 'shame job' a lot when younger members fall out of line within the community.

Cummeragunja represented change and adaptation to the white man's ways but provided a space for the continuation of the old way of life. As Uncle Ronald Morgan pointed out, assimilation began from the entry of white men to our shores.[19] For men like Ronald's father, Bagot Morgan, it was a case of survival and response to rapidly changing circumstances. Bagot 'encouraged many of the Aborigines to come and live on Maloga, to give up their ways of living, and learn of the white man'.[20] The trade-off for learning the English language was that the old language fell out of practice; it came back in the cultural revival of the 1980s. Fortunately, some words, stories and songs in the original language had survived. In Cummera dialect we use Aboriginal words for some body parts, such as 'moom' for bottom, and we use 'jiliwa' for toilet. A person who is 'goolin' is upset about something. We talk about a 'guthup', a person who is too flash. We also use the term 'poor' for someone who has died, not to reflect their status but as a mark of respect for the person who has gone back to the Dreamtime. These expressions reflect cultural beliefs that bind us.

Although we speak our Cummera drawl within the community, we have no trouble code-switching to standard English. Granpa James ensured that we could speak and write in powerfully expressive English, as our leaders like Uncle William Cooper, Pastor Doug Nicholls and Marge Tucker showed.

The achievements of political activists such as Uncle William and Uncle Shadrach James have been well documented. Yet Cummera people achieved also on a day-to-day level, whether it be the women who 'made do with whatever they had, twenty cents of bone for a soup'[21] or the men who built their houses with unpaid labour.

Cummeragunja is remembered by many Yorta Yorta with happiness. Ronald Morgan's comment that 'the people of Cummeragunja were not without their recreation' is an understatement: Cummera was never short of entertainment. Besides regular concerts and dances, there were processions in which were shown dresses that women had skilfully put together.

From all accounts, music flowed through Cummera like Dungula itself. While individuals such as singer Jimmy Little went on to achieve national fame, on the local level the Cummeragunja Church Choir was, in the humble opinion of Uncle Hilton Walsh, 'one of the greatest choirs you could ever imagine'.[22] It toured the region during the World War II years.[23] The choir sang hymns first learned at Maloga Mission, as well as Negro spirituals such as 'Shall We Gather at the River', introduced to them by the Fisk Jubilee Singers from Tennessee.[24] Merle Jackomos recalled that at Christmas festivities, families would share a meal at the bend of the river and sing hymns while the kids were swimming.

~

Our history of Marngrook highlights how traditional skills elevated the local Cummera team to 'Invincibles' status in the local and regional competition. Between 1921 and 1931 the team won six premierships, before being forced to withdraw from the league after a new rule was introduced banning players over the age of twenty-five. In trying to rationalise such a rule, one is faced with the 'damned if you do, damned if you don't' syndrome. Being marginalised from mainstream society on the reserve but willing to compete as equals on the football field resulted in the Invincibles being penalised because they were too good for their opponents. It reveals how high the systemic barriers were in the racial equality equation.

At the centre of this story, the Invincibles created a line of champions that has continued for more than a century. Names like Sir Doug Nicholls, Eddie Jackson, Billy Muir, Robbie Muir, Shadrach James Junior, Andrew Walker, Nathan Lovett-Murray, Jarrod Atkinson, Djaran Whyman, Chris Egan and Jy Simpkin are standouts who played at the top AFL level. The Invincibles also produced stars such as Bobby McDonald, Lynch Cooper and George Nelson in running and Barney Walker in boxing. The team gave the people of Cummera great pride. As well as fielding football and cricket teams and many champion foot-runners, Cummeragunja held an annual sports carnival at Christmas that included bike riding, woodchopping and athletic events. The women fielded a cricket team.

The Invincibles story provided the impetus for the current Rumbalara Football Netball Club in Shepparton, which has teams competing in local and regional competitions. The club has won a total of twenty premierships between its various football and netball divisions and has become a hub for the Yorta Yorta community in the region, fielding thirteen teams with over 250 young people participating from week to week.

~

The walk-off was a desperate action by a community who loved their home. Even when they were not living on Cummera, Yorta Yorta people and residents were always coming back there. Men often had to leave in order to find seasonal work and would then come back to support their family. Generations of people who grew up at Cummera and spent their lives elsewhere are buried there in accordance with traditional customs of returning to the Country of your Dreaming.

Cummera's legacy is one of survival and continuity as well as pride and determination. The increased numbers of Yorta Yorta people who have come back to the reserve to live demonstrate that in many ways, the Yorta Yorta and former residents never completely left. However, there is a contradiction: Cummeragunja was a home that Yorta Yorta people were forced on to, but that they chose to fight for when it was taken away from them. Then the authorities controlled their lives so much that they decided to leave. Under the tyrannical rule of McQuiggan, a productive and exemplary farm in its heyday had turned into more of a concentration camp.

In 1988, as we marked 200 years since the British invasion, we also celebrated the fiftieth anniversary of the walk-off, calling our event the 'Walk On'. In 2009 it was repeated for the seventieth anniversary and in 2019 for the eightieth. These re-enactments are a reminder of our people's determination to reclaim Cummeragunja as part of our ancestral heritage and our ongoing struggle for land rights and human dignity.

The historic walk-off of 1939 brought unprecedented press attention and debate in the NSW, Victorian and federal parliaments. In 1940 the NSW Government replaced the Aborigines Protection Board with the Aborigines Welfare Board, which resulted in a change in policy direction from protection to assimilation into mainstream society, where Aboriginal people were to be assisted in housing, education and employment. In reality, however, there was little, if any, support and those people who moved from Cummera ended up on the fringes of local towns or camping on the riverbanks or near rubbish dumps. It was on one of those riverbanks that I was born.

PART II

From Riverbank to Town Life

5

Riverbank Mooroopna

I was born on 16 March 1943. My birth certificate records my parents' residential address as 'Riverbank Mooroopna'. It may seem strange—even unusual—for someone's birthplace to be given as a riverbank. Remember, however, that before I came along, it is true that thousands of generations of our people were born on the riverbanks of Yorta Yorta Country. If we factor that into our timeline of history (60,000 BP), there were some 2,400 generations of Yorta Yorta people born on Country before me. Gently delivered into the loving hands of their mothers and carers, they grew up as proud Yorta Yorta people. There were rituals to celebrate the arrival of newborns onto Country that continued at Maloga and Cummera to the mid-twentieth century and beyond. Women had their own midwives to help in the delivery and care of children.

The names of those dear souls are still remembered in the community today. We will never forget dhama winyarrn like Aunty Nora Nicholls Charles. Dear Aunty Nora's name is revered in our oral history for her loving care in delivering many of the babies on Cummera. She told me about her life on Cummera as a midwife and about the babies she delivered in her time:

> Trevor Morgan was born in a bag humpy,[1] that's where I delivered him, in a bag humpy. I delivered forty babies at Cummera [laughs]. Georgie and Brenda [Nelson] were my babies. I did midwifery for seven years. I used to always take the girls into Doctor Graham [Echuca] to see if I could handle it. And if I couldn't he'd order them

> into the hospital then. He didn't care what matron said, because I wasn't qualified you see. And he was thinking of me, and if the patient was all right, he said 'Oh, you can manage it, but if you want me, he said, ring me and I'll come out'. I managed all right, but this is what used to go on those days. I used to go up to the punt, to those bag humpies up there—[some of the children] were born in a bag humpy at the punt. But I used to be across the river on stormy nights in the little boats and up the river, down the bend, in those days. I didn't mind, I liked the job. They were too shy to go to the hospital. The last manager stopped me from doing the job and he said, 'They'll have to go in there [hospital] now.'[2]

I was privileged to share some of Aunty Nora's warm, caring spirit when I was growing up in Itchica. She was a regular visitor to our family. My grandmother Nanny Lou shared many stories with her about dear old Cummera, with a melancholic longing for the old days. Lola James (a great-granddaughter of Granny Kitty) told me:

> Granny Kitty and her daughter Ada Cooper were also well-known midwives at Maloga and had a lot of knowledge of traditional medicines. Granny Ada delivered both white and Aboriginal babies. There was a white doctor who used to go to the mission, but he always called Granny Ada in to give him a hand. If he had a white mother to deliver that he was worried about, he'd send a rider to the mission to give Granny Ada a horse to come and help.[3]

My birth was different. My mother had already given birth to three children before me: Dimpsie, Fay and Clive. With Mooroopna Hospital being only a stone's throw from the river camp, my mother chose to have me there. And with me in her arms, she returned not to a comfortable house in Mooroopna with running water and equal comforts, but to our fringe-camp riverbank address.

The riverbank on the flood plain between Mooroopna and Shepparton, which we called the Flat, is where my life and entry into the Yorta Yorta world began. We lived on the edge of gubbah (white people) society, seeking freedom and liberty from segregation and reserve life. I enjoyed living there with my cousins and family. The memories of the Flat culture have stayed with me. I certainly take pride in knowing that the riverbank is my place of birth.

Before I tell you about my childhood, I want to tell you why the Flat is an important part of our history. It is linked with other Yorta Yorta cultural sites and is directly connected with Cummeragunja. People moved to the Flat after the walk-off. Moving there was a chance for our people to regroup. Having to leave their home place of Cummera was a heartbreaking experience. The Flat would have been chosen because of its significance as a traditional gathering place for clan groups. Like many of the traditional camp sites along the river systems, the Flat was culturally important and part of the enormous timeline of Yorta Yorta occupation and use of traditional lands. It provided food, fresh water and forestry materials for establishing a community.

Growing up in a fringe camp like the one on the Flat taught me many things. I became acutely aware of the separate worlds that divided Koori kids from gubbah kids, and the wealth and privilege those kids enjoyed. Why were we treated differently to gubbah kids, who never had to justify their daily existence? Why didn't we have shoes and nice clothes and a proper home to live in? Why were we camped on the fringe and not living in town? Questions like these constantly challenged my thinking and sense of being. Deeper insights came as the hunger for knowledge grew within me.

The courageous freedom fighters of Cummera had helped to bring about some change in government policy. That policy had used the word 'protection' to justify decisions to segregate and control Aboriginal people through the reserve system. It changed in 1937 from protection to assimilation. This meant Aboriginal people were to be assisted to transition from the reserves to town life. Governments were supposed to provide housing, health, education and employment services for Aboriginal people—things that white people enjoyed and many took for granted.

Aboriginal people were ambivalent about the new policy of assimilation. Although they believed they were entitled to government services, 'assimilation' was seen as an attempt to erase their culture through the process of cultural absorption. As Uncle Doug Nicholls said in 1969, 'Let us enter your society on our terms, living side by side with you but remaining at all times a cultural group with our own proud identity.'[4]

Uncle Doug certainly put identity politics on the map there and then and was way ahead of his time.

At this time, many Aboriginal people were pushed off the reserves onto the edges of white society. Racist attitudes in the broader community denied them housing and equality: there weren't too many white people who wanted us living next door to them in towns. As one can imagine, living on the Flat under those conditions and external factors created of inequality and racial tension made life very difficult.

The prejudice and hostility towards Aboriginal people moving into towns was palpable. In 1957, the McLean Inquiry found out about the Flat's isolation and impoverished conditions and challenged the morality and humanity of local governments and township residents.[5] Families living on the Flat were not getting basic human rights and entitlements. They could not get unemployment benefits, maternity bonuses or age pensions. The Flat being a fringe camp showed that the assimilation policy was a dismal failure and had not helped Aboriginal people transition from the reserves into mainstream society. It was one of the many disasters of governments' policies on Aboriginal affairs.

It is significant that the Flat was on the edge of two of the most prosperous towns in the Goulburn Valley, Mooroopna and Shepparton. The location itself created a public awakening.

~

Despite all this going on around us, it was an unforgettable experience growing up on the Flat. One thing we learned very quickly was the need for solidarity. We learned the value of 'brother's sister's keeper' protection.[6] We learned to stick together as a close-knit kinship group. Indeed, it was a powerful survival mechanism.

I lived on the Flat until I was seven. Growing up there left me with much to reflect on—the good, the bad and the ugly all rolled into one narrative. As kids we had a sense of freedom and enjoyment of the river and the bush. We could go hunting. We visited our relatives, who looked after us like our own parents. We could swim in the river. We went to school together as one mob in solidarity.

Some of the elders taught us how to find bush tucker. They taught us how to get witchetty grubs from the trees. We would bring them back and cook them on the coals; when cooked, they tasted like almonds and were very moreish. In my later studies of traditional food nutrition, I found that a witchetty grub is equivalent to the calory intake of a pork chop. I forget how many we ate each time, but I know they were a regular and nutritious protein source.

We supplemented our food intake with rabbits and sometimes a kangaroo, and there were plenty of fish and crayfish in the Kaiela River. The bush tucker foods were complemented by fruit that families brought home from working in local orchards and canneries. Plenty of apricots, clingstone peaches and pears were added to our bush food. It was a healthy diet for young active fellas growing up on the Flat. I don't think anyone went without, and the cultural protocol of sharing and caring helped to balance the food distribution.

Looking back, I can see that the Flat was a place of its own character and making. All the houses were made of bush timber and second-hand materials. Kerosene tins were flattened out and used for cladding. The walls were lined with potato and flour bags, painted with a mixture of paint and flour made into a pasty white liquid. The number of people living together in tin-hut humpies as an extended family group on average was up to twelve. This included your parents, brothers and sisters, cousins and grandparents, and sometimes an aunty and uncle.

Living spaces would be partitioned off with hessian bags for sleeping and living quarters. We all slept in small beds. Sometimes there would be two or three in one bed, sleeping head to foot. The floors were just hard dirt, but they were clean, tidy places. The women kept the houses clean and we would always be sweeping the yard outside with gum-leaf branches used as brooms. My cousins were meticulous with this. They kept the hut neat and tidy by sprinkling water on the ground to keep the dust down.

There were many amazing people on the Flat who stood out for the way they adapted their survival skills to the imposed conditions of life. One old fella who fascinated us as kids was a tribal man by the name of Alfred Bull. We called him Old Bull. He was a long-grass man who camped on his own in the bush. I remember him when we sat around the fire at night. He liked his tobacco and would light his cigarette by grabbing a hot coal between his toes from the edge of the fire and lifting it out. Like his ancestors before him he never wore shoes, and his feet were so hardy and tough he could walk over hot coals. He always slept in the long grass. As kids we were always on watch for where he might be camped. Sometimes we used to see him on our way to school in the morning, sleeping with one leg propped over the other sticking out of the grass. He would be lying back in peace enjoying the freedom of his surrounds and the singing of the lovely birdlife.

Old Bull was an iconic figure in the Flat camp. He provided free entertainment and always kept us on the alert for what his next trick might be. There were many other talented people who could sing, play the guitar or spin a yarn. They helped to keep the spirit of the camp alive and together as one.

Certain rules helped to keep the unity of family life. We younger members were guided by our elders, who made sure we did our daily duties for the upkeep of the Flat. There were strict rules that included keeping up the fresh water supply for the community and helping to collect bush materials for the huts. There was no pipeline from the main town supply, so we had to develop our own system. Our elders put 44-gallon drums along the bank and our job was to keep them full. We did this by bucketing the water from the river with a rope-pulley system. The bucket would run down the rope into the river, and when it filled, we pulled it back up. The elders kept a close eye on us to make sure the drums were full, since they were the only fresh water supply for the community. The bucket-and-pulley system was sufficient and provided good exercise for us young, energetic lads living on the edge.

The physical and hunting activity helped us to develop natural muscle definition. It also kept us fit for playing sport and for physical work in the fruit industry. The solidarity of working together and contributing to community wellbeing also helped us to develop important leadership skills. Indeed, our survival was dependent on keeping the old ways of communal life going. The value of sharing and caring for each other got us through some rather trying times.

~

The kids from the Flat went to the local Mooroopna Primary School. That's where I started my formal education. The fact that we walked to and from school from the bush with no shoes was something the gubbah kids quickly cottoned on to. I'm sure they would have loved to do the same—but it was bloody cold in the winter.

Our forebears being largely denied proper education made us the first generation of kids to enter the public school system. Racism was mostly in our faces. Some teachers tried to deal with the reality of race relations, but others left it in the too-hard basket. The idea of Aboriginal studies and cultural awareness in the school curriculum was non-existent, and the humiliating experience of stereotypical images of Aboriginality coming at you was a constant. Being called 'dirty blacks from the Flat' was a common taunt that we took home from school. We were fortunate, however, that our families were a close-knit group who were always around for support.

My mother shared with me her experience of the hard times and the happy times on the Flat, and the value of helping each other to get by when hardship and racial barriers confronted residents trying to gain economic equality. She talked about how prejudice affected the kids going to school:

> We lived on the Flat when we first moved to Mooroopna and that's when the women were working in the cannery. We were able to support our families with the work we found, and in those days when we were on the Flat, we never had the conveniences like today. We used to have to come home from work and bucket water up from the river to do our washing. They were real hard times, but we were happy and used to help each other.
>
> [The Flat was where] they were prejudiced against [us]. The children going to school had problems and they used to come home upset and say that the white kids would be calling them names and throwing their colour up to them. They were always coming home with a problem saying that they had a fight with someone over their colour. Mr Gallagher was the schoolteacher there then and he was a fine man who tried to prevent a lot of the sorts of attitudes that kids had when our children first started going to school. We grew up with

his own children and they mixed in with us. My two brothers George and Keith Nelson played football with them.[7]

I moved off the Flat when I was seven but can still picture my mother and father and relatives there in the camp on the riverbank. Mum worked on her feet all day in the cannery, coming home to wash and cook for a large family, while my father worked in the forests cutting wood and shearing sheep to make ends meet.

Mum had the courage to support us when we faced racism. Her message to us was always 'You're as good as them'. She also passed on to us that we must stand up for ourselves and fight racism.

Racism at school and in the town was deeply entrenched. It manifested at different levels and was always at the back of your neck. Being relegated to the status of fringe dwellers, excluded from the social and economic fabric of the town, was in itself a blatant act of racism. And it was entrenched in government policy. Uncle Shady (Shadrach James) nailed it in a letter he wrote to the minister for home affairs in 1932:

> The whole attitude of the white man towards the Aborigine has all along been to dispirit, to humiliate him, to extinguish his self-respect; in short to kill his hope. To his natural disabilities the white man has added other disabilities, which make the conditions of life very hard for him, and the very atmosphere in which he lives seems hostile and they have no will to live.[8]

Our own personal space and security were supported by the degree of respect we gained for ourselves as a group. The Flat mob were exceptionally talented performers in sport, and many became champion boxers, footballers, runners or cricketers. This gained a degree of respect and allowed for many lasting relationships to be forged with gubbah kids and community members. It was a long way from formal reconciliation, but some big chips were being knocked off along the way.

Lots of work went into addressing racism during our time on the Flat. Many of our wonderful leaders didn't take a back step when calling it out. This helped to expose the damaging effect of racism in the public eye, which in turn inspired us as the younger generation to stay strong.

~

Life on the Flat was a hard slog. People living there had come from the reserve without trade qualifications and did not have access to mainstream services. At the time, the Goulburn Valley enjoyed the economic status of being the 'food bowl' of the nation. This was a key factor in the migration of families from Cummera to the region after the walk-off. The labour force from the Flat provided the backbone of the local farming and fruit industry. Employers needed Aboriginal people to work in these and other labouring industries.

Aboriginal workers made a significant contribution to the social, economic and cultural fabric of the towns and to the regional economy. Men from the Flat found seasonal work picking fruit and cutting timber, while women found work in the canneries. Cannery work was hard. The women were forced to stand all day at a conveyor belt full of fruit, using a small tool to take the stones out. The women in the canneries faced a lot of hostility. My grandmother Priscilla Nelson James shared with me her stories about the lack of equal pay and employment discrimination:

> When we left Cummera we moved to Mooroopna, but we couldn't get a house, and we went down and camped on the river. But they were so hostile here in Mooroopna towards us. They didn't want us blacks to be working in the cannery … the manager at the cannery … was hostile towards us. Then it came! Uncle Shady was such a clever boy, you know! He got in touch with them [the cannery owners] down in Melbourne, and they called them up and they had a big meeting down there, and they said to Shady [who had given them the names of the people who were put off]: 'You go right back to Mooroopna, and you tell them there at the cannery to reinstate them at once', and they would be in touch with the manager.
>
> Next day Shady brought the news and we all went in a body to the cannery. Oh, and they came out all being really nice to us, saying, 'Oh yes, come on what work would you like to do?' and we went back there and never had any more trouble. It was Shady who got it fixed up in Melbourne for us. They wrote to the cannery and said, 'You reinstate those women immediately, they're just as good as any white woman you've got working in that cannery.' And then after we went there and worked and my goodness, we were the best workers in the cannery! We always got first preference after that. Those early days on the Flat settled deep in people's hearts and minds.[9]

Uncle Shady followed the path of his father in higher education and studied law at the University of Melbourne. Like his father, too, he was very active in justice matters and represented his people on many legal and political issues. To the local Aboriginal people, he became spokesman, lobbyist, legal adviser and letter writer. His work for Aboriginal women in the canneries is a hallmark of his brilliant advocacy skills. The cannery issue is one of the many political struggles he fought with the support of other capable Cummera leaders of the time. He became secretary of the local branch of the Food Preservers' Union of Australia, a position that strengthened his advocacy, and was also vice-president of the Goulburn Valley District Council. His contribution to Aboriginal affairs shines through in a photograph of members of the Australian Aborigines' League. In the photo he is standing proudly in front of the League members with his small briefcase.

In his role as secretary of one of the important Aboriginal organisations that sowed the seeds for Aboriginal justice matters in the early 1930s, Uncle Shady was a brilliant writer and spokesperson for his people, with a vision on truth justice matters that still reverberates in the community. In a letter to Prime Minister Ben Chifley on 2 April 1946, he wrote:

> Life's true worth is not measured by its material resources but by the character of its people and I say to the people of Australia, let not the shocking treatment of the Aborigines as it stands today mar forever your character, but arise, awake, shake off the reproach and shame and be not recreant to your highest duty to protect the people you have so grievously wronged.
> P.S. Would it be possible Sir to meet with the Minister for the Interior and express my views personally on this subject.[10]

As a young lad growing up in Mooroopna and Itchica I was fortunate to listen to and learn from Uncle Shady's charismatic leadership. He is one of the iconic ancestors that inspired my generation in the struggle for racial equality, self-determination and sovereignty in the twentieth century and beyond.

~

Local employers were quick to seize the opportunity of having a readily available labour force. Indeed, many got rich by hiring Aboriginal workers under piecework conditions. Piecework agreements meant that workers were paid according to production rather than set wage conditions, and you had no leave entitlements. Your salary was based on the amount of fruit you picked and the number of cases you filled. The cases, or boxes, were made in connected farms. This way of paying workers made more money for the employer, who would make money selling the fruit without having to pay workers entitlements like annual leave. Nor would the employer have to put money into health and safety measures.

Constable Albert Haag of the Mooroopna police force raised the issue of inequality of Aboriginal workers in his report to the McLean Inquiry, claiming that Aboriginal people were often exploited by local employers.[11] It was ripe time for picking, as they say. This system, with the blackfellas bending their backs for the boss man, was an overpowering image in the plantation labour economy. Nevertheless, it is true that employment in the fruit industry was very much a catch-22. Given the limited opportunities and the barriers, the fruit industry was the only backstop available. Aboriginal people worked long and hard hours on the plantations to support their families. The piecework arrangements suited workers who were good pickers, and they could make good money. My cousins were renowned for their ability to consistently pick large amounts of fruit, and they were paid well during the season. There was a camaraderie between workers, and their Koori humour helped them get through the hard labouring work in the summer heat.

When I was thirteen, I had a summer job on a tomato plantation with my brother Clive. We spent our summer holiday picking tomatoes because we needed money to buy school clothes and books for the next year. There was no Abstudy or education assistance in those days. 'Working for the man' is an experience we often reflect on with mixed feelings. The plantation was owned by a member of the Aborigines Welfare Board. He employed many Aboriginal people on his tomato and box-making estate and was a big powerful man who liked to have control over his workers. The way he used the fear of child removal to control our lives in the plantation system is beyond my sense of humanity. One 40-degree day, me and my cousin chose to go for a swim in the lagoon for relief from the stifling heat of the tomato patch. When we returned, who should be standing waiting for us but the big boss man of the plantation. For seeking relief from the burden of hard labour in the hot sun, he threatened to remove us to a children's home. This frightening memory has stayed with me ever since.

The Aborigines Welfare Board largely consisted of non-Aboriginal people. They were chosen to give advice on local issues and to have input on decisions and policy matters. The Board was the precursor to other larger government bureaucracies that assumed control of Aboriginal affairs at state and federal levels. It had taken over from the Protection Board to carry out the assimilation policy and was responsible for the administration and care of the Flat community. It was constantly watching over the lives and movements of residents. Welfare officers and police often came without invitation to check on people and how they were living.

We were afraid of the welfare agencies and their powers, which included the taking of children. We were painfully aware that children had been forcibly removed from their parents at Cummeragunja under the Protection Board. As mentioned in Chapter 4, my aunty Margaret Nelson had been removed with other girls from Cummera in 1917 and never returned. This left a lasting distrust of government officials.

The fear was ominous and ever present. Child removal continued on the Flat and was reported by the McLean Inquiry in 1957 when former Victorian police magistrate Charles McLean examined the powers of removal under the operations of the *Aborigines Act 1928*. His report stated that 'twenty-four of the younger children were, at the instance of the police, taken from [their] "homes" and committed to the care of the Children's Welfare Department [in Melbourne] by the Children's Court'.[12]

I clearly recall the shock waves that ripped through the hearts of our close-knit community and often think that I was lucky not to be taken. The memory of these heartbreaking experiences remains in the records of the Stolen Generations and the *Bringing Them Home* report of 1997. It was not until 2022 that Victorian survivors of the Stolen Generations received some justice through the state government's

Reparations Package.[13] The forced removal practices remain under scrutiny and are part of the Yoorrook Justice Commission.

~

In 1958, following the McLean Inquiry report about the impoverished conditions of the Flat, residents were rehoused on a transitional housing estate at Rumbalara. This was one of the main recommendations of the report. The houses that were built were small brick dwellings. There is one still standing today, and you can see the twisted thinking that was behind the design and scope of the housing project. Those houses weren't built for decent living and perpetuated the practice of discrimination. After they were built it was discovered that the plan for the estate had neglected to include a laundry, baths or proper washing facilities for residents. The size of the houses was inadequate: they needed to accommodate the average-sized extended family of nine to twelve people but were small, poky places that often ended up overcrowded and without sufficient recreational space. Families had to manage and do the best they could to get by.

When the general public are exposed to the history of the Flat and the administration of Aboriginal affairs in postcolonial Victoria, it is a huge wake-up call. When I'm teaching the Oncountry Learning course, I like to take students to Rumbalara to see and hear the story of the housing project. Their reflections on the mindset of the project range from total shock to bewilderment that such discriminatory policies and utter contempt for humanity could exist.

Rumbalara has grown into one of the major Aboriginal health and community service organisations in Australia. Its name comes from the Yorta Yorta word for 'rainbow'. At the end of the rainbow, as the saying goes, there is a pot of gold. That is the vision that drives Rumbalara's success today. It has gone from a collection of small concrete dwellings to a major organisation that offers health, dental, justice and community service programs and employs over 300 people.

6

Off the Riverbank to Itchica

We moved off the Flat when I was seven. For my parents, moving off the riverbank with a young family and leaving close relatives behind was a big decision. The isolation and conditions of the Flat were one thing, but the key factor was the lack of proper infrastructure. Local towns were privileged to enjoy such infrastructure and took it for granted. The paternalistic overlordship of the Welfare Board forced people to find other alternatives, if they could.

My family was fortunate to have the resources to move from the Flat to the township of Echuca. This came about through the efforts of both my parents, particularly my father's shearing skills. My father, Clive Atkinson, and my grandfather Henry Atkinson were both top shearers. Puppa Henry saw the transition in shearing technology from the blade to the handpiece—I think it was called the bogey in shearing language. It was a heavy piece of machinery with combs and cutter blades that you held in your hand all day.

Puppa was a gun shearer, renowned for his strength and ability. As a shearer, he was known as Harry Atkinson and was the head ringer in all the sheds of the district. For many Aboriginal shearers, the ability to shear quality and quantity was a meal ticket to substantive equality and greater acceptance. Moreover, it was a skill revered by sheep station owners.

The owner of Moira Station who came after O'Shannassy was Franc Falkiner, in 1899. He was quick to capitalise on the deadly shearing skills of Puppa Henry. Uncle Fred Walker told me the story of Puppa's shearing ability at a contest at the Moira Station shearing shed. In its heyday, it was one of the bigger sheds, he said, with a 'fifteen men stand'. Before that, when shearing was done with the old single-blade tool, it was much bigger. Uncle Fred recalled: 'One of the best shearers was Henry Atkinson who was backed by Falkiner, who put 50 quid on Puppa Henry to compete against anyone anywhere for quantity and quality.'[1] In those days £50 was a lot of money to put up for a shearing contest. By today's calculation, it would be thousands of dollars. I never got to the bottom of the story of the winner, but I know that Uncle Freddy had a lot of faith in Puppa Henry's ability. I'm pretty sure he would have backed him all the way.

Shearing was a skilled trade that many men from Cummera picked up through their work on the pastoral stations. Some of the larger stations, like Moira, Madowla and Perricoota, benefited greatly from the labour and domestic services of people from Cummeragunja. Aboriginal shearers mastered this skilled trade and were in constant demand. Unlike in other labour industries of the time, Aboriginal shearers were able to get equal pay for their work. It was probably the only industry where an equal wage was a due entitlement for Aboriginal workers. They could compete equal to, if not better than, their gubbah counterparts when they stepped onto the board. In shearing language, the board is the platform on which the actual shearing takes place in the shed. Once you were on that board, you were entitled to be treated equally. There was no preference or special treatment; you were one with all comers, as the saying goes. It was a different story when you stepped down from the board into public life, but when you were there, you were entitled to the same respect and payment per sheep as other shearers. This could be substantial if you were a top shearer. Cummera shearers gained a good reputation for quality and quantity shearing, which increased demand for them in the industry.

Many of the top Cummera shearers left a legacy that is continued by their offspring. That is the case in our family and many others. There was a code of ethics that shearers worked by, and this was strengthened by the Australian Workers' Union, which supported equal wage justice for Aboriginal shearers. Some of our leaders, like Uncle William Cooper and Jack Patten, were key advocates for Aboriginal workers' rights of the time, through active union leadership. Uncle Fred told me many stories about Cummera shearers, praising how deadly they were. He named the Atkinsons, Coopers, Walkers and Morgans as top shearers, adding that they were also pretty to watch: 'They were all good shearers. They all made good money too! Yes, they would buy a new horse or get a couple of new wheels for their buggy so they could travel around the sheds. Some of the men would also find work harvesting when the crops were ready.'[2]

Uncle Fred's description of being 'pretty shearers' to watch is a quaint image. It turns the trade into a spectacle, watching shearers go head-to-head. I picture him sitting back admiring their abilities. And, of course, he was related to those top shearers. He was a gentle and caring man himself, and I enjoyed spending time with him sharing and recording his stories.

~

My parents wanted better conditions and opportunities for our family, including the right to housing and education. They heard of residential land available for purchase in Echuca South. The story goes that my father hopped on his bike and rode from Mooroopna to Itchica—over 70 kilometres each way, most of which was a dirt track! With the money saved from their shearing and cannery work, he and Mum purchased two small blocks of land in Premier Street, not far from the Yakoa wala. Having purchased the land from a local real estate agent, Dad rode his bike back to the Flat to organise our move. We didn't have transport at the time, so they must have engaged someone with a vehicle to take us from Mooroopna to Itchica.

The land transaction was not an inherent native title right or a grant of land based on prior rights: it was a freehold title purchased from hard-earned cash. My father never took a backward step in reminding people of the treacherous history of land ownership by the British Crown. Of course, he didn't know the language of land rights at that time, but in terms of moral justice for land theft he wasn't backward in coming forward for what he believed.

Our father built the family house in Itchica using skills he had learned at Cummera, where most of the houses were built by Aboriginal people. Our home was an important stepping stone for our family. We were among the first generations of Aboriginal people to move into the towns after the walk-off and the fringe camps. After a century of being excluded from towns, segregated on reserves and seen as inferior, this was a huge change for our people. Does it seem strange to you that the whole community of Cummera people had been banished from society for generations because of discrimination? It was certainly a puzzle to my generation, one that would later take me around the world looking for answers. But for now, the question was whether we would be welcome in the towns. It was the destiny of our family to overcome the obstacles and make a go of living in gubbah society, and Mum was just the woman to take on this challenge head-on and succeed.

Our home also provided accommodation for my grandparents Puppa Henry and Nanny Lou, who had camped on the riverbank at Barmah after the walk-off. My parents were conscious of their needs as elders. When elders lived within a family group, they shared stories and passed on knowledge. I was blessed to have this experience when our various grandparents lived with us, including my great-grandmother Granny Mag Nelson, a Waveroo person of the Upper Murray region. After her marriage to Henry Harmony Nelson, she lived on Cummeragunja in Yorta Yorta Country. She lived with us in Itchica until she passed in 1952 in her late eighties.

Puppa Henry and Nanny Lou had no means of support on the riverbank except for what Puppa could bring in from his fishing and leeching skills. Being a sharp-eyed bushman, he was able to find work catching leeches in the wetlands, which enabled him to bring in some money after he retired from shearing. The bloodsucking leeches were in demand for medical treatment in hospitals, where doctors used them as an alternative for treating infections, and for draining fluids from injuries. The leeches were put on the affected area and would suck the blood or fluid from the injury, eventually dropping off dead once they were full of the infected fluid. This was a valued method of treatment in the medical profession.

Puppa developed a clever technique for catching the leeches. He rubbed fish fat on both sides of a flat board to attract them. When the board was placed on the water, leeches would gravitate to the bottom side of it. Puppa would flip the board over to scrape off the leeches. While they were being scraped off, more leeches would be sticking to the other side of the fatty board. It was an innovative double-sided technical operation that ensured continuous scraping of leeches off the board. The leeches were emptied into a stocking with a wire rim that stopped them from escaping. Once the stocking was full, it would be sent off to the local hospital for distribution to the major hospitals. Long and firm nylon stockings were an important commodity for the leeching industry. I don't know where Puppa got his from, but he seemed to have a regular supply and managed his small enterprise with grace and fortitude.

A photo of Puppa Henry in the limelight during his leeching career is illuminating. It makes us admire his bush skills and his capacity to seize opportunities when they arose. He made the best of them. The leeching trade also takes us into the natural diversity of the forest wetlands and the adaptive skills of our people. They were quick to use traditional and adaptive strategies for harvesting river resources like fish, wildlife and other bush tucker.

My father told me that Puppa Henry was a very strong man for his size, weight and age. He was renowned for his strength in hitting the 'high striker' contest at shows. This was a strongman attraction at public events like the yearly Boxing Day carnival in Itchica. It has a lever with one end holding a puck attached to a tower with a bell at the top; contestants strike the other end using a sledgehammer. The aim is to try and send the puck to the top of the tower. If the lever is struck with enough force, the puck rises high enough to hit the bell. Operators traditionally enticed people to try their luck on the high striker with language like: 'Step right up and test your strength!' or 'This is a test that separates the men from the boys'.

It was on this call, I'm told, that Puppa Henry would step up to the plate. He was able to hit the puck and ring the bell every time, sometimes even damaging the puck with his awesome power. I've seen the high striker mechanism in action at many Boxing Day carnivals and always imagine the accolades Puppa would have got for ringing the bell so many times. That would have been a hard act to follow. Go, Puppa Henry—you were a legend of your time.

~

The family home in Premier Street was small beginnings, and the extended family soon increased to eleven people, including Puppa Henry and Nanny Lou. Life was moving on and there were now seven children. They included Dimpsie and Fay from Mum's first marriage, who were living in Mooroopna with their Nanny Priscilla, and Clive Junior, me, Marlene, Veronica and Graham from our father, Clive Auldenby Atkinson Senior.

It was a cultural tradition to carry the names of our ancestors. We inherited middle names from our grandparents. Dimpsie Albert was from his father's first name; Fay Priscilla was from her grandmother Priscilla James; Clive Henry was from Puppa's first name; Wayne Roderick was from Puppa's middle name; Marlene Lorraine was from her Aunty Lorraine; Veronica Odette was from her Aunty Lula; Graham John was from his Uncle John; and so on.

After the extended family settled into the new abode, our father saw the need to build a larger home on the front part of the land. He worked on the building himself and got help from other workers he knew in the neighbourhood. In a rather uncanny twist of neighbourhood diplomacy, my father was able to negotiate the purchase of the front room of the house across the road, which was being renovated. His grand plan was to detach that room and reconnect it to the new building on our block. Moving the room across the road was done by wooden rollers and jacks and a lot of heavy lifting. It was an awesome task and remains a vivid memory for us kids. We sat on the floor of the room with excitement as it moved slowly across the road. 'Hey, look we're moving!' we would shout as it travelled to its new abode. After much sweat and labour, the room was attached and became the front room of our home. It accommodated the family and was our entry point to Itchica mainstream society from the Flat on the Mooroopna riverbank.

We always kept in touch with our relatives on the Flat. About eight years after we left, in 1958, they were moved to the transitional housing estate at Rumbalara (see Chapter 5). Some were accommodated in a low-rent housing estate in Mooroopna. These were commonly known as 'Commission houses' and were provided by the government for low-income families. Many of our people are still living in Commission houses today. In the transition from the fringe to mainstream society, the gap in Aboriginal socio-economic status narrowed marginally, but there were still many living in poverty conditions.

Other changes started taking place in the family structure as we settled in Itchica. In the early 1950s, my father found a small place for Puppa Henry and Nanny Lou to live: a small wooden cottage in Hovell Street, Echuca East, with a stove and a red-brick chimney. This little pad had a profound effect on my life as an Atkinson sibling. I developed a close and loving relationship with Puppa and Nanny and went to live with them in the early 1950s. I was around nine then, and in primary school at Echuca 208. I think they pulled me their way for comfort and care under their eldership status. Moving between family groups, living with cousins on the Flat and spending time with your grandparents was nothing new to our cultural way of life.

At the time, I didn't think it was going to be for so long, but as it turned out I did not fully return home to my family until I was thirteen and at Echuca Technical School. Over that time I kept in touch, returning to Premier Street for short stays. It was in the loving care of Puppa and Nanny, however, that I was nurtured. I returned home for good when Nanny was called back to the eternal Dreamtime in 1956, four years after Puppa's passing.

Puppa and Nanny's home in Echuca East was an old weatherboard house with a rusty tin roof that often leaked. There was no electricity, but it had a wood stove and an open fireplace in the lounge. At night we lit a kerosene lantern and candles for some light. A rusty old iron was parked on the side of the open fire, and I would use it to iron my clothes for school the next day. There was no TV or radio—we would just sit around yarning and listening to stories by the fireplace. For a while Nanny Lou had a relative staying with us from Coranderrk. Her name was Aunty Lou Edmunds, and she was a quiet soul who kept to herself much of the time. She often yarned with Nanny Lou in language, which would have been a mix of Dja Dja Wurrung and Woiwurrung they had learned from their ancestral Country. It was lovely to listen to them yarning away in the lingo, as we say.

Nanny Lou would often visit her relatives at Coranderrk. Her sister Caroline Morgan had lived there after moving from Dja Dja Wurrung Country, but passed in 1938, before I was born. This was after the Loddon Aboriginal Protectorate Station at Franklinford in central Victoria closed in around 1850 and the surviving Dja Dja Wurrung people were moved to Coranderrk. There was a close relationship between Cummera and Coranderrk before and after colonisation, and in 1982 I was able to follow up these connections in my research and record some stories in my oral history project.

Nanny had other regular visitors who would come and stay. I remember a man by the name of Mer deen, who I think was an Indian hawker. He used to come and park his horse and cart in the block next door. Many of his people were travelling around doing odd jobs like sharpening knives and scissors, and selling haberdashery. Mer deen would come and sit on the back verandah with his bubble pipe. I would watch him closely, fascinated by the pipe bubbling as he took long draws of smoke and then puffed it into the air where it twirled and disappeared. I don't know what the old fella was putting into that pipe other than tobacco, but it had a nice aromatic smell. I was often tempted to try it out while he was away, but I never did—I was frightened I might get caught and scolded by him or Nanny.

This story reflects the deep sharing and caring nature of Nanny Lou. She welcomed visitors who were adjusting to the new and distant world of Australia. Some of the Indian travellers gravitated to the edges of the reserves, where they set up camps and cooked food. My mother told us stories of the attractive smell of curried food that drifted across the reserve, and about the rotis they cooked on a hotplate, which were like our damper bread. I know that some of the Indian travellers married Yorta Yorta people and had families who are prominent members of the community today. I don't know what happened to Mer deen, a gentle soul of no fixed abode who left a vivid impression on me. The bubbling pipe on Nanny's back verandah and the aromatic smoke floating through the air are part of a legendary story of kindness and sharing.

My life with Puppa Henry and Nanny Lou was a profound experience that shaped my identity, my sense of being and my life. Puppa was such a gentle man, with so much cultural wisdom and knowledge. Coming from the bush where he was born in the Moira Forest in 1870, he had plenty of quality time to spend with me when I was a child. Nanny Lou took me into her arms—some of my family say she spoilt me a bit. I think I also tested the boundaries of freedom there, compared to a home in which my parents held a tighter but still caring rein on us kids.

I did stretch the boundaries too far when I spent a day on the river hunting and fishing in preference to school. This is when I would often return to the family home for short stays. I nearly broke Nanny's dear heart when I wagged school and turned up on her doorstep for protection instead of going home and having to face the switch. I would be covered in dirt from the bush and hungry, but she couldn't let me stay: she was bound by my parents' rules about school and had to send me home. I remember my sorrow in having to leave and go home to face the music. As I walked away, I waved to Nanny as she stood next to the mailbox on the fence line. Her lovely grey hair and face still come to me. She waved goodbye with her gentle hands as I turned the corner for home, and I waved back with tears in my eyes. When I returned, Nanny Lou said, 'Don't you ever do that to me again, son, it broke my heart. After you left, I went inside and cried my heart out for having to send you away.'

This was a big wake-up call for me. I was mortified and sought repentance for stretching the boundaries so far without proper care for her love and kindness. It was a shame job on me and one that I never forgot, a big lesson learned about respect, care and compassion for our elders.

Nanny Lou taught me many things about being humble and caring towards others, particularly our loved ones. She sang beautiful lullabies in language to put me to sleep. And I remember the smell of Puppa's old flannel shirt when he would tell me stories. They would send me to sleep, and Nanny would come and gently pick me up and put me in her bed for the night.

Many of my early growing-up days were filled with stories of the old tribal times hunting for bush tucker and ghost stories about sinister creatures that lurked in the bush, like the hairy becker, which sent shivers up my back. 'Don't go to those places at night or the hairy becker will get you!' was the underlying message. This was a common trait of blackfella culture wherever I travelled. The dooligah, the hairy becker and the gidatji man had intrinsic powers. These were social control messages designed to keep you safe and inside when it got dark. I remember huddling together with brothers and sisters on our way home in the dark and our bikes hitting the wall as we raced to get inside, frightened of the hairy becker.

Living in town was a big change for the elderly people. They had grown up living off the fat of the land and the rivers. The variety of bush tucker from the forest wetlands in Yorta Yorta Country was reliable and bountiful, and many of the old people who moved into towns pined for their traditional foods. Puppa Henry kept in touch with the old ways and was able to get the bush tucker he liked. One of his favourites was the turtle. In Yorta Yorta law you can't eat the long-neck turtle because it is one of our totems. You can only eat the short-neck, which Puppa would bring home and cook in the oven. Nanny Lou would freak out. 'Puppa, take that turtle out of there, it's stinking the house out,' she would say. The transition from traditional cooking methods in the open fire pit to cooking inside in the oven put her on edge. The smell soon settled, however, when the turtle was ready to eat, and the nourishment of the turtle helped to calm the storm of it being cooked inside the house.

To cook the turtle, Puppa taught me to wait until you could hear the breastplate crack in the oven. The cracking sound indicated that it was cooked. This tucker, Puppa told me on many occasions, would grow hairs on your chest. I always kept a tab on that yarn and eventually found out it was true. We are all hairy sorts of fellas in one way or the other.

When the turtle came out of the oven you didn't need a plate, you just rolled it over on its back and ate it off the shell. There were special parts that were called thunder and lightning—these are the glands in the four quarters of the turtle's body. They are full of bitter brine and you must pick them out before you eat the highly nutritious djitiga.

While I'm writing this, my mouth waters for the taste of freshwater turtle and I empathise with the way our elders pined for their traditional foods when they moved into towns. The nutrition, flavour and nourishment of the turtle is an example of the variety and abundance of traditional foods that have sustained our people from time immemorial.

~

Puppa was a wonderful teacher. He would take me to places where he explained the behaviour of insects such as ants, including how they get food and how you could read changes in the weather from watching their movements. He also told me stories of when he was the head stockman on Moira Station in Franc Falkiner's time. His job was to ride the station boundary, keep an eye out for predators of the stock, and check the fences. At the end of the journey, he would report any problems or damage to the station overseer. The station covered a large area, and he would camp at different places along the way where he knew he could get bush tucker. One of his favourites was the Gulpa River, an anabranch of Dungula and the northern boundary of the station. This was near Mathoura, where his mother Louisa was born, and he used to visit. These were treasured stories that I kept in my mind and followed up when I was older. I used to like visiting the places he told me about and where he would have camped, to get a feel for his presence on Country.

Puppa kept in close touch with his cousins who also moved to Itchica from Cummera. When he wanted to visit someone, he would say to Nanny Lou, for example, 'I'm just going to see Uncle Frank.' Frank was his first cousin on his older brother Bill Atkinson's line. He would hop on his bike, which had a hessian carry bag he'd made for bringing home food and other goodies. He especially liked a drop of sweet fortified wine. Off he would go to a place called Lenny's Gift Wine Shop in Itchica. He would take an empty bottle for a refill and have a sip on it later, making sure he was out of reach of Nanny Lou's sharp eyes. She didn't like goopri at all.

It was 1952 and Puppa was now in his early eighties. Time was catching up with him. The hardworking life as a shearer, stockman and bushman had taken its toll, and his call to the Dreamtime was not far away. It came when he had to go to hospital in Itchica. I went back home while he was there and one night Nanny, Mum and Dad returned from the hospital with the sad news that Puppa had passed. I could hear Nanny Lou wailing her heart out in grief, the pervasive sound of sorry business at Aboriginal funerals. Sorry business has to take its natural course. It allows for the grief to be shared openly with family until it is resolved.

Puppa was buried in Echuca Cemetery in 1952. Nanny was now on her own, still grieving. This gave me more reason to stay and look after her, cutting wood and doing the shopping and other odd jobs around the house. It was hard for her trying to get through the week on a pension. She had to pay rent and buy wood for the kitchen and open fire, food for the week and often clothes for me for school. I wanted to help bring in some money and got a weekend job selling footy guides for the Echuca Football League. On Saturdays before the game I would go around the pubs selling the guide, and after that I would do the boundary umpiring for Echuca South. This gave me an extra five bob as pocket money, and a bit extra to help with Nanny's pension. It was a hard struggle moneywise, and our material possessions were the bare minimum. But the love and care I got from Puppa and Nanny was more than money could ever buy.

One of the special things I enjoyed was the lovely bread and butter pudding that Nanny Lou would cook for me when I got home from school. She used to cook it in an enamel dish, and with great difficulty I still try to make this special pudding. Every pension day she would come and meet me in the park next to the school with pies and lemonade to share. When the school bell rang, I would look across and see her lovely shining white hair as she waited for me in the park with bag in hand. She was tall, always nicely dressed and wore a blue overcoat in the winter, which made her stand out in the crowd.

It took a long while for Nanny to get over Puppa's passing. In the evening she would often have conversations with him, telling me his spirit was restless, still lingering before it returned to the Dreamtime. This continued for some time but eventually ended when Nanny told me with relief that Puppa was finally back home in Yorta Yorta Dreamtime. Little did I know that she would be joining him soon.

After Puppa's passing, Nanny became sick with a disease we called tick toller rue. It was a nasty, painful thing she had to deal with. For relief she would hold a hot water bottle against her face. Sometimes I could hear her groaning in the night from the excruciating pain she was suffering. She eventually had treatment for the condition in Bendigo and recovered. Another bout of ill health came as a shock when she was diagnosed with breast cancer and lost one of her breasts. Her recovery appeared to be going well but the cancer became terminal and she was hospitalised in Itchica. I returned home and used to visit her daily on my way home from school. It was sad to see the cancer taking hold and the sickness making it hard for her to communicate in her loving and jovial way. I visited her up until her passing in 1956, just four years after Puppa. She was buried with him in Echuca Cemetery, together with her twin brother, Alf (Gingo) Morgan, who had died in 1949. All three are buried in the same grave. I said goodbye to Nanny Lou when we saw her in her coffin before the burial. She was at peace, free of pain and ready for her journey back to the Dreamtime. Her beautiful face lying in peace with her lovely shiny silver hair will stay with me forever.

Returning home after Nanny's care to my parents and siblings was a big change. The freedom I had enjoyed under my grandparents came to an end. It was time to knuckle down under my parents' expectations of family life, work and education. I was aware that education was one of the main priorities that had taken us off the Flat, and that the valuing of education went back to Maloga and Cummera where Granpa James was the head teacher. This was where the value and inspiration of education came from, and it continues to influence our family and the Yorta Yorta community today.

7

The Journey of Education

After spending a year of primary school in Mooroopna, I started at Echuca 208 State School when I was seven. Primary school education at 208 Echuca was a new world for Aboriginal kids, particularly when we entered the school grounds. Most of the kids there were of English or Irish background, while other ethnic groups from Greece and Italy had started arriving after World War II. Aboriginal kids were only a small percentage of the population, representing the family groups who had moved to Itchica after the Cummera walk-off.

As a result of the demographic spread of the Aboriginal population in Itchica, it turned out that our family was related to most of the Aboriginal kids we went to school with. This influenced the way you were treated at school and in the classroom. Family groups who moved to Itchica were related on the Atkinson, Walker, Charles, Morgan, Davies, Jackson, Firebrace and Egan lines. They shared ancestral connections with the original ancestors of the Yorta Yorta, Dja Dja Wurrung, Wamba Wamba and Wurundjeri people of Victoria and New South Wales. This included the Moonahcullah Mission near Deniliquin. They had close connections with Cummera through intermarriage, sport and cultural exchanges. Most of the Aboriginal community chose to stick together. This eased the pressure of trying to adjust to the new world surrounded by the pressures of assimilation and systemic racism.

It was a hard slog for Aboriginal kids coming from the reserve system, whose school experiences had been shaped by the segregation policies of the day. Trying to adjust to the town world and concentrate on your learning was a strenuous call. Within the grading system there was a special grade for students who weren't performing well in the general school system. It was mainly for Aboriginal and non-Aboriginal kids who needed more support.

Looking back, I can see more clearly just how the education system was structured in its teaching practices. Aboriginal kids in the special grade were exceptionally talented in the creative fields of art, sport and hands-on work but seemed to have less interest in the formal learning process. They often struggled with school because of the prejudices that other kids and some teachers held towards them. I think the special grade was a more adjustable environment for Aboriginal kids. My experience in Grade 4 brought this home to me. By then I had made friends and managed to hold my own in the school grounds. I sat with non-Aboriginal kids in the early grades. But when I fronted Grade 4, I got a huge shock.

The teacher said, 'No. You can't sit with your friends in this class, you must sit with your cousin.' My cousin was a girl, and we knew each other through our family connections; our grandfathers were brothers on the Atkinson bloodline. Being the only two black kids in the class, we had to sit together, but other kids could sit with their chosen friends. Classes were gender based, and children sat with their own gender. We were the only ones sitting at a mixed-gender desk, not allowed to sit with our own friends. This meant we were the only two in the class who were denied the same rights as the rest of the class, and it was because of our Aboriginality.

When I get a chance to reflect on this experience with my cousin, we always have a good laugh at the two of us sitting there. She reminds me of the teacher's bullying tactics and getting slapped on the head. He was a grumpy old man who not only set us apart but also kept a watch on us. He would hover over us and give me a slap on the head just to let us know he was the boss. I remember confronting him after I left school and asking him why he had treated us that way. He had no comeback and was shaking with remorse—that's where I left it, with some degree of retributive justice.

Battling against the odds at school became nearly an everyday experience for Aboriginal kids. The load you regularly brought home to your parents was seeking relief and emotional support. I was lucky to have strong-minded parents who stood firm on racism and discrimination in or outside of school. My mother was strong and comforting when we brought home hurtful experiences. If it happened at school with a particular teacher or in the schoolyard, she would be there to sort it out. She was a passionate barracker for us on the footy field and was well known there for her voice against vilification. Many people learned quickly not to mess with Mumma Atkinson. She gained a reputation for not taking a back step from racism and for calling it out when it happened. Her passion for justice and freedom from discrimination was equalled by her respect and warmth towards people from all walks of life. This was an important part of our upbringing. Learning how to deal with the hurt that comes with racism required unconditional support. Mum was very proud of her Aboriginality, and she taught us how to deal with racism.

'There must be a better way,' I would say to myself after coming home from school after a bloody encounter with a racist kid. Mum had a way of dealing with racism that she had learned from her own strong family upbringing. She taught us to be proud of our Aboriginality and to look the person in the eye and tell them, 'Yes, I am a blackfella and I'm proud of it.' Turning the racism back on the person and not wearing it yourself was a form of reverse psychology. *It doesn't belong to you; you don't have to wear it; it's the mindset of others and not you.* It is a good social tool, and an effective way of dealing with the put-down nature and effects of racism. I practised this alternative to physical confrontation and found that it helped. However, saying you don't have to wear it by changing your approach is one thing, but the reality is that racism continues to manifest in many negative ways and is deeply entrenched in society.

The rest of my primary schooling wasn't as frightening as Grade 4. Skills that helped me gain greater respect and acceptance came from the creative and sporting fields. Students often revered the artistic abilities of Aboriginal kids and how they could draw and paint and share stories about their history in their artwork. In sport we were some of the best runners and footballers and could hold our own when it came to boxing. I had learned much from my days on the Flat. Many of my cousins were top boxers who went on to become professionals and popular performers in the travelling boxing tents. At the annual Show Day and Boxing Day carnivals, there would be a line of boxers standing up on the board open to being challenged 'for a round or two for a pound or two', as the saying goes. Jimmy Sharman's boxing tent was a major attraction for boxing enthusiasts, and those carnivals were big days for many of our people, who would travel from Cummera and local towns to watch their favourite boxers in action. Most were related to each other and the people attending, which made it like a large extended family gathering.

The footy ground was another sporting arena dominated by Aboriginal kids, who seemed to have an innate ability to excel over and above their opponents. The top players were sought after by local clubs when they finished school. I think our achievements on the sporting field may have affected our performance in school. Sport and creative work were a break for many who found academic learning too alienating. In that context, I made an extra effort to excel in sport rather than in the classroom. Being good at sport gained the attention that came with performing well. Our families gravitated to the sporting events to watch us play. To know that your mob were there to encourage you gave you extra incentive to perform well, and you got an ego boost from the praise that followed.

These days I have students who have written convincing papers on why Aboriginal people are so good at footy. The hand-eye coordination skills and the ability to read the game—often called 'magic'—are talents people admire in Aboriginal players. Whether our footy skills are a carryover from life before colonisation is now being debated.[1] People who write about the sporting ability of Aboriginal players have explored whether this 'magic' stems from the hunter-gatherer lifestyle and our game of Marngrook. Important skills were needed to live closely in tune with their environment and to hunt for food. For survival, you needed a sharp eye and the ability to read Country. Also, hunting and ceremonial performances produced the physical fitness that suits competitive sport. These are skills that could have shaped the ability of Aboriginal people to perform so well.

~

Being in Grade 4 with the racist behaviour of that teacher was one of my worst primary school experiences. But reaching Grade 4 reminded me of my parents' education. They were only allowed to be educated to Grade 3 (8–9-year-old level) under the prevailing Protection Board and Education Department regulations.

My father often shared the frustrations and desire for a better education than what he was restricted to on Cummera. He told me the story of asking his teacher why they weren't allowed the same level of education as white kids in the towns:

> He [the teacher] was only allowed to teach us to 3rd grade. He said, 'You boys would be clever alright, but I'm not allowed to teach you any more than 3rd grade.' He said, 'That's why I've got to send my children across to Barmah School, over to Victoria.' So that's what I found out, that we weren't allowed to be educated any higher than the 3rd grade because it was the rules that teachers had to go by. The people that went to school under Granpa were better educated than us. They didn't want to educate us fellas for some reason. I don't know they might have thought we'd cause trouble or something if we became too aware of the real facts.[2]

My father's frustration at being denied the right of education and his desire for knowledge and empowerment have stayed with me. Becoming aware of the facts showed me the repressive nature of the reserve system. It stayed uppermost in my mind and was one of the incentives for me to study history and human rights at La Trobe University later. Examining the violations of human rights our people suffered on the reserves, including the right to education, became a work in progress for me. Education is a fundamental right that belongs to all people, without distinction of any kind—race, colour, sex, language, religion or political opinion. Our parents not being able to realise the ability that the schoolteacher saw in them was a turning point for my generation because it motivated them to ensure we got the education they had been denied. And it motivated my journey into higher education after primary and secondary schooling.

There was no Aboriginal history taught to us in primary school except for the odd line in Anglo versions of our history. The idea of visiting the rich Yorta Yorta cultural heritage sites of at least 60,000 years was not in the school curriculum. Instead, we got versions of colonial history and stories of Captain Cook 'discovering' Australia. Sometimes when Aborigines were mentioned, the whole class immediately turned to look at you. If you were game enough to challenge the false assumptions of Australian history made by teachers, you were likely to be told to keep quiet or were ignored. Thankfully, there were a few more enlightened teachers who had some contact with Aboriginal people. They listened to Aboriginal stories and helped to balance the degree of knowledge deprivation that existed.

The inclusion of Aboriginal history in school curriculums remained a void for decades. Much of the eventual change came about in the 1970s through the Echuca Aboriginal Co-operative (now Njernda Aboriginal Corporation). Njernda workers and elders pushed for greater inclusion of Aboriginal history and culture, and the employment of teacher aides in schools. They provided support for Aboriginal kids, introduced Aboriginal history and culture into the education program, and took kids to visit Aboriginal places and significant sites. This helped to build confidence in the Aboriginal kids attending school and to raise the level of awareness about local identity and Aboriginal history. My daughter Gabby was a teacher aide at Echuca Primary School for a while, which was a challenging experience for her.

~

Thinking about growing up in Itchica brings back memories of the good times and hard times we faced in adjusting to town life. As an extended family we had many visitors coming and going. We enjoyed spending time with the cousins who stayed with us; they were on the Nelson and Atkinson family lines. Brian and Carmel Nelson lived with us for a time and their eldest brother, George, lived with us for many years and was like an elder brother in the family. He was very gifted and became a champion runner who trained the Stawell Gift winner of 1974. He also looked after us when we were going to school and lived with us after he married Brenda Morgan, who is a daughter of Uncle Ronald Morgan and Ella Cooper of Cummera.

Our favourite visitor was Uncle Bill Onus. He is Mum's first cousin on the Henry and Granny Mag Nelson Dja Dja Wurrung and Waveroo lines. Uncle Bill was of Dja Dja Wurrung and Yorta Yorta ancestry, a man of many talents and a visionary thinker. He was also an experienced filmmaker, president of the Aborigines Advancement League of Victoria and a strong advocate for the Yes vote in the 1967 referendum. He was an immensely powerful and eloquent speaker and was well informed on Aboriginal affairs. His command of the English language was strong, which I assume reflected his early education at Cummera and his higher education in Melbourne.

Uncle Bill was a role model for us younger generation growing up in Itchica. I liken him to some of our outstanding leaders of the time who had a significant impact on our thinking and upbringing. His love for culture, serenity and the bush was awesome. He encouraged us to do the best we could in life and to always walk tall and be proud of our identity. His advice was honest and uplifting.

When Uncle Bill stayed, he loved to spend time with Mum. They would have catch-up yarns that stretched into the night. In the morning, he would gather us young fellas into his van and head bush to his beloved rivers Dungula and Kaiela. Once we were on the river at a special site, Uncle Bill would quickly change out of his city clothes into tribal dress. He would put on his lap-lap with a cord belt, strap his tomahawk to his waist and off he would go into the bush. He was a big strong man with lots of hair on his chest and shoulders. I wish I'd had a camera back then to take photos of his transition from city life to tribal ways. It was a startling experience for us young kids.

As he headed off into the bush, he would call us: 'Come and I'll show you how our ancestors lived before the white man came.' His message rang loud and clear, and off me, Clive and Graham would go, following Uncle Bill and his son Lin on men's business up front. We followed in a line, watching as we journeyed back into our ancestral past, ever cautious, listening all the time to Uncle Bill's strong voice echoing off the river and back into the bush. It was challenging initially, but the underlying message was truly clear. He invited us young fellas to get rid of the white man's clothes, quickly reminding us that our ancestors never wore such clothes. We got the message and joined him in the cultural immersion journey. As country kids we were a bit shy, but we knew and trusted where Uncle was coming from. Off came the clothes, down to our jocks and bare feet. 'Don't forget this is how it was not that long ago,' Uncle reminded us. He then took us on a journey of discovery. We tracked through the bush with Uncle showing us different ways of getting bush tucker—the bush tucker that had sustained our people for so long—and sharing his eloquent Dreaming stories.

One of his special hunting skills was to look for sawdust at the bottom of trees then trace the dust back up to the witchetty grub hole, cut a small notch in the tree with his tomahawk and carefully prize the grub out of its hole. The grub wire he wrapped around his belt was part of his prized portable toolkit for hunting and getting bush tucker on the move. After he got a handful of grubs, he would light a small fire and cook them in the coals. Given their moreish taste it was easy to consume at least a half a dozen, which was a substantial meal of high-quality food. The fish and crayfish we got from the river supplemented the diversity and richness of our diet.

We kept close to the river and were able to teach Uncle's son Lin to swim and to be aware of the dangerous river undercurrents. This helped to consolidate the close kinship ties and connections to Country we held as cousins. At the end of each cultural excursion we waited for Uncle Bill to come back from Melbourne, which he did regularly until he passed away in 1968. In later years, Lin always talked about our happy days on the river and how we had taught him to swim. The things we did with Uncle Bill brought us out of our town habits and back to the reality of our rich cultural heritage. Indeed, they were a wake-up call for us to think more about our cultural identity. Uncle's knowledge of cultural traditions, storytelling and the value of the old ways will stay with me forever.

What came home to me from Uncle Bill's leadership was the cultural knowledge he was imparting to us as the younger generation of Yorta Yorta growing up in mainstream life. He saw many changes taking place in our way of life and in the older ways of our people. He saw us slowly being absorbed into the new world and clearly knew that the end goal of the assimilation policy was cultural erasure and absorption. I could sense that by taking us under his wing with care and powerful teaching, he was trying to ground us in our own cultural identity. He wanted us to be proud Yorta Yorta men of the next generation, able to walk and talk in both worlds. The underlying message was: 'Yes, it is fine to walk in the new world, get a good education and learn new skills, but don't ever lose the inheritance with which you have been blessed.' He often talked of how the culture was handed down from the Dreamtime, which he called Alcheringa. This was the name of an ABC-TV documentary series he hosted in the 1960s that re-created the world of Indigenous culture before European invasion.

The short film *Elders* produced by Tony Briggs in 2019 conveys the storylines held by our elders. It brings alive the way old customs are used to teach younger generations about their identity and bush culture, and is a tribute to the wisdom and teaching of our elders past and present. I was invited to play the role of one of the elders in the film, and it reminded me of the wonderful experiences we had as kids under the mentorship of Uncle Bill.

Uncle Bill was a man of many talents. He had a boomerang shop in Deepdene, an eastern suburb of Melbourne, where he made boomerangs out of the natural bends of wood from river gum trees. He was a deadly boomerang thrower whose performances were highly acclaimed. In honour of Uncle Bill's work and his inspiration to my family, I wrote a story about his boomerang-throwing magic. The story came from a visit I made to Jagiellonian University in Krakow, Poland in 2019. While there, I was asked to view what appeared to be a lookalike boomerang, made from mammoth tusk, stored in the School of Archaeology. It had come from the excavation of a cave site in southern Poland and was dated around 23,000 BP. This was a good opportunity to share the story of Uncle Bill's expertise. His skilled boomerang-throwing attracted many people to come to watch his performances, and the story of how he threw a boomerang at the grand old Tivoli Theatre in Melbourne is still revered. To demonstrate the boomerang's returning capacity, he would cover it with luminescent paint. In my story, he throws the boomerang from the stage of the Tivoli out over the audience. As it swirls over their heads it creates a spectacular image. With the lights out and the luminescent colours radiating the boomerang's magical powers, the audience is mesmerised. They are thinking, 'Can this be real?' With masterful skill the boomerang returns to the stage and Uncle Bill catches it in both hands and politely bows. The grand applause is his reward for such a dynamic cultural performance.

Being able to throw a stick of wood is one thing, but for it to come back into the hands of the thrower in a theatre is a hallmark of Aboriginal ingenuity. The proposal that Ngarrindjeri inventor David Unaipon put forward 100 years ago for building a boomerang-powered flying vehicle was tested recently by engineers at the University of New South Wales and found to be practical.[3]

For me, these are treasured memories of Uncle Bill's knowledge and love for culture. I share the stories in honour of his admirable leadership as an elder and his caring spirit for us as young kids growing up in Itchica. Thanks, Uncle Bill, in Yorta Yorta woka.

~

The next big step in my education journey was to secondary school at Echuca Technical College. Echuca Tech was mainly a boys' school that focused on teaching trade skills. Having a trade up your sleeve, as we learned, was a meal ticket to a career in the skilled industries. Some girls went to the tech to learn sewing, but most of the girls from primary school went on to Echuca High and Catholic schools.

The step up to tech school was also a step up in maturity, from youth to adolescence. It was a more competitive environment and there was a diversity of kids from surrounding country towns, many from farming families. The tech school provided agricultural education at a time when agriculture was the mainstay of the regional economy. A class in agricultural skills was available for students to combine with technical training. This was the new environment for my generation of Aboriginal kids. In the early 1950s we were the first to gain entry to secondary school education in mainstream society.

My older brother Clive, younger brother Graham and I all went to Echuca Tech, while my two sisters Marlene and Veronica went to high school. My older brother Dimpsie and older sister Fay had left school; Dimpsie was working on the railways and Fay was working in a local fruit shop. Clive was an exceptionally talented artist, and tech school gave him the chance to make a name for himself in art. He started off as a sketch and landscape artist. Later, he graduated with a diploma in graphic art and design. He gained many accolades for his painting of a bridge over the Campaspe in West Echuca and was invited to design the emblem for the tech school. He was then awarded a scholarship for art, which put him on track for bigger and better things in the art world, and turned his hand to Aboriginal art and design work. I think he was the first Aboriginal student to win a scholarship for art. That made him and our family very proud.

Another very capable Aboriginal artist from Echuca Tech was Paul Egan. Paul was an excellent sketcher who used a lead pencil to draw images from comics and magazines. Clive and Paul both excelled in sport, too, and were very good at running and football. They represented the school in interschool sporting carnivals. I played footy with Paul at school and we both played in the Echuca South premiership side in 1967. He was a big strong man and a top player like his older brother Bob Egan; Bob played for Echuca. Paul's name was Andrew Paul Egan and his initials were APE. At school he got the nickname 'Ape', which was taken by him not as offensive but in good humour—not like the name that was directed at Adam Goodes when he played for the Sydney Swans, which had a more derogatory meaning. Paul had a similar build to Adam and could hold his own on and off the football field.

I was still living with Nanny Lou in my first two years of tech school, until she passed away. At primary school I did exceptionally well in the creative and sporting fields but lost interest in the academic side. (This would come back to revisit me when I returned to study later in life.) At tech I performed reasonably well in the creative and hands-on technical classes and did some artwork, but my main interests were in technical drawing, carpentry and clay modelling. At first, I had my eyes set on doing a trade in carpentry, but other things in the outside world attracted my interests. When I reached Form 3, which was equivalent to the Junior Technical Certificate, I left school. Unlike my brothers, I chose to get a job without a trade. The Junior Tech Certificate was a ticket to an apprenticeship for five years and from there you were a fully qualified tradie. A trade, whether it be chippie, plumber, fitter and turner or mechanic, was a good back-up to have. Both Clive and Graham did apprenticeships in their respective fields of printing and fitting and turning. Later in life they used these skills to advance their interest in other fields, including printing, art and Aboriginal affairs.

We had to deal with experiences of racism at tech school. Aboriginal studies were not in the school curriculum except for passing remarks about Aboriginal history. Like in primary school, this attracted the interest of other students, who would immediately put you in the spotlight. One encounter I clearly remember is a confrontation with a teacher in our clay modelling class. He seemed to have it in for me from the word go. I was pretty good at clay modelling and had one of my creations, a dog, displayed at the school open day. This didn't stop the intimidation and negative vibes from the teacher. I mentioned it to Mum and she was quick to sort it out there and then. She visited the teacher and put him in his place, which paid off for me in the end.

My days at Echuca Tech are full of good memories of the friendships I made. I got to know some non-Aboriginal students well in class and outside of school, and through me they became more aware of Aboriginal culture and history. Some of them liked the cultural spirit of our family and our love for telling yarns. One of my closest friends, who has since passed, was Paddy Malone. With a name like that you immediately knew he was of Irish background. Paddy was a loved member of our family. There was something about him that was like our own mob. The ability to stand outside yourself and crack a joke, no matter how daunting reality may seem, is, I believe, both an Irish and an Aboriginal trait. Our shared ability to laugh is something I've learned more about over the years. I've learned that being able to crack a joke is a survival mechanism you can fall back on to balance the daunting reality at your feet. It is also about learning how to hold the legacy that you carry. I can see more clearly how this dynamic manifests itself in our own mob when we get together.

I also formed an alliance with some Italian friends who I played sport with at Echuca Tech. Through this relationship we forged a formidable force against racism. We gained much respect for calling it out when it happened to both the Italian and the Aboriginal people. We forged mutual relationships between our cultures at school as well as in the seasonal industries and shearing sheds. We were also welcomed into each other's homes.

The cross-cultural relationships my family and I forged with non-Koori people need to be mentioned. Our family seemed to make friends with people who found solidarity in the cultural spirit we shared. Our mutual acceptance and trust grew out of non-Kooris learning to walk in both worlds as equals, free of preconceived ideas about Aboriginality. It was a two-way process that bridged the gap between white and black. We were cutting through cross-cultural differences and coming together as one.

It is common among Koori people to say, 'Oh, he/she's spent so much time with us learning our ways that he/she is a Gubbahriginal', meaning one of us. This is a cultural rather than a biological status that emerges and is used within family groups. Mind you, the process to earn such a title takes time. No one can claim it straight up. It is sacrosanct and is earned through acceptance and trust over a long period. In this context, our friend Paddy Malone was a prime example of the Koori-gubbah relationship. It was so strong that he was often called Uncle by younger members of the family.

Some of my university students today find it hard to come to grips with the fact that there is so much joking and laughter when the mob gets together. 'That is what survival is all about,' I say. It is a cultural value we draw upon to ease the reality of constant struggle. 'The struggle continues' is an Aboriginal saying that reveals the endurance of struggle. It is the nature of the business and the messaging that portrays our existence. I think that is why many people like our dear friend Paddy Malone and others find solidarity with our mob. They seem to gravitate to the wisdom of our comparative ways. Drawing on our strength to find relief and solidarity with the mob is a cultural practice. Over the years I have found many commonalities among people who have experienced similar histories. I have also found that it is closely related to cultural and socio-economic factors.

Looking back, my tech school days were a steep learning curve. The environment and way of learning could have been much better. I struggled with how some of the academic subjects were taught—it wasn't a learning environment that suited my needs. The fear of failure was a constant impediment to learning. It was on that basis that I decided to drop out at the end of Form 3 and search for greener pastures in the workforce.

This decision was also influenced by my family commitments. Things were becoming a struggle for my parents. The need to enter the workforce to help bring in money to support our family outweighed my education at that point. Like my father, the hunger for learning was still in me, but it would have to wait to be fulfilled in another time and place.

8
Working Man Blues

At the age of fourteen, I already knew what hard physical work was about. My father used to take me into the shearing sheds with him to teach me how to shear. He wanted to pass on the trade that had been handed down from Puppa Henry, to keep it going.

However, he wasn't the best of teachers in the shed because he was too busy wanting to get his tally up for the day. His patience was a bit short and when he put the heavy vibrating shearing machine in my hand, I was anxious about its power. I needed to get used to it, but time was of the essence in the shearing shed. It was a very competitive industry and once you were up on the board with the bogey in your hand, it was all about speed, quality, quantity, and a lot of sweat along the way.

I started off as a rouseabout, picking up wool and keeping the pens filled for the shearers. Sometimes my father would call on me to help him hold back the neck of a ram so he could complete the long blow or stroke up through the neck without cutting the sheep. The rams were strong, and you had to pull hard to get their necks back.

The shearing shed is where I learned a lot about shearing culture. Many of our cousins were top shearers, and they respected my father. They knew he was a clean shearer who had mastered the trade very well from Puppa Henry, the head ringer. One thing I liked about the shearing culture was the lovely food the owners provided for smoko. I also liked sitting back listening to the shearers sharing their stories.

You needed to be tough and powerful to survive in the shearing industry. There were reasons to like and dislike a life of shearing.

My father used to bring shearers home who we were related to. Some of them were the best in the country, renowned for their ability to shear up to 300 sheep every day. Top money could be made if you could stick at it. That was the career path my father encouraged me to follow.

However, my dislike of shearing also came from the culture it created. When the local season finished, shearers were on call to work in sheds further away. Sometimes it would take them away for months. Women were left to look after the kids and keep the household going. Isolation from home was a big factor. Alcohol and gambling were other factors that were part of the shearing culture and would determine how much a shearer brought home from the long runs.

There were many times our father was away doing long runs in the Western District and in New South Wales. My mother talked about being a shearer's wife. Sometimes my father is said to have returned with less in his pocket than was expected for the amount of time he'd been away. I think that happened more when shearers were away and less at home. When they worked closer to home there was more accountability for their pay packet.

The other hard part of shearing was the competitive nature of shearers themselves, who were often eager to test each other out with their fists. I've heard many stories. I've seen how some of the tougher ones not only held the title of being the best shearer but also the best with their fists, as the head of shed.

The other drawback is that shearing is a seasonal industry. Unless you left home to extend the season, you had to find other work to cover the off-season. Some years my father found work cutting wood, picking fruit or working in the laundry at Echuca Hospital. Our mother worked at the hospital as one of the cooks.

These were the factors I considered when I thought about going down the shearing path. After watching closely and listening to all the stories from the top shearers who visited our home, I chose a different direction.

Before I found my career path, I tried my hand at other jobs. Not having a trade up my sleeve from tech school was a drawback in one sense, but if you could do a man's work you could get a man's pay. I worked doing hay carting and driving trucks to pick up and stack the hay. I didn't need a licence to drive the truck around the paddocks, and the driving skills held me in good stead for other work. When the hay finished, I got a job milking cows on a dairy farm in Echuca Village, the heartland of the dairy industry. In the early 1950s, the industry was enjoying its most productive economic period and there was a lot of demand for workers on the farms.

I learned much about dairy work and picked up some farming skills. I used to ride my bike from home to Echuca Village for the morning milk at 6.30 a.m. and return home for lunch. Then I would ride back for the afternoon milk at 4 p.m. and return home in the evening around 6 p.m. I rode around 20 kilometres each day. My wage for dairy farm work was eight quid, which is about $16 now, for six days a week and long hours. Riding a bike for that distance certainly built up my stamina and helped in my sporting activities. I was playing basketball for a team called the Rebels and footy for the Echuca South Football Club. In my spare time I did some running along Yakoa to keep fit.

After spending nearly twelve months on the dairy farm, I got a job in town working in a dry-cleaning shop and another at a roadside cafe pumping petrol. The cafe, on Ogilvie Avenue, was called the DKO. It was leased by my older sister Fay and her husband, Les. Both jobs were a stopgap while I was waiting to get a position at the rice mill. Working in town was a relief from the number of kilometres I had been travelling back and forth to the dairy farm. The money was less, however. The combined jobs brought me around five quid or $10 per week.

One of my mates, Paul Burchill, was working at the rice mill at the time. He told me about the jobs going there, which were paying the basic wage. The basic wage, as it was called then, was about fifteen quid a week, which is equivalent to $30. It was more than double the wage of an apprentice, which is what my schoolfriends were making in their respective trades. Paul told me to go and speak with the manager.

When I fronted up to the rice mill the boss sized me up and asked, 'Can you do a man's work?' This was the criterion for being paid the basic wage. My answer was honest and straightforward. By now I was sixteen and had developed physically and got stronger from my other jobs and sporting life. I looked him in the eye and said, 'Yes, I can.' I told him I had been doing a man's work since I was fourteen and then asked him what a man's work was. He replied, 'If you can lift a 78-pound [35-kilogram] bag of rice and do shift work hours.' That's what constituted a man's work for the rice mill and the basic wage.

The job in front of me seemed awesome! I just had to pass the challenge of whether I could lift a bag of rice that weight and stack them four high on a pallet. I remember Paul giving me a trial run and teaching me how to use my body to lift such a weight. I was used to lifting heavy weights in the fruit-picking and shearing sheds, and had also done some heavy lifting on the dairy farm carrying bales of hay and bags of feed for the pigs. Now was the big moment, and with Paul's patient advice I was able to lift a bag of rice with no great difficulty. Later on, it became a contest to see if you could lift one over your head like a weightlifter, but I won't go into the Koori saying for that.

Having met the first challenge with some degree of confidence, I was ready to enter the world of rice production in the Echuca Rice Mill. The rice was being grown and harvested in the Riverina district of New South Wales around Wakool, Moulamein and Deniliquin. It was a new introduced cash crop to Australia that needed lots of water. The rice was harvested and transported by rail to places like Itchica, Deniliquin and Leeton to be milled. Much of it was for internal consumption and a lot was exported overseas.

The mill was a 24-hour operation that worked in three shifts. The day shift was 8 a.m. to 4 p.m., the afternoon shift was 4 p.m. to midnight, and the midnight shift was from midnight to 8 a.m. Some called that the horror shift, working from midnight till dawn and fighting the fatigue of irregular sleep. To my surprise, many students worked at the mill. Leaving school to get the basic wage was an attractive option and helped to put more money in your pocket. I was pleased with the wage I was getting at the mill, and my parents were pleased that I was bringing in money to support the family income.

After doing a range of mill work, packing and lifting bags and loading out produce for export, I soon had enough money to buy a car. I was going on eighteen. My first car was a classic two-tone green FJ Holden sedan, and I drove it until I could get my licence when I turned eighteen. These were things you could get away with in the country in those days. But you quickly learned not to push the boundaries too far. I think the local police were surprised when I fronted for my licence, because they had often seen me cruising around town in my FJ Holden with mates on board.

The rice mill helped me get on my feet. Eventually I was promoted to the position of assistant miller. My job was to assist the head miller, who oversaw the management and operations of the mill. We had to keep the machinery running smoothly and deal with any technical malfunctions. I learned about the workings of rice production and machinery operation, and about the management and care of the shift crew. I got some important skills from the mill.

After working the three different shifts for nearly five years, I left to find daytime employment. It was hard having to fight sleep on the midnight shift when your body should have been naturally resting, and I was ready for work in the outside air after overexposure to rice dust, loud machinery noise, and irritation from the dust, which created itch.

My next job was with a wholesale retail merchant delivering goods to grocers and supermarkets in Itchica and surrounds. Lumping a bag of spuds around on your shoulders was like mill work, but not as heavy as a 78-pound bag of rice.

~

The most significant event that happened for me in 1964 was meeting my first wife, Wendy Forbes. Wendy came to work in Itchica in the early 1960s with local radio station 2QN, a branch of its head station in Deniliquin. We met through her relatives in Itchica, who often visited our home. On one occasion she happened to join their visit, we met, and all is history from there on. We had similar tastes in music and sport and generally had a lot of common interests. Before meeting Wendy, I had seen her playing in one of the local basketball teams and noticed that she was new to town. Our meeting grew into a close relationship and from there we got engaged; we married in mid-1965.

It wasn't long before Wendy and I had two lovely daughters. Yolanda was named after one of Wendy's close friends who was a dancer with a touring Haitian group; Wendy had known her in Sydney before she came to Itchica. Our next child, Gabrielle Iris, takes her middle name from my mother. Gabrielle was born the same year Echuca South won its first premiership in the Echuca League—a wonderful double for the year 1967.

After the grand final win, I exercised my cultural rights and went missing for a couple of days to celebrate. It was called 'walkabout' in the old days and that term is still used when our people seek to exercise that right. Sounds like a good idea but doesn't always work when you have important commitments.

It was time to settle down to family business and parenting, providing a home and care for our two growing girls. We were able to get a small flat to kick off, then we moved to a low-rental Commission home, and from there to a house in Echuca South. My having a steady job was a big bonus: it helped bring in reasonable money to keep the household going. Wendy was doing casual work, waitressing and making clothes. Later she worked as a receptionist in the local doctor's surgery.

In 1970 we were able to move into the house my mother had been living in. A tragic accident had left her a paraplegic, and she moved from the family home into the care of my three sisters, Fay, Marlene and Veronica. For the next thirty-four years they and their husbands took turns looking after Mum in their homes, which was a family way of taking care of our mother, who was using a wheelchair. Another generation of grandchildren benefited from a grandmother's love and learned to share the nursing care.

~

Working a day job in the clean air allowed me to pursue my interests in sport and music. Our family came from a line of top musicians who had been strongly influenced by the musical talents at Cummeragunja. My mother was a very good singer, dancer, pianist and ukulele player. With these talents in the family line, she encouraged and mentored us kids in our music. Her mother, Priscilla Nelson James, and Aunty Becky James Murray, sisters on the James-Cooper line, were qualified musicians, and Granny Priscilla told me the story of how Cummera influenced their music abilities:

> Aunty Becky and I were taught music. We both learnt from a music teacher that used to come to Barmah and then after that he came over to our place at Cummera and taught us there. My father [Granpa James] had a piano there for us and we both learnt music theory and then we were able to teach our own people. We organised the concerts and plays that were part of our entertainment on Cummera. And then later we used to travel around to the surrounding towns and put on our concerts for the white people.[1]

Aunty Becky shared her story of how she was taught music by Mr Haslem in Itchica. She was so proud to tell me about her Diploma of Music: 'That's my certificate there in the frame on the wall. But I also got other certificates too! After Mr Haslem, I was taught at Nathalia and then I became a qualified music teacher and trained them all at Cummera for the concerts and the plays we presented.'[2]

Aunty Becky also talked about the famous Cummera Choir that still sings at functions today:

> We taught them all to sing in their different harmony sections, and when we used to sing, they could hear us at Barmah. Our voices used to carry down the river. The Maloneys who owned the hotel at Barmah would come out and sit along their verandah … and they used to say to us how lovely it sounded and how our voices used to float over the water from Cummera.[3]

Wonderful stories like these bring home the sense of community life on Cummera and the role that music played in people's daily lives. We were lucky to inherit the love of music. The influence of our parents, grandparents, aunties and uncles was outstanding. We watched and listened to their deadly music performances and from this, we followed on and developed our own music skills.

Growing up, we were lucky to have an additional music mentor in our cousin Uncle Archie Walker. Uncle Archie's family carried on the lovely music from Cummera. We used to sit around watching and listening to him play, and eventually we played with him when we reached a higher level of music ability. He was very versatile and played guitar, steel guitar and piano accordion.

Music was a big part of our family life. With a stroke of good fortune, it elevated us into the limelight of Itchica's social life. It also helped to break down the barriers of socio-economic class and acceptance. We got wide acclaim playing for functions and gigs and other major public performances.

Our mother believed in what we could achieve and encouraged us to do our best in whatever we chose to do. 'You can do anything you want,' she would say, 'if you work hard and put your mind to the goal you want to achieve.' We always remembered that what mattered most was the pride of who we are and where we come from. The influence of our ancestors and our heritage was always at the heart of what we did. Doing things with respect and cultural integrity was the most important thing.

It was against this background and encouragement that my brothers and I formed our first band, called The Shades, in the early 1960s. My brother Clive played guitar, I played bass and guitar, and my younger brother Graham played drums and guitar. We were joined by our mate Paul Burchill, who played with us and also became our brother-in-law after he married our sister Marlene. We were very much a family band and stayed that way for most of our music career.

We also had two top vocalists. Having two versatile singers up front helped to diversify the material we played, elevated our performances and got us a broader audience. One vocalist was a young girl, Gwen Firmer, from the farming district of Koyuga. She had a top voice and could sing a variety of tunes, from rock to laid-back songs like the 1962 Ruby & the Romantics hit 'Our Day Will Come'. The other vocalist was Brian Meldrum, Ian 'Molly' Meldrum's younger brother. He lived in Kyabram and liked the music we were playing. He was a very good vocalist and also played the mouth organ, which enriched the sound of the band on some of our Beatles and Rolling Stones numbers. Brian later became a sports journalist with the *Herald-Sun*; he kept in touch with us over the years. He was a very talented and likeable person. Being Molly's brother, he attracted a lot of accolades for our band. With all that talent on board our hopes were high, and our ambition was to one day hit the big time. 'Look out,' was the message, 'The Shades are coming!'

My life was moving at a fast pace: family, working, footy, basket-ball and music. The Shades were on the rise during the 1960s music revolution. This was the beginning of the Beatles era. There was a quantum shift in music from America to the Mersey sound that came out of Liverpool. We were playing gigs in Itchica and surrounding towns. Practising and learning new tunes and keeping up with popular tunes of the day kept us very busy. We put a lot of work into doing the top tunes well, and this increased our professional profile. We had regular bookings for gigs. One of our big leaps forward came from winning a Battle of the Bands contest in Benalla in 1968. I forget how much money we won, but I know it went towards buying more band equipment. The silver trophy is stored with The Shades memorabilia.

The award led to increased demand for bookings, not to mention extra money in our pockets. We travelled for gigs not just in Itchica and the Goulburn Valley, but also, in the early 1960s, we were proud to be the first Aboriginal band chosen to play at the Koori NAIDOC Ball in Preston in Melbourne. The band at that time was made up of local musos of the calibre of Harry Williams on lead guitar, my brother Dimpsie on guitar, Graham on drums and myself on bass and vocals. Our frontline vocalist was the late Bertie Williams, and many guest artists also did vocals on the night. What a night it was. Looking out from the stage at the crowd dancing and singing to our music is a wonderful memory.

We got to do a few NAIDOC Balls. Our largest one was at the San Remo Ballroom in Carlton in 1987. We had a big line-up that included Clive on guitar, Paul Burchill and Robby Walker on guitar and vocals, me on bass, guitar and vocals, Allan Richards on piano and vocals, and Graham on drums. We used to call this 'the big rig' for the big sound we got. The extra brass and instrument sounds were created by Allan through the three-deck keyboard he played. Robby was in the limelight as a top guitarist playing Clapton and Santana tunes. 'Playing up the neck to the double adapter' is how we used to describe his style of playing.

Playing for a packed crowd who gravitated to the floor to dance to our music was icing on the cake. Our music was largely rock'n'roll and blues, intermingled with some popular country and Koori tunes. This put us on the map as a professional band with a broad diversity of musical styles, and we became a backing group for featured artists. We backed many topline Australian artists at the Astor Ballroom in

Shepparton, including The Seekers at the height of their brilliant career, Lucky Starr, Greg Anderson, Peter Doyle and a Melbourne band called The Phantoms, who played covers of songs by the famous Shadows instrumental group of England. All these artists and bands were the topliners in the music scene of the 1970s and early 1980s.

While music put us on the map as a group, we had other work to do in our respective journeys of life. Bringing in money from playing in the band was a handy supplement to our regular employment.

Music is still a central part of our family, and the guitar is never far away when we have family gatherings. I play regularly with my brother-in-law Paul and other musos. My main claim to fame was winning the Victorian Koori Country Music Award at Mooroopna Country Music Festival at Rumbalara in the early 1980s. This took me to the Australian Indigenous Country Music Festival in Sydney the following year, where I was runner-up for the Australian Indigenous Country Music Award.

We actively encourage younger members of the family to follow music as a career path. This has included mentoring our niece Lou Bennett in her successful music career. Lou is a talented musician who plays keyboard and guitar and sings nice vocals and harmonies. She started her career in The Shades, extending our repertoire to include Tracy Chapman covers. Lou's music took her to Melbourne, where she was instrumental in forming the famous Tiddas band, who achieved national and international fame with their original and exceptional harmony-style music, much of which Lou composed. She lived with us when she came to Melbourne from Itchica, and we played a lot of music together, including at Koori functions, before she headed off to form Tiddas.

Simon Johnson, my oldest brother Dimpsie's son, is another talented musician carrying on the family tradition. He plays bass and guitar and has sung harmonies with popular Indigenous artist Troy Cassar-Daley. Dimpsie played guitar with a variety of country bands in Mooroopna and Shepparton.

Music is a universal language that can take you anywhere in the world. When Cathy and I are travelling, I'm always on the lookout for a music shop to drop into for a chat and often hire a guitar to keep the dexterity in my fingers going. I was lucky to be able to play with renowned Victorian singer-songwriter Shane Howard in one of Ireland's top gig pubs in Galway, the Crane Bar. Shane often plays there as a guest artist when he returns to reconnect with his Irish heritage.

Music is the doctor, as the saying goes. That is something I can vouch for as a remedy for easing the soul and the mind and keeping a sense of balance when trying circumstances come along.

~

In between music, I decided to stop delivering spuds to shops and tried a different path of work, getting a job in the local meatworks. Slaughtering was not my forte, but somehow I ended up working in the blood and guts of it all on the mutton chain. The pay was good and the work was more like a sport than a job. We had to work flat out on a production line herding sheep to the slaughter and putting them through to the end of the line. I was told there was a good career path in the meat industry if you could stick it out. I spent a couple of years balancing the meatworks with the bookings we got for The Shades.

I was also playing footy with our beloved Echuca South, only a stone's throw from where we lived. The connection with Echuca South was a carryover from when we were kids looking for places to hang out. We gravitated to the footy ground and watched our Aboriginal player relations, including my brother Clive. I followed him and we both played with South. Graham joined later, after a stint with his mates at Echuca East. At one stage there were that many Atkinsons on the field it was hard to pick who was who. Sometimes people would call me Clive or Graham because we looked much the same on and off the field. I got the nickname 'Kanga' because I had the ability to jump high to mark and palm the ball to what they now call onballers—back then, they were rovers. Dimpsie played as a rover with Mooroopna in the Goulburn Valley League. Our mother was a passionate barracker and always there to encourage us. Sometimes she would nearly jump the fence if anything untoward happened on the field.

Between work, music and sport, we were an active family. We left no stone unturned as we contributed to mainstream life. We also kept a close link with the rivers and continued to fish and bring food home for the family. The connection was in our blood, and we made sure we kept it going.

After an industrial relations dispute at the meatworks over workers' rights, a group of us walked out in solidarity. We were remotely based, without union support. I finished my stint in the meat industry bearing no grudges and learning about rights-based workplace issues. Later, the call for justice and human rights became a common theme for me in my formal studies. My experience at the meatworks helped me to become more informed about workers' rights and the need for solidarity and fairness in dispute-based resolution.

I also learned some German from one of the workers. It helped to break the monotony of the repetitious daily work. At the time I didn't realise I might have had a flair for language, but it certainly helped to pass the days working on the chain gang.

My next job was away from factories and back to outside work: I got a job in Itchica driving a truck for Readymix concrete. I worked there for a couple of years as a company driver. It was more likeable than the meatworks and allowed me to get out and about. I made a diverse range of friends in that industry. My manager was the best boss I've ever had—mainly because we both played footy for Echuca South. He was good mates with other Aboriginal players in the team. He was jovial and easy to get on with and had a great sense of humour. Indeed, he often used to get up and sing with our band when we played at his local pub. With his rich, husky voice he could knock out a great version of 'Ghost Riders in the Sky'. His nickname was Spider because of his long gangly arms and his football style. I pay homage to him and his family and remember them dearly. I even taught his son how to throw a boomerang in the back paddock, which he always remembers when I see him.

Driving for Readymix took me into surrounding towns and to some large construction sites. The outside work suited me and helped to expand my knowledge of the construction industry. The Barmah Bridge was one of the main sites I delivered concrete to; it was built in 1966. I used to have a good laugh when the Italian workers on site would ask if I was Italian. I also used to run into former schoolmates doing their apprenticeships. They would often ask me how much I was getting compared with their low apprenticeship wages.

My Readymix driving job changed rather dramatically when the company drivers were replaced by owner-drivers. The irony is that this meant I went from delivering concrete to being on the receiving end as a concreter. I got a job with one of the contractors and learned the trade of concreting. It wasn't long before I reached the tradie title of 'trowel hand', which enabled me to do the finishing-off work after the concrete was laid. I soon learned enough about the work to be able to do weekend jobs myself. My old Gubbahriginal mate Paddy Malone came on board and worked with us for a while, and we did extra jobs in our own time. It was fun working together, putting in the hard yards and cracking jokes along the way. Paddy continued to work in the concreting industry, while my life took a major turn in the early 1970s.

~

Life as a local Yorta Yorta man living in a rural town of people from largely Anglo-Celtic backgrounds had its ups and downs. Tensions, conflicts and confrontations over Aboriginal matters were part and parcel of country life. Despite all that, I always kept in touch with what was happening in Aboriginal affairs.

The resounding Yes result of the 1967 referendum raised our hopes for a better and more equitable future for our people. Our hopes were further raised in 1972 when Gough Whitlam came to power. His policy commitments to land rights and self-determination were commendable. Indeed, it looked like a new day was dawning for Australia and its First Peoples.

Some changes started taking place in the administration of Aboriginal affairs. The old Welfare Board mentality was replaced by a larger bureaucracy called the Department of Aboriginal Affairs (DAA). It replaced welfare officers with social workers whose role was to visit communities and provide support for families dealing with hardship. Under the new DAA structure, they were also given powers to advise communities about opportunities in the areas of Aboriginal affairs and education. The time was ripe for change and reform. To deliver the new policy commitments, local community-based organisations began to spring up in regional centres where there were sizeable Aboriginal populations. The Echuca Aboriginal Co-op in Itchica was set up in 1974 (it changed its name to the Njernda Aboriginal Corporation in 1990). Local co-ops, as they were called, provided an important community base. They became major service delivery providers in health, education, housing, employment and other services, and assumed responsibility for land and cultural matters. Njernda was granted some farmland as freehold in the late 1970s. At that time there was no process in Victoria for claiming land on the basis of prior rights.

These changes showed me there were pathways to consider in Aboriginal affairs policy direction. The self-determination policy was aimed at empowering Aboriginal people so they could have greater control of their own affairs through employment, education and training. Education programs were being set up to provide knowledge and skills for those who had left school early and wanted to return to study. These new opportunities for community and educational growth attracted me. It was time for change and time to feed the lingering hunger within me for further knowledge and higher education. I knew I had valuable work experience in my favour and was confident it would hold me in good stead with the discipline required to return to formal study. I already enjoyed an active social and family life and was ready to knuckle down to the task. I was confident I could do it and was highly motivated to give it my best shot.

A window of opportunity opened for me when I heard that a national education program for Aboriginal people was happening in Adelaide. It was called the Aboriginal Task Force and was at the South Australian Institute of Technology. The program was open to Aboriginal and Torres Strait Islander students from across Australia, many of whom were public service employees working in DAA and welfare agencies.

I contacted the program to discuss the entry requirements and support for mature-aged students wishing to return to study, and in 1974 quickly went from a life of hard work in Itchica as a jack of all trades and master of some, to life as a full-time student. The storyline now takes us from Itchica to a new world about to open in time and place.

Rainbow Serpent mural by Yorta Yorta artist Robin Bailey at the Dharnya Centre in Barmah. Courtesy Robin Bailey.

Traditional fishing at Maloga. Courtesy Norman family collection, State Library of South Australia, Ref: PGR422/3/802.

Yorta Yorta women's camp winyarrn mana with possum skin clothing, Moira. Courtesy Norman family collection, State of Library South Australia, Ref: PGR422/3/805.

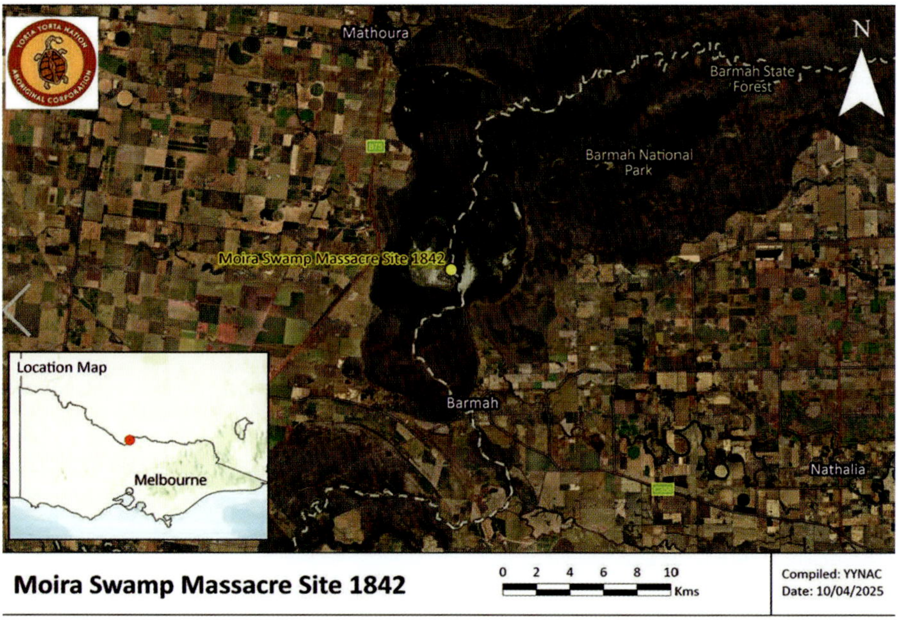

Moira Swamp massacre site in Moira Forest where 26 Yorta Yorta people were killed in 1842. Courtesy Wayne Atkinson.

Maloga mission community in 1883 with Granpa James in waistcoat and tie (centre). Courtesy Norman family collection, State Library of South Australia, Ref: PRG 422/3/644.

Cummeragunja Church. Granpa James is behind the piano and his daughter Priscilla is seated at the piano. Henry Nelson is seated at the far left. Courtesy *Living Aboriginal History of Victoria*.

Australian Aborigines League Victoria founders, from left: Shadrach James, Ebenezer Lovett, Annie Lovett, a son of Claude B Smith (a white supporter), William Cooper, Claude B Smith, Sarah Cooper, Hyllus Briggs, Caleb Morgan, Anna Morgan, Martha Nevin and Doug Nicholls.
Courtesy Koori Heritage Trust Melbourne.

Left: Thomas Shadrach James, 1859–1942. Courtesy Atkinson family collection.

Right: Henry Nelson family, from left: Grandfather Henry Nelson, Priscilla Nelson James, Margaret Nelson (Stolen Generation), Granny Mag and Uncle Bill Onus.
In front are George Nelson Jnr, Ruby Muir and Iris Atkinson Nelson on Granny Mag's lap.
Courtesy Atkinson family collection.

The Invincibles Football Team, Cummeragunja, 1927. Courtesy Rumbala Football Netball Club history display, Shepparton.

An elder of the Mooroopna Flat being visited by one of the Welfare Board Members. Courtesy *Living Aboriginal History of Victoria*.

Puppa Henry Roderick Atkinson leeching in the Barmah wetlands, 1940s. Courtesy *Barmah Chronicles,* GM Gibbins, 1991.

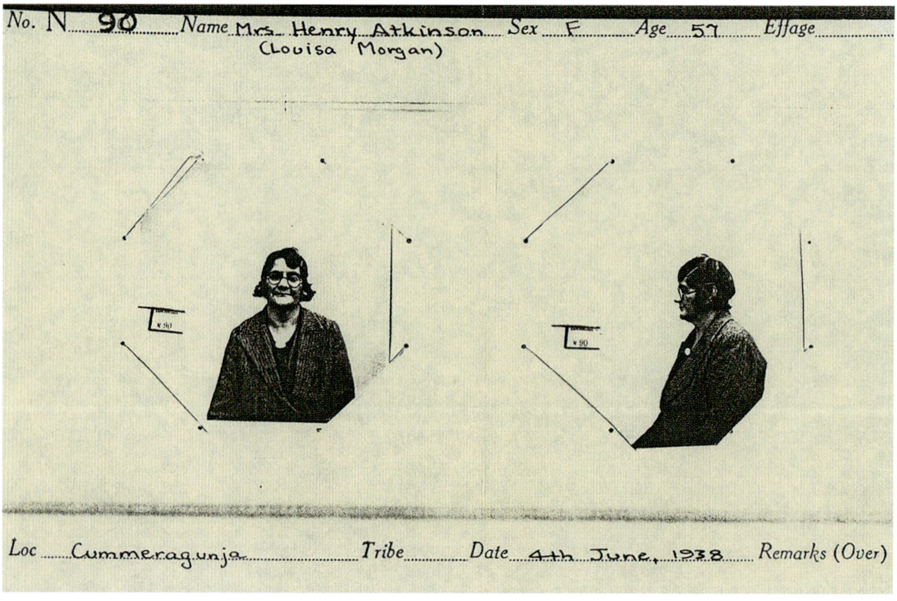

My grandmother Nanny Lou as photographed by Norman Tindale at Cummeragunja as part of the Harvard Project, 1938. Courtesy Tindale Collection which has been returned to the Yorta Yorta Nations.

Family at Premier St, Echuca, 1950s. Back: Wayne, Clive and cousin Brian Nelson. Front: Marlene, Veronica and cousin Carmel Nelson.
Courtesy Wayne Atkinson.

Uncle Bill Onus throwing a boomerang in 1941. Courtesy Mitchell Library, State Library of New South Wales.

Atkinson children in Echuca.
Back: Clive, Veronica and Marlene. Front: Graham and Wayne.
Courtesy Atkinson family collection.

Echuca South Football Team premiers, 1967. Back: Wayne is second and Paul Egan is third from left. Middle: Jack Sullivan is far left and Henry Atkinson is far right. Courtesy Atkinson family collection.

The Shades band: Paul Burchill, Graham, Wayne, Lou Bennett, Brian Meldrum and Clive. Courtesy Atkinson family collection.

Task force graduates, Adelaide, 1977. Edmund Wanganeen, Wayne, Kevin Dann, Joyce Trust, Ian Trust, Freda Thornton, Laurie Poland, Cyril Archer and Andrew Wilson. Courtesy Wayne Atkinson.

Wayne's daughters Gabrielle and Yolanda, Echuca, c. 1978. Courtesy Atkinson family collection.

Atkinson family in Echuca. Back: Clive, Wayne, Dimpsey and Graham. Middle: Faye, Veronica and Marlene, with Iris seated in the front. Courtesy Atkinson family collection.

My mother Iris waving with Aunty Geraldine Briggs and Aunty Marj Tucker, Elders Camp, Camp Jungai, 1984. Courtesy Wayne Atkinson.

Interview with Uncle Albert Mullet
in Bruthen, Gippsland, 1989.
Courtesy Wayne Atkinson.

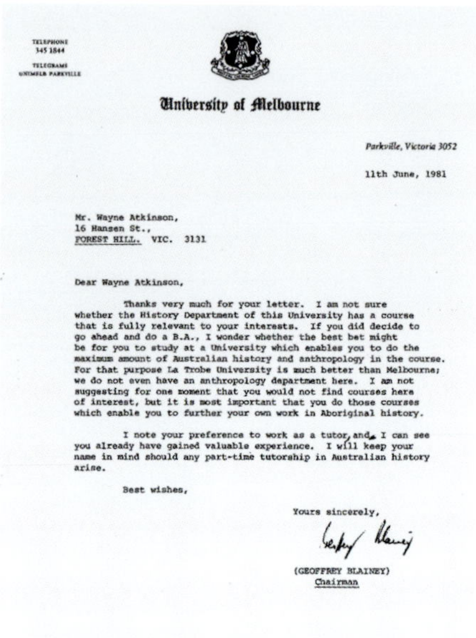

TELEPHONE
345 1844

TELEGRAMS
UNIMELB PARKVILLE

University of Melbourne

Parkville, Victoria 3052

11th June, 1981

Mr. Wayne Atkinson,
16 Hansen St.,
FOREST HILL. VIC. 3131

Dear Wayne Atkinson,

Thanks very much for your letter. I am not sure whether the History Department of this University has a course that is fully relevant to your interests. If you did decide to go ahead and do a B.A., I wonder whether the best bet might be for you to study at a University which enables you to do the maximum amount of Australian history and anthropology in the course. For that purpose La Trobe University is much better than Melbourne; we do not even have an anthropology department here. I am not suggesting for one moment that you would not find courses here of interest, but it is most important that you do those courses which enable you to further your own work in Aboriginal history.

I note your preference to work as a tutor, and I can see you already have gained valuable experience. I will keep your name in mind should any part-time tutorship in Australian history arise.

Best wishes,

Yours sincerely,

(GEOFFREY BLAINEY)
Chairman

Geoffrey Blainey rejection letter, 1981.

Wayne and Cathy during overseas study in Canada, 1982. Courtesy Wayne Atkinson.

Oncountry teaching at Cummeragunja School with Yorta Yorta elder Aunty Liz Hoffman and Wayne in the middle, 2003. Courtesy Wayne Atkinson.

Yorta Yorta gathering at the 80th Anniversary of the Cummeragunja Walk Off, 2019. Courtesy Wayne Atkinson.

Koori Mail

The Voice of Indigenous Australia

THE NATIONAL INDIGENOUS NEWSPAPER – 100% ABORIGINAL-OWNED 100% SELF-FUNDING

EDITION 511 WEDNESDAY, 5 OCTOBER, 2011 PUBLISHED SINCE 1991

Phone: (02) 66 222 666 www.koorimail.com Recommended price $2 (GST-inclusive)

NSW-Qld knockout league clash set to be a reality

THE game fans of Indigenous rugby league have longed for looks set to become a reality.

Reliable sources have told the *Koori Mail* a state of origin-style match up between the winning teams of the NSW and new Queensland Murri Aboriginal Knockout carnivals will be a part of next year's NRL season-opening All Stars event. The Indigenous All Stars versus NRL All Stars game is set down for Saturday 4 February at Skilled Park on the Gold Coast.

The exact time and venue for the proposed 'Aboriginal Knockout' clash has yet to be confirmed.

The *Koori Mail* understands the decision to hold the game comes on the back of the successful inaugural Queensland Murri Carnival played on the Gold Coast (see our report in sport).

Fans have been clamouring for such a NSW-Qld clash for years.

Keep reading the *Koori Mail* and koorimail.com for more news as it comes to hand.

● See more rugby league reports in our sports section

Bolt guilty

Columnist breached discrimination laws

ABORIGINAL pensioner and activist Pat Eatock (front) celebrates outside the Federal Court in Melbourne last Wednesday, following her racial vilification win against controversial newspaper columnist and commentator Andrew Bolt. The Sydney-based 73-year-old is pictured with her daughter Cathy Eatock and witnesses for the case Graham Atkinson, Wayne Atkinson and Geoff Clark. In his judgment, Justice Mordecai Bromberg found assertions by Mr Bolt that some 'fair-skinned Aborigines' were choosing to be Aboriginal and using their Aboriginal identity to access benefits and advance their careers breached the *Racial Discrimination Act 1975*, sparking a flurry of national debate about freedom of speech versus freedom from racial prejudice.

● See pages 6 and 7 for the full story.

● Deadly Awards rock Sydney Opera House – Pages 49-52

Bolt case, *Koori Mail*, 4 October 2011, from left: Cathy Eatock, Graham, Wayne and Geoff Clark, with Pat Eatock seated in front. Courtesy *Koori Mail*.

Canoe Tree yama muttar in the Moira Forest with ring bark markings from the Forest Commission. Courtesy Wayne Atkinson.

Barmah–Moira Forest Wetlands during replenishment of Dungula dharnya biyala (river redgums). Courtesy Wayne Atkinson.

PART III

Reclaiming Culture

9
A New World in Adelaide

This part of the storyline takes us from when I left Itchica in 1974 and moved with my family to a new world of ambition and discovery in Adelaide. The experience of Adelaide set me on a path of education that brought home to me the value of education as an empowerment tool. It allowed me to reach my full potential as a Yorta Yorta man and enabled me to gain knowledge and skills that I could apply to my people's struggle for justice, equality and self-determination.

I also learned the value of listening to the history and stories of our own people. This led me to record oral history from our people, and to learn more about our timeless past and the lives of our people on Cummera and Coranderrk. From this profound journey of learning I was able to develop oral history programs that celebrate and record our culture and stories. Reclaiming culture and the campaign for ownership and control of our heritage is where the storyline leads on this journey.

My hunger for knowledge and belief in the value of higher education came from my ancestors. I was raised within an extended family kinship network that taught us to be proud of our Aboriginality. It helped to transcend the put-down culture of those outside our group, and to walk tall and proud wherever we chose to go in life. It has continued to hold us in good stead through the many trials and tribulations that we face as First Nations peoples.

At the time I chose to seek further education I was thirty-two and married with two school-aged children (ten and eight). After weighing up the variables of moving and the advantages of a more secure future, we moved to Adelaide in 1975. Education and finding new pathways in employment and family security were my main goals. We found a new home in Elizabeth South, an outer-northern suburb of Adelaide. The kids found it strange at first, but they soon adapted and made new friends. The open class learning style in South Australian schools suited them well. Elizabeth was largely a decentralised town. Back then it was a vibrant car manufacturing centre, with a majority of workers coming from England and a small population of Nungas who worked in the factories. Others commuted to Adelaide by train for work and education. I was one of many students from all corners of Australia arriving for the Aboriginal Task Force education program.

Our arrival coincided with four other important events of the time in Australian history. First was Cyclone Tracy's catastrophic hit on Darwin in December 1974. People were still suffering from the shock and effects of the cyclone when we moved. Many were seeking health care and accommodation in Adelaide, and some were Task Force members. Second was a political measure that helped me with my studies. The National Employment and Training System was introduced by the Whitlam government in 1974. It provided an allowance for people to return to study to improve their education and skills for the workforce. The scheme also provided a living-away-from-home allowance that allowed me to return to study in Adelaide with the Task Force program. Thank you, Mr Whitlam. The study allowance was equivalent to what I'd been making as a concreter in Itchica: about $60 per week.

The third major event was the enactment of the *Racial Discrimination Act 1975* by the Whitlam government. At long last we had a human rights mechanism enshrined in Australian law to protect people against human rights violations, discrimination and racial vilification. (I will return to the impact of this law in Part V.) Last, but not least, was the dismissal of the Whitlam government in November 1975, which reverberated through our lives over the next two years with marches, protests and recriminations. This introduction to politics and actions outside the study program was a steep learning curve for our study group.

~

Fronting up for the first meeting with other Aboriginal and Torres Strait Islander students was like a new world beginning for me. The South Australian Institute of Technology (SAIT) on North Terrace was a lovely red brick building in the style of an English academic institution. Our study area was on the top floor with a good view of Adelaide, the first city I—a shy country lad from Itchica and Dungula—ever lived in.

Our initial introduction to the course was encouraging. The teachers were enthused about running a course of such historic significance. There was no formal Welcome to Country with smoke and clap sticks, but there were Nunga elders who welcomed us with open arms. They shared many stories and encouraged us to make the best of our studies. Our orientation to the world of academia was smooth and welcoming. It was quickly followed by an introduction to the study program.

The course was divided into two parts. The academic learning was mostly social sciences and humanities, while important cultural learning took place between us as Aboriginal and Torres Strait Islander students from different geographic and cultural backgrounds. Looking back, this was a unique experience that enriched us all in our comparative cultural backgrounds, self-esteem and confidence as First Nations people. The course was well structured and designed to cater to our study needs. It allowed people to come back to formal study and work at their own pace as they transitioned to tertiary-level education. Subjects included Sociology, Psychology, Politics, Social Work, Welfare Dimensions, Aborigines and the Law, and Community Development. We also had English and History classes, and guest lecturers taught an Aboriginal Studies component.

There was plenty of support along the way. Many students, like me, were away from home in the absence of equivalent Aboriginal tertiary education programs in our own state. The academic staff were tuned into our needs and diversity. While there were no Aboriginal lecturers, most staff had previously worked in Aboriginal affairs; we also had a variety of top-profile Indigenous leaders and activists visit as guest speakers. David Gulpilil was then at the height of his brilliant dancing and acting career, and came to entertain us with a magic performance, even playing Beatles songs through his didgeridoo.

We did have an Aboriginal counsellor who provided support for students and their families. In my second year an Indigenous lecturer from Victoria, Johnny Austin, came on board and taught Indigenous Studies, Legal Studies, and Politics. We were the frontrunners, but it would take many years before equal opportunity policies kicked in to give Aboriginal and Torres Strait Islander people equality within academia.

Each day you woke up looking forward to what you were going to learn. There were people from traditional backgrounds who spoke their own language and were willing to share cultural knowledge, while students from regional and urban backgrounds had a vast range of stories and common experiences to share. Our knowledge embraced language, culture, oral knowledge, secret-sacred business, and shared experiences. Overall, this remains one of the big takeaways from the course for me and I'm sure others. What we learned from each other was the high point for me. There were so many talented people around, and sharing sport, music, culture and our own histories helped to inspire our learning. The combined music, sport, community activities and studies kept us active and together as a group and helped us to bond as one mob.

In sport we had our own basketball teams that competed in the local men's and women's competitions. A lot of top footballers came from interstate and played senior footy with clubs in the professional South Australian, Victorian and Western Australian football leagues. They were sought after by local clubs and some played locally, attracting a lot of interest from the community who would turn up to watch.

On the music side, it wasn't long before the guitars came out and we formed a Task Force band made up of musos who played in bands in their own communities. The tunes I had up my sleeve from The Shades days were very handy. I played bass and guitar and sang vocals, and we had Kevin Dann from Broome on lead guitar, Billy Harrison from Adelaide on vocals, Jimmy Martin from Broome on drums, Steve Alberts from Broome on guitar and vocals, and Cyril Archer from Derby as our front man. Some of the women joined in on vocals and did guest spots at our gigs. We played at our own social events on campus and at community gigs in Port Adelaide, and were the feature band for Orientation Week. Me and Jimmy Martin also played with another top Adelaide band, which added money to our study allowance. The guitar was always being passed around in our recreation pad. There were lots of musos and renditions of songs going down, with a bit of country, rock, blues and some originals the main repertoire. The legendary Task Force Band were renowned for knocking out deadly tunes and bringing people together.

The Task Force gave us three different qualifications. First was a Task Force Certificate, which provided basic skills in literacy and welfare-oriented programs. This was relevant for those choosing to work in community organisations. Second was a Certificate in Community Development, which was equivalent to a Higher Secondary Certificate. The third and highest qualification was an Associate Diploma of Social Work, which could be used as a stepping stone to a university degree.

As we settled into the course, many of us found some of the Western theoretical constructs a bit over the top. They were too abstract and difficult to grasp, so we engaged a tutor to help decipher the jargon. It was a teaching requirement that lecturers had to adapt their language and teaching styles to cater for the cultural background of the learners. This made us realise the power we had as a student group. We had the right to raise teaching and content issues with the Academic Board. We could ask questions and challenge the way knowledge was being conveyed in accordance with our cultural values. Keeping it simple and breaking down academic language so that we could fully understand and learn together was a mandatory requirement.

We learned much about political activism and strategies that could be used to bring about change, particularly from guest lecturers in the Community Development subject. The textbook for that course was American activist and political theorist Saul Alinsky's *Rules for Radicals*.[1] His rules are effective empowerment tools for breaking down the barriers of inequality. Alinsky's aim with his rules was to bring about a more fair and just society by challenging agencies that promote inequality. For him, direct action was a political strategy designed to bring about change, and the means engaged in the process justified the ends being pursued—a tall order, but a plausible Western theoretical construct that provided strategies to think about. We had a lot of discussion about whether we could achieve real change in the power dynamics of Aboriginal Affairs policy through Alinsky's *Rules for Radicals* theory.

It was a time ripe for radicalism within universities and in the actions of public protests. You had to be radical to be able to get your message across and create change. Standing up in a lecture and challenging a view got you an ego reward from your peer group and was a way of releasing the fire in the belly for change that many of us had.

I was familiar with some home-grown political strategies that could be termed radical and driven by direct action. Yorta Yorta leaders had contributed to substantive changes before and after the 1967 referendum. Listening to the powerful voices of elders like uncles William Cooper, Bill Onus and Jack Patten and aunties Marge Tucker and Geraldine Briggs made you sit up and take notice. Their voices came from the grassroots, or what's called base-camp politics.

One very prominent Aboriginal visitor who put fire in many of our bellies was Charlie Perkins. He had already put the power of direct action in our minds from his courageous Freedom Ride campaign in regional New South Wales in 1965. Many in our group, including myself, would have joined him if we had the chance again. At the time of Charlie's visit there were hardly any Aboriginal people studying at universities in Australia. In addition to graduates Charlie, Margaret Valadian and John Moriarty, my younger brother Graham was doing a degree in social work (he graduated in 1977). That showed the extent of exclusion of Aboriginal and Torres Strait Islander people from mainstream higher education in Australia in the mid-1970s.

When Charlie visited us, he and John Moriarty were both employed in the Department of Aboriginal Affairs in Canberra. DAA had a bad reputation. It was regarded by many as a paternalistic structure run by mostly white career public servants. It overlorded the advancement of Indigenous Australians for most of the 1970s and 1980s and continues in similar structural and systemic forms today, for which it receives much criticism. Charlie talked about his frustrations working within such a daunting bureaucratic structure and told us about some of the confrontations he'd had with one of the head bureaucrats of DAA, Barry Dexter. Trying to create change within such a system was a heavy load to carry. Charlie gave us an insider's view of how the structure worked, breaking it down into its main functions and describing whose interests it really served. Most of the money—or at least two-thirds of it, according to Charlie—was absorbed into what he called 'The Industry' and bureaucrats' salaries. That is, it went into the pockets of those who chose to ride on what was quickly becoming an Aboriginal industry in itself (and has stayed as such, on a much larger scale).

Fifty years down the track from Charlie's Task Force lectures, the same issues vindicate his assessment and remain systemic barriers within the Aboriginal Affairs industry. His words come back to revisit us in current-day analysis of Indigenous Affairs policies and practices. The extent to which our affairs continue to be dominated by non-Indigenous interests was brought home in the report of the Royal Commission into Aboriginal Deaths in Custody, published in 1991. The 2024 final report of the Productivity Commission review of the Closing the Gap Agreement was even more scathing of the failure of governments' ability to deliver (see Chapter 22).

Charlie's lecture was certainly one of the most enlightening experiences we had. His way of teaching was excellent, coming from the heart of lived experience and his combined studies and knowledge of the economics and politics of Aboriginal Affairs. The lecture left its mark on me. Thanks, Charlie, and rest peacefully.

The ideas and discussions were interesting in those precious days as we were forming our dreams and visions for a better future. The insider/outsider view of achieving structural change in the system was a hot topic in our studies of the theory of change in politics. In our discussions, many believed that to change the system we needed to get inside and change it from within. The outsider view advocated for change by direct action and collective organisation. Putting theory aside, the irony of both views is that change is bloody hard no matter what approach you choose.

The insider/outsider view is still a dominant and divisive discourse in Aboriginal affairs today. Self-determination and community control is the only way, in my view. From my experience, the most practical option is the chipping-away philosophy, using base-camp politics to advance the cause. It is slow and tedious and needs a lot of patience, but knocking off the big chips inspires you to keep going. There are many examples we can reflect on from our own communities that demonstrate the success of community-based action. I believe that simple strategies shared from our past have led to more change than imported ideological theories.

~

The key things I came away with from the Task Force program were a big smile, an air of self-confidence, a high level of self-esteem and, most importantly, reaffirmation of my Aboriginality. I was ready to take on the world and break down those barriers that had been put in our way for so long.

It gave me the confidence to speak for myself. I was able to challenge underlying prejudices, stereotypical notions of Aboriginality, and casual racist jokes when they arose. I was aware of the odd racist one-liners that were often used to get a laugh. Those who made these jokes didn't think their words were offensive, and those of us on the receiving end would often cop it sweet to keep the peace. Sometimes you forced yourself to laugh along with the snide remarks to break the simmering tension. It wasn't comfortable, and you wanted to be out of that space. But people became more conscious of what they were saying when I was around. I would express an informed view on Indigenous matters and challenge some of the narrow-minded views portrayed in the media and social interactions.

Learning to adjust your survival skills to cope with racism and vilification is difficult. The reality is that racism is so deeply entrenched in human socialisation that it's hard to get rid of. The Task Force gave me insight into the value of knowledge and being able to challenge inner prejudices that one may have picked up in one's own upbringing. Some of my small country town views were challenged. I became aware of sexist and misogynous behaviour that I needed to confront. I was aware that change from within starts at the individual level: it's about yourself and the changes you need to deal with.

Learning in a secure environment made me more aware of the issue of knowledge deprivation, which certainly applied to my life before Adelaide. If you have been deprived of knowledge, then it is hard to know, isn't it? But a balance can be found. A simple proposition that reaches out to the more informed may offer a challenge to those who are deprived. Seeking out knowledge and becoming more informed is a healing process that starts from within. Self-education is a powerful way of overcoming the deprivation gap. An understanding of this framework helps to tackle and deal with learned prejudices and attitudes in a more balanced and objective way

The Task Force gave us valuable skills in literacy and knowledge that could be applied in our own communities. I'm sure we also gained personal growth and self-development skills through the social sciences and humanities courses.

~

There is a room at the top of the building on North Terrace that holds personal memories for those who ventured down the path of group dynamics. An extraordinary learning curve took place in one of our psychology subjects. We did therapeutic work on dealing with aggression and on the subject of unresolved anger. The lecturer concluded, after knocking around with our mob, that we as Aboriginal people (including myself) carried a lot of unresolved business within us. Finding a way to deal with anger—how to control it, manage it and get rid of it—became the key challenge. For this, we were introduced to the concept of gestalt therapy.

Gestalt therapy has a here-and-now focus on a person's awareness of their world and their relationships with others. It is sensitive to the ways that past experiences and fears may be affecting your life. Our tutor used this therapy for dealing with the lingering anger he found in our group. If not controlled, as we know, unresolved anger can cause tensions, alienate people and impact on others, including family relationships. It's easy to say that you are better off without it, but that is easier said than done. Underlying factors for the anger we may carry need to be considered. When you look at the nature and history of Indigenous-European relations in Australia, there are many causative and related factors. I won't go into that except to say that yes, many of us did carry anger to varying degrees. What I witnessed in that little room upstairs under the guidance of our therapist, however, was full-on anger expressed in many, often scary ways.

The idea behind gestalt therapy is to bring out the causes of anger and face them. You can then work out the anger through what is called two-chair work. That is, you put whatever caused the anger in the chair in front of you, and then you address that chair. You create dialogue with the nature and source of the anger you're dealing with. In releasing our anger, we could use foam battens to go to town on the cause of the anger. We could literally bash the hell out of the chair in front of us. The idea of this therapy was to release the anger, unleash it, get it out, and hopefully leave it behind. I can remember many floggings going down in that room. It was a rather gruelling and emotional experience, but the therapist skilfully took us through and was able to empathise with us during the process. At the end of the emotional encounter, we were totally exhausted. It took time to desensitise and come back down to an even keel.

We had time to reflect on the process as a group. It did help to face a lot of the unresolved frustrations and anger we carried around. However, it is still a vivid memory and often revisits many of us, including myself. I know of others who have, like me, journeyed back to the Room at the Top to reflect on our experiences. I often think about the issues we dealt with and the stories we shared. It had a bonding and trust-creating effect on us as a group. While those stories are kept in our secret, sacred memory boxes, we all have compelling memories of what we shared and left behind.

My journey of re-entry to education through the Task Force ended in 1977, but the connection with place and the brothers and sisters I studied with continues to this day. Many have since passed on, but we still have a national network of Task Force members who keep in touch—I recently visited and paid respect to dear friends in the Top End in Broome, Derby, Wyndham and Kununurra.

~

Unfortunately, while I was focused on my studies things didn't work out so well for my wife and kids. Elizabeth was too far from the city, making it difficult for Wendy to find work and for the kids to adjust to school. The transition proved too difficult for us as a family, and towards the end of 1975 Wendy and the girls returned to our home in Itchica. They were happy to be back in their own comfort space while I finished my studies in Adelaide. It was an awkward adjustment to make partway through the Task Force course, but my determination to complete the journey of education I had started helped to get me through the trying circumstances. We were lucky to have support staff to help us through difficulties, and I was disciplined in my work as a mature-age student.

I found accommodation in North Adelaide at Lincoln College, a residential college for students, which gave me space to concentrate on the study program. I returned home to Itchica to spend time with the family during term and Christmas breaks and then hitched a ride back to Adelaide with local trucks that travelled back and forth from Moama. Missing family and the kids was always in my mind. It was one of the hardest adjustments to make. I had to keep reminding myself and reassuring my family that the sacrifices would pay off in the long run. A better future would come at the end, and I would be home.

I graduated from the Task Force in mid-1977 with an Associate Diploma of Social Work. Graduation was a grand occasion shared by family and community members who came over from Itchica and Melbourne to celebrate. I went on to become one of the first to test the status of the associate diploma after graduating, when the Victorian Tertiary Education Accreditation Committee recognised it as the equivalent of two subject credits towards a Bachelor of Arts at a Victorian university.

Other students returned to their jobs in Aboriginal Affairs across the country or continued their studies in the degree program that developed. Many graduates became outstanding leaders in their communities in politics, health, media, archival research, land rights and cultural heritage control. Some became senior administrators in Aboriginal community organisations and national peak bodies. Those who gained national acclaim include:

- Pat Turner, CEO, Aboriginal and Torres Strait Islander Commission (ATSIC) and National Aboriginal Community Controlled Health Organisation (NACCHO)
- Jack Ah Kit, member for Arnhem and minister in Northern Territory Government
- Tom Calma, Social Justice Commissioner, Australian Human Rights Commission

- Freda Thornton (Glynn), co-founder of Central Australian Aboriginal Media Association (CAAMA), Alice Springs
- Stephen Albert, first chairperson of National Aboriginal Education Committee; actor in the stage and film versions of *Bran Nue Dae*
- William Tilmouth, Central Australian ATSIC Regional Chair; founding chair of Children's Ground
- Arnold 'Puggy' Hunter, inaugural NACCHO chairperson
- Andrew Wilson, Senior Aboriginal Access Officer, State Records of South Australia
- Cyril Archer, manager of Aboriginal Hostels Ltd; community leader in Derby, Western Australia
- MaryAnn Bin-Sallik, PhD in education, Harvard University; dean, College of Indigenous Education and Research at University of South Australia; dean, Faculty of Aboriginal and Torres Strait Islander Studies at Charles Darwin University
- Ian Trust, executive chair of Wunan Foundation, East Kimberley region, Western Australia.

The list goes on, including those who became PhD graduates, professors, lecturers and tutors in universities, TAFE colleges and community-based education programs. Many others achieved their chosen careers in fields such as international studies and human rights advocacy.

The Task Force was a successful model that influenced many changes in Indigenous education in Australia. The calibre of its graduates speaks for itself. If left to develop at its own pace and build on those achievements, the Task Force could have reached the level of an Aboriginal education program of national and world-class status. That is the dream for me as I reflect on what it achieved and what I learned. The factors that ended the Task Force program at SAIT when it was at its best are another story to be told.

I must pay tribute to the leadership of former South Australian premier Don Dunstan, who supported the vision of higher education for our people. And heaps of gratitude go to the Nunga community, elders, leaders and support groups who made it possible.

10

Indigenous Studies at Monash

In mid-1977 I returned to my family in Itchica. How would I apply those two-and-a-half years of intensive study that had changed my life and worldview?

I was offered a position in the Centre for Research into Aboriginal Affairs at Monash University in Melbourne and given the job of coordinating the Indigenous Studies program. The program featured many of the top Indigenous speakers from across Australia, including Harry Penrith (known as Burnum Burnum), Cheryl Buchanan, Gary Foley, Chicka Dixon, Kevin Gilbert, Kath Walker (Oodgeroo Noonuccal) and Jirra Moore. It was run concurrently with the University of Melbourne's Indigenous lecture course.

My job was to pick up the visiting guest speakers from the airport and introduce them to the class, and to coordinate the program between the two universities. I also worked on developing research projects and applying for research funding. The Task Force had inspired my interest in oral history, and I aimed to apply for a research grant that would enable me to work on recording the relationship between Cummeragunja and Coranderrk reserves. I was already partway there with research I had done while studying under the mentorship of our history lecturer at SAIT.

The job at Monash also opened other unexpected opportunities, such as when I was seconded to DAA to work on the National Aboriginal Conference (NAC) elections in 1977. I already had a good insight into the workings of DAA from our brilliant lecture by Charlie Perkins, but to join the bureaucracy that had come under the spotlight so much in our studies was a venture beyond my expectations. 'Really? Could this be true?' I said to myself as I pondered the scope of the task ahead. I did have a backstop, however, in that my younger brother Graham was working there at the time. This was some consolation for me as a newcomer to the world of DAA and the paternalistic image it had.

My secondment was for three months to work as liaison officer on community consultations for the NAC elections. The NAC was a national organisation established by the Liberal Fraser government in 1977 to replace the National Aboriginal Consultative Committee (NACC) established in 1973 by the Whitlam Government. The NACC had held national elections to elect forty-one representatives of regional electorates, but its mandate did not align with the expectations of Aboriginal leaders, who challenged its advisory status. They wanted responsibility for funds, and rights as a representative body based on the principle of self-determination.

When the NAC replaced the NACC, its powers were again curtailed. In fact, it was another advisory body to DAA. Its members were democratically elected by Indigenous people from regional and urban electorates across the country. Victoria and Tasmania were combined to represent the southern region of the NAC electorates. Nationally, there were thirty-five members elected to the NAC. Being another elected body with only advisory status was problematic.

My cousin on the Atkinson line, Paul Kirby of the Wamba Wamba tribal group, was also working on the elections. We conducted consultations for Victoria and Tasmania. The area was divided into five regions to elect four representatives from Victoria and one from Tasmania. The process was run by the Australian Electoral Office and was one of the first democratically elected advisory structures in Australia. The Aboriginal and Torres Strait Islander Commission (ATSIC) followed over a decade later. These are the origins of government structures designed to establish a link with the community through advisory bodies.

The secondment was a big step up from concreting and being a student. I was on the front line of DAA, the Australian Electoral Office and the regional elections. Paul and I worked well together. We learned much about the nature and extent of community engagement procedures, family group networks and the diversity of Traditional Owner territorial groups. Covering both states in the consultation process was a big task. We needed to contact the broad range of Aboriginal people across the length and breadth of Victoria and Tasmania. Consultations took us to the heart of local community-based organisations and beyond. I learned a lot about grassroots consultation. We visited individual families and people camped in the bush and on riverbanks. When we were on Country our job was to disseminate information as we travelled. We organised meetings to explain what the NAC was about, tapped into public events, and did a lot of work to promote the elections. We also had to coordinate the elections with the Electoral Office officials working through the process.

Working on the elections was a groundbreaking experience for both of us, putting our profiles out there in the community. We gained invaluable knowledge that could be used in future consultation processes, as well as a broad understanding of the spread and location of communities, organisations and kinship affiliations across the region. Later in life I was able to apply the lessons from this secondment experience to my work on statewide consultation processes at the Koori Heritage Working Group in 1982–83, the Koori Oral History Program between 1984 and 1987, and the community engagement process for the Yoorrook Justice Commission in 2021–22.

The NAC did put the federal government on notice with its recommendation for a treaty. Land justice in Victoria was on the agenda. The NAC used the Yolŋu word makarrata to describe the nature of the treaty needed. However, relations between the NAC and the government deteriorated into political mayhem. It faced the same fate as its predecessor and was eventually abolished by the Hawke Labor government in 1985. ATSIC was established five years later in March 1990; it was abolished in 2005.

The history of these three attempts by the NAC, the NACC and ATSIC to establish a representative Indigenous structure is relevant to debates about treaties, self-determination, sovereignty, and the referendum on the Voice. The rise and fall of those structures in such a short period sends a big message for future actions. All three were certainly active in giving advice, but when the advice was not listened to or acted upon, they remained powerless. How can advisory bodies have the power to bring about change in the administration and control of Aboriginal affairs?

No doubt, the transition from being called a committee to a council to a commission involved quantum steps in representative democracy. They all fell short, however, because of their subordinate relationship to government. Government controlled their funding and ability to fully represent Indigenous self-determination rights and interests. The constitutional amendment for the Voice faced the same fate of being confined to an advisory body controlled by the government. The demise of the previous structures shows that just giving advice at this point in our history is not good enough. An extraordinary number of reports, royal commissions, inquiries and recommendations for reform and structural change attest to that, and it all came home in the failure of the Voice referendum in October 2023. The lack of detail in the role, structure and powers of the Voice and the history of advisory bodies created a political quagmire to find a pathway through. I will return to the disappointing outcome of the Voice referendum in Chapter 22, with an alternative pathway proposal.

My secondment to DAA for three months culminated in the NAC elections. On completion of this remarkable journey of learning, I returned to Monash to reconnect with my research project on oral history.

11

A Picture from the Other Side

My interest in oral history was initially encouraged and nurtured by one of our exceptional teachers at the Task Force, Rosemary Ingoldby. Rosemary was one of the senior figures in the course and her teaching approach was strongly influenced by her connections with the Nunga community in South Australia. Much of her learning came from her involvement with the Raukkan community at Point McLeay, where she had been a community worker in the 1960s.

Rosemary was aware of the enormous depth and richness of oral knowledge held by the communities we students represented. She saw this as an important source of cultural and historical knowledge in our studies and encouraged us to tap into this knowledge to balance the ledger of the written record. She clearly pointed out that most of the history had been written by wudjelas or gubbahs, excluding the rich and diverse oral knowledge of Aboriginal and Torres Strait Islander people. She argued that early European ethnographers were notorious for interpreting traditional culture through their own blinkers and exhibited attitudes of bias and racial superiority. Thankfully, there was a shift in Indigenous history analysis and writing in the early 1980s. This came largely from historians who challenged past trends and tried to look at events from the side of the victims of the frontier experience.

Rosemary's teaching was influential on me. Her views on the recognition of oral history as a valid source of knowledge in the articulation of our history hit home. Indeed, it was her inspiration that put me on track for further research and studies in oral history. Gaining further education was a powerful game changer. There was no going back to old modes: it was a new journey with other challenges in front of me.

Returning to education had brought me back in touch with my own mob and how I could contribute to the struggle for justice. The Task Force experience filled me and my fellow students with visions and aspirations for a better future. We believed we could bring about change for the betterment of our people. This was uppermost in my mind when I finished that journey of my studies. It was further strengthened by the 'what do we want, when do we want it, and what have we got' call for land rights.

After completing the Task Force and working at Monash, my life changed dramatically on two fronts. My marriage had suffered while I was studying in Adelaide. Living away from home for extended periods put a strain on the relationship, and my returning to Itchica with hopes of finding work in Aboriginal affairs was a huge adjustment for the family.

After great difficulty, our marriage ended—on amicable terms. Parenting responsibilities for my two lovely and growing daughters continued at another level. I now had more time to spend with them, making up for lost time. I moved to Melbourne and found a base where I could keep in touch with family and have a home for the kids. They had regular visits for weekends and holidays, where they got to broaden their outlook and experience city life.

Adjusting to Melbourne after Adelaide gave me a chance to refocus on work. While at Monash, I applied for a research grant from the Australian Institute of Aboriginal and Torres Strait Islander Studies (AIATSIS) in Canberra. In 1978 I was successful in receiving a grant to complete an oral history project on Cummera history and its relationship with Coranderrk in Wurundjeri Woiwurrung Country. The idea for this project came to me while I was a student in Adelaide. We were encouraged to find out more about history from our own communities and from the Aboriginal viewpoint. So during the end-of-year break, I and other students would collect information from our communities that we would then share and discuss in our history classes. These discussions helped to answer a lot of the questions we had as Aboriginal people about our backgrounds, our identity, and the history behind us as a people.

I wanted to find out more about the history of Aboriginal missions and reserves. I already knew some of the history as told to me by my parents and grandparents who had lived on Maloga and then Cummera. The next place I looked in was books. I would like to give special recognition to earlier Aboriginal writers Ronald Morgan, Theresa Clements and her daughter Marge Tucker, and Sir Doug Nicholls, who through their efforts to record their history as they saw it gave me a lot of inspiration for the project. Special recognition also goes to Dr Diane Barwick, Mavis Thorpe Clark, Nancy Cato and Frank Endacott for their research and consultations in this area of history. However, most of the books I looked at had been written by non-Aboriginal people who had never lived on a reserve. Their accounts of reserve life were so far removed from actual life experience that they did not provide the answers I was looking for. The language was complicated, there was no gut feeling, and the written record had few Aboriginal voices. This didn't cut it for me. The rich oral history tradition that shared knowledge of events of the past was excluded, so that's where I wanted to begin.

I wanted to get a picture of reserve life from the other side of the story, thus the project was named *A Picture from the Other Side*. I tried to keep it simple and straightforward, using Aboriginal viewpoints to go deeper into reserve life at the personal level. Developing a road map for the inclusion of oral history as a valid source of knowledge was a big challenge. I had to learn new skills for recording and documenting information. I wanted to lead the way with goopna ngarwu and break new ground for the concept of storyline history. Picking up the storylines and following them through in time and place is a concept I used later in life when teaching students on Country.

The greater part of Yorta Yorta history is based on the practice and use of oral tradition. Indeed, it is the oldest and original method of acquiring information globally. Written history evolved from this source of knowledge. Historians used oral sources to write about the early wars in Europe, and the Bible is said to have been written from oral sources. In this context, written history is relatively recent in the Indigenous world. The pen and paper were introduced in the days of the reserve system, starting in about 1876. While the Yorta Yorta adapted to the written word, they retained a rich repository of oral knowledge.

'Oral tradition' is the umbrella that covers all forms of knowledge passed down by word of mouth. 'Storylines' is used to describe the way Indigenous stories relate to each other like veins running across the land. They are passed on by word of mouth and are communicated through other mediums of art, language, music and ceremony. Oral tradition teaches foundational stories to present and future generations. Learning from and understanding oral knowledge continues to be part of the discourse of Indigenous cultural studies.

Much has changed in the role that oral history plays in passing on knowledge within First Nations communities. Colonisation, frontier violence and forced removal policies impacted heavily on cultural practices. This came home to me when I contacted and interviewed people for the project. Initially I sensed there was an inner fear about sharing the depth of cultural knowledge held by our elders, fear carried over from the forced assimilation policies that tried to suppress Aboriginal culture and render its value as inferior.

Government policies may have made our practices seem dormant, but they were awakened by the cultural revolution that started in the late 1970s. Working on one of the first Indigenous oral history projects in Victoria gave me a chance to seek out and document the cultural protocols involved in the relationship between what I call the knowledge seekers and the knowledge keepers. Under Indigenous cultural and intellectual property rights, knowledge keepers have ownership of their recorded oral interviews.

I soon became aware of the fragile path I was treading. Those who had previously sought information from Aboriginal communities had left a legacy of anger and mistrust. It was an eye-opening experience to learn of the damage done by career-minded gubbah researchers. Most of their research seems to have been done to further the interests of their CV. They were writing to serve the curiosities of the academic world rather than applying knowledge to strengthen and empower community aspirations.

Fortunately, research practices have improved. Some Aboriginal and Torres Strait Islander people gained access to AIATSIS resources, past practices were exposed, and ethical changes were introduced to research policies. The question of who owned the material was controversial until it was enshrined in human rights mechanisms and intellectual and cultural property rights instruments. These mechanisms now protect ownership and cultural property rights.

I was fortunate to know people in the community I could sit down and have a yarn with. I also had access to my parents' generation who had lived on Cummeragunja up until the walk-off in 1939. Growing up in the extended family network on the Flat and living in Itchica had kept me in touch with our oral history. While I had learned about cultural protocols and the ethics of research from Task Force members and previous research studies, I must say I learned a lot more in the real world. I learned about developing trust with the community, showing I respected elders as the knowledge owners and returning copies of the stories I collected to them when the project was completed.

When I first took my project to the Yorta Yorta, most thought it was needed, but there were those who were sceptical and cautious from past experiences. The Norman Tindale research project was still uppermost in people's minds at Cummera. This was a joint Harvard and Adelaide University project over fourteen months in 1938–39, during the period of assimilation policy. It included 2500 case studies and the collection of thousands of genealogies and photographic images from south-eastern Australia, including Cummeragunja. There is a shock wave when you learn about the motives of the project's findings. The data was used to argue that Aborigines could be biologically absorbed into the white race without any fears of later throwback to darker skin colour. The assumption was that the Aboriginal population could become white and be fully absorbed into the general population over five generations. The researcher in charge of the project was Norman Tindale. We approached him and got copies of the data he collected. They included genealogical data and images of people on Cummera with frontal and side profiles to demark their Aboriginality.

I got a chance to catch up with Tindale in person when he spoke at a conference at AIATSIS in Canberra. Many people had the same concerns about his data: it had been stolen from Aboriginal people without their knowing what it was going to be used for and was still sitting in archives that were not available to those he had researched. In the late 1980s we managed to get the return of the Tindale collection, and it is now stored in the Yorta Yorta Nation knowledge database.

The issue of putting Aboriginal people under the microscope for scientific interests goes back to Daniel Matthews' time at Maloga. On 11 July 1880, he recorded in his diary a visit by Dr Canvin of the French warship *Rhin* accompanied by Count L Samoiski. They spent the night with Matthews, who said that Canvin 'made critical physical examinations of the Blacks for scientific purposes being under instruction from the French Government'. People became fearful of him 'when the Doctor measured their heads and compared with coloured discs the different shades of their skin'.[1]

Against such clandestine and prejudiced practices, I needed to ensure my project methodology was sound. I learned much about the process of eliciting information from people who held sensitive stories regarded as secret sacred knowledge. This had to be treated with full respect and confidentiality. I found that the fear barrier instilled in people's lives was a personal thing that could not be passed over. It took a long time to break through the pain of mission and reserve life and get to the other side. It started to become easier when elders could see that my generation and those after were becoming more aware of our culture, identity and history. We wanted to know more and to learn the full story from them.

As I approached the end of the project, I was joined by Cathy Guinness. She accompanied me on some of the oral history journeys and became my partner in life. Our first journey at that time gives an idea of our early days together. Cathy recalls:

> It was in Adelaide through the Task Force that I first met Wayne, and several years later we decided to share our lives together and I came over to Melbourne to be with him. Wayne was still recording stories of his elders when I joined him. We were not to know it at the time, but the history he learned through this project became the foundation of his life's work. That he included me in this journey was also a hint of what was to come. It seems to me as I look back that it was extraordinarily generous of him to share his Koori community with me, a gubbah. Would my presence deter people from being up-front as they told their life stories?

My own background was a big contrast to Wayne's. I was born in England and came to Sydney with my family when I was seven. My father was chaplain at Sydney University, and it was here that I graduated in Science. Then I spent three years back in England, where I worked with West Indians in their struggle for fair treatment in housing and employment. I also completed social work training.

On returning to Australia, I worked as a community worker with Aboriginal communities in New South Wales at Wreck Bay and Roseby Park. I was then attracted to South Australia by Don Dunstan's progressive Aboriginal affairs policies. Under his leadership I was involved in empowering Aboriginal councils on reserves. How would they regain their power after such a long era of oppression?

Thus began my lifetime search to understand the processes of decolonisation. I was keen to see the changes brought about by the independence movements after World War II. This search took me to Papua New Guinea, Africa and India. I loved learning about diverse cultures. I then turned to teaching Aboriginal Studies at the tertiary level. To prepare for this I completed a Diploma of Education and a preliminary Master of Anthropology.

These jobs gave me the opportunity to visit and work with communities on the Aboriginal reserves throughout South Australia. I organised student visits to these communities to learn directly from Aboriginal people, and I employed Aboriginal visiting speakers in the Aboriginal Studies courses. I knew how much better learning was when the teachers were themselves Indigenous. By the time Wayne and I met, I had eleven years' experience working with Aboriginal communities.

My travels with Wayne for the oral history project were a great introduction to Victoria and Koori communities. I had often experienced Aboriginal suspicion of gubbahs and understood where this came from: Kooris have had so many negative experiences, what with racial abuse and discrimination as well as the more subtle assumptions of white superiority based on racial stereotypes and class differences. The power of social workers and police over them was all too often part of their history. There was every likelihood that in Victoria, where I was unknown, I would be seen in this light. There was certainty that I would get it wrong from time to time as I quickly learned local Koori protocols. I could not be sure whether I would be on the receiving end of suspicion about my motives, so I played it safe and offered a listening ear. I tried hard to avoid being a know-all or, on the other hand, showing my ignorance. As it turned out I need not have been so wary. People knew and trusted Wayne and generally just accepted me as his partner.

Wayne was a natural interviewer. He always enjoyed being with older people, founded on the deep love of his own grandmother and grandfather. He has a gentle and empathetic nature, and now he added to that the skill of recording the interview unobtrusively on cassette tapes. He also developed the delicate art of guiding the conversation without cutting into the flow of people's stories.

I listened without much understanding as elders reminisced about people I didn't know, but this was a start for me. I gradually formed a picture of the vibrant Cummera community and of the oppression that led to the walk-off.

~

When Cath joined me, we travelled around Victoria visiting communities and meeting elders. The first stop on our journey was Bairnsdale for an interview with an elder, Aunty Mally Cooper, who had lived at Cummeragunja in her younger days. Aunty Mally welcomed us both in and sat us down with a cup of tea. After we exchanged news of relatives, I set up the small microphone and eased Aunty into the research questions. People felt good about sharing their experiences, knowledge and wisdom with those like us who were interested in learning. Aunty was Gunditjmara from western Victoria who married a Yorta Yorta man, Blue Gum Cooper, from Cummeragunja. I was related to Aunty's husband on the Cooper ancestral family group line. Cath was quick to learn that when we get together, we always talk about our genealogies and how families are connected through bloodlines, and our shared experience of missions and reserve history.

Saying farewell to Aunty, we set out on the Omeo Road up into Victoria's High Country. I wanted to introduce Cath to my Victoria. We stopped for a cuppa in Omeo and then drove on through Hotham Heights to Mount Buffalo. Here we discovered how very much we each treasured the bush, and how easily we adjusted to life out of the back of a van. I have a vivid memory of our bush camp at the base of Mount Buffalo—the simplicity of pulling up in a quiet spot, letting down the tailgate that was our table and chairs, and lighting a fire for cooking and keeping us warm. There is nothing like an open fire in the bush to create an inviting, cosy space for reflection. The next day we drove up the mountain and did some spectacular walks in the national park, taking plenty of photos to capture the experience.

Next stop was Myrtleford, tobacco country, to interview Uncle Dinny Roach. He and his wife lived in a small old workers cottage on the edge of the town. Uncle was a great storyteller. He had been a timber cutter in his time and was a solid strong old man. He entertained us with hair-raising stories about travelling on the undercarriage of trains, watching the sparks fly as the train struck metal and stone. He'd had no money for fares. Those were the days of surviving with irregular manual-labour jobs and an itinerant lifestyle. It was only later that Archie Roach became famous with his song 'Took the Children Away' and later still that I learned Dinny was Archie's uncle.

Back in Melbourne, it was time to write up the project. The work that went into putting oral history back up front was one of the magical moments of my career path. I began my manuscript with evidence from the memoirs of Theresa Clements and Ronald Morgan and then summarised the non-Aboriginal sources. Numerous documents record happenings before living memory. I examined the events as they were recorded through the eyes of the early squatters, protectors and missionaries. I went into the archives and examined the records of government reports, together with more recent studies by anthropologists, archaeologists and historians.

The bulk of *A Picture from the Other Side*, however, is the history of Cummeragunja as told by the people who lived there between 1880 and 1980, with special attention on their movements back and forth to Coranderrk. From over fifty tape recordings and interviews with elders who had lived on the reserves, I gathered a rich store of details about their lives. Although most of the report is about Cummera, I was fortunate to interview Priscilla McCrae, Dan Atkinson, Ivy Simpson, Bevan Nicholls, Merle Jackomos and other survivors about their memories of Maloga. Marge Tucker and others told stories about bush tucker, and Ivy Sampson spoke about Aboriginal cures. My grandmother Priscilla spoke to me about Yorta Yorta language and recited the lines of a corroboree song. She said:

> Our people, my mother Ada [Cooper] James and her brothers, and Theresa Clements, used to speak in the language. That's how we picked up a lot of it. If anyone was here talking with me, I could answer them … We used to say, if our mother was going out, Muma, woka nyini yana? Where you going to?[2]

When some of the younger generation, like my niece Lou Bennett and others, got on to the tapes they were amazed by the stories and language. This motivated Lou to write songs using our language and to pursue her career and a PhD in linguistics. She is now a senior lecturer in the School of Social and Political Sciences at the University of Melbourne, teaching language and taking students to Yorta Yorta Country where she uses Yorta Yorta language. All this—including a dictionary of the Yorta Yorta language, much of which I drew upon in writing this book—came from the revival of language from oral history tapes.[3]

A Picture from the Other Side is full of fascinating testimonies about schooling, Aboriginal initiatives that were blocked by government, troubles with various officials, and the breaking-up of Maloga and, later, Cummeragunja, including the walk-off in 1939. There was a sense of urgency to record while there were many elders still alive who retained knowledge of our history. It is the story of a people who managed to withstand the oppressive laws, restrictions and conditions of reserve life and survive. I was proud to record the stories of our people, who had retained their identity, pride, sense of humour and wisdom.

A significant outcome was returning a copy of the manuscript to those I'd interviewed. This was done conditional upon the manuscript being deposited at AIATSIS in 1981. The narratives are an example of the rich oral history of our people and the power of the storylines. The taped materials, transcripts and manuscript are in the institute's archival system and can only be accessed with permission and there are restrictions on their reproduction, use and publication. Due acknowledgement is made where extracts are used in this book.

The most exciting part of the project was when I gave a copy to my mother who then shared it with family members. She read it and said, 'Son, it was just like sitting in a large room listening to the voices'—that is, the voices of all the people to whom she was mostly related. She could visualise them and remember how they spoke. I was so glad she enjoyed the manuscript. While I was not born on Cummera, I was aware of the affection that people had for it with the way they embraced each other and shed a tear for the memory of dear old Cummera. I could see the passion for it when I would take my mother back to visit her birthplace and her loved ones. Time moves on, but the love for dear old Cummera will remain forever.

The biggest takeaway from the project was the feedback from the elders and my receiving a Commonwealth Overseas Study Scholarship. This allowed me to travel to North America to learn more about how First Nations Peoples there were recording and presenting their histories.

For Cathy, this was also a time of great change:

> Wayne's manuscript was completed during our first year together in Melbourne. The acknowledgements include 'many thanks to my closest friend Cathy Guinness for her support and skilful assistance with compiling and editing of the manuscript'. Collaborating in this way felt like the start of a strong and equal partnership.
>
> While this work was progressing, we moved house. We had been staying with Wayne's younger brother Graham in Blackburn and spending the weekends entertaining the children of their previous marriages and often other cousins as well. We moved into a small house in Forest Hill where Wayne's girls would have their own room when they came to stay for the weekend or holidays. I was now a stepmother and adjusting to the two girls whose upbringing in Itchica had been so different to what I was used to. This was the start of a lifelong friendship with Yolanda and Gabrielle.
>
> At the end of that first year, I wrote to Adelaide College to tell them I would not be returning. I had hedged my bets and taken a year of unpaid leave in case it didn't work out in Melbourne. Life with Wayne was much too interesting and challenging to return to my old job. From there, I was in it for the long haul.

12
First Nations Kinship

For me, the 1980s began with renewed vigour and inspiration. In 1981, after completing *A Picture from the Other Side*, I was very excited to be granted an Aboriginal Overseas Study Award by the federal Department of Education. From July to October that year, Cathy and I travelled to North America and met with First Nations peoples to learn about their oral history and American Indian Studies programs. The inspiration I gained put me on the path of much bigger and more enlightening education. The North American experience also allowed me to expand my knowledge base and helped put me in a position of authority regarding oral history method and practice in Australia. I wrote papers and gave guest lectures, which contributed to putting oral history on the map in Victoria and New South Wales.[1]

The main interests of our study visit were in programs organised and run by First Nations communities on reservations. We also visited programs run by First Nations people in universities and schools. By visiting these programs, we hoped to gain insight into how people first got them going, what methods were used in collecting and documenting oral history, how American Indian Studies was being taught, and what sort of funding and assistance was available. More importantly, it was an opportunity to compare the history of colonisation, land rights and treaty agreements in Canada and the United States with those in Australia.

From working at Monash to producing a project that culminated in an overseas study visit—what an unexpected reward! Apart from my time in Adelaide and my move to Melbourne, I hadn't travelled much at all. For a country river boy at heart, this was a big leap. In fact, I had only been on a plane once before, in 1980 for a flight to New Zealand for a cultural exchange. My brother Clive and our friend Paddy Malone had travelled to England and Europe in the 1960s and my younger brother Graham served in the Royal Australian Regiment in Vietnam in the early 1970s. My sisters Fay, Marlene and Veronica had not travelled abroad at that stage and my older brother Dimpsie was very much a local lad except for a boxing tournament in New Zealand, as Fay recalls.

Other Victorian Aboriginal people had visited America before our research journey in 1981. Mollie Dyer, who founded the Victorian Aboriginal Child Care Agency (VACCA; now the Victorian Aboriginal Child and Community Agency) in 1976, had been inspired by a visit to the Yakima Nation in Washington State. My brother Graham, who was a director of VACCA, had also visited First Nations communities; he was able to help me with contacts in America. After tech school he had trained as a fitter and turner but was drafted to serve in the Vietnam War in 1965. When he returned from active service in Nui Dat Phuoc Tuy Province, he was offered a scholarship to attend university. His Bachelor of Social Work from the University of Melbourne led to work at DAA and VACCA.

Flying into the clouds to explore another part of the Indigenous world and visit the Traditional Owners of the United States and Canada was an exciting proposition. I made sure I did my homework. I read Dee Brown's *Bury My Heart at Wounded Knee* at least three times and absorbed lots of other materials on North American Indigenous relations. I was basically looking for answers to a broad range of questions. Uppermost was the question of British colonisation and its impact on First Peoples. I wanted to understand the roots of their oppressive policies. Of special interest was the history of the reserve system. I already knew that the legal fiction of terra nullius had been used to justify our dispossession, but that was only the start of a bigger picture. I wanted to get to the source of the policy of segregation and control as it was practised and refined in other British colonies before it reached Indigenous Australia in the eighteenth century.

During my study tour I was very fortunate to have the company and support of Cathy, who, under her own arrangements, accompanied me on the journey. As she recalls:

> In my second year with Wayne, we found ourselves travelling to the other side of the Pacific. If you want a decisive test of a relationship, I reckon a challenging journey in a new country is a pretty good one. Happily, we did pass the test. Our first adventure began in Phoenix, Arizona when we hired a car. It was stiflingly hot, and this was the first left-hand drive and the first air-conditioned car we had driven—essential when it was regularly over 40 degrees. Giant cactus grew from the sandy desert, and we had been told to be wary of rattlesnakes and scorpions. We were in the south-west, an area of large First Nations reservations that had been won after many long struggles. They were now held under treaty agreements and systems of self-government.
>
> Although when we had meetings with official contacts I was just the partner, I was aware of how much I contributed. We would need to get around unfamiliar cities by public transport. So, my addiction to maps and timetables became very handy. Each evening would find us not relaxing in front of the TV but reflecting on our day and recording the events. These discussions were a great way of consolidating discoveries made.

In Tucson, Arizona, our most significant meeting was with Vine Deloria. His radical teaching was mind-blowing. Here was an Oglala Sioux man who was professor of political science at the University of Arizona. Back home in Australia the few Aboriginal Studies programs at universities were run by non-Indigenous lecturers; indeed, there were hardly any Aboriginal academics at this time. Deloria had established the first master's degree program in American Indian Studies in the United States.

Deloria, a lawyer by training, had a major impact on us. We attended a lecture he gave about riparian water rights. At first glance this would seem to be an obscure topic, and it was certainly technical in its details. Deloria not only explained the importance of these inherent common law rights but told the students in no uncertain terms that they must be better informed than the bureaucrats and experts on the other side of the fence—beating them at their own game is another way of putting it. Deloria called for the enforcement of treaty provisions. Asserting Indian sovereignty, he argued for the people's inherent right to their own political and cultural existence.

As we travelled from one First Nation to the next, the advantage of treaties became more and more evident. Their economic and cultural wellbeing depended on land ownership. Despite the failure of governments to fully honour treaty rights, the treaties had at least provided the foundation for First Nation negotiation powers.

Deloria inspired my next steps in education. Being able to sit in on his lectures at the University of Arizona in Tucson changed my thinking and encouraged me to return to study. He wrote several well-known books, including *Behind the Trail of Broken Treaties* (1974), *God is Red* (1973), *Custer Died for Your Sins* (1969) and *We Talk, You Listen* (1970). Chapter 4 in *Custer Died for Your Sins*, 'Anthropologists and Others', is a critical analysis of anthropology as a discipline and of its role with regard to First Nations communities.[2] Anthropologists, he says, are 'the most prominent members of the scholarly community that infest the lands of the free and in the summertime the homes of the braves'.[3] Deloria's wit was sharp and clever; so, too, was his teaching.

The most inspiring message I took away from Professor Deloria was his relationship with and respect from his students. You could have heard a pin drop in his lectures. His call for students to study hard and to learn the history better than the white man was riveting. He demonstrated the value of legal training and political analysis when many Aboriginal people back home were being trained for welfare work. No reflection on welfare work, but this led me to think more about the value of legal and political studies when I returned.

~

Our first foray into a First Nations reservation was to the White Mountain Apache in Arizona, a land of mountains and rivers. We were welcomed by Edgar Perry, the Apache director of the White Mountain Apache Cultural Center. He told us about their oral history project with its extensive collection of taped interviews that were being transcribed and translated into English. The material was going to be used for teaching Apache history in schools. It was part of the cultural museum, supported by a comprehensive research library. The whole centre was funded by the tribal council. We were impressed and inspired by this wholly Indigenous centre. We had seen nothing like it in Australia at this point.

We then travelled north to Navajo and Hopi land. We were starting to realise how significant it was that these Nations were living on their own treaty lands and prospering from their ownership of the oil and other products of the land. The Navajo Nation runs its own government, schools and industries. Our first stop there was the Navajo Community College (now called Diné College). The buildings themselves were striking, reflecting Navajo tradition and philosophy. A modern octagonal building stood next to a traditional hogan that had been used as the basis for the architectural design. The Nation also had a media station with its own radio and TV programs.

What a profound contrast this community-owned and -run Navajo reservation provided to Cummeragunja. Owning the land and its resources was a basic requirement for Navajo development. This realisation led us to learn more about the treaties with First Nations that distinguished North America from Australia. Why was Australia the only British colony where treaties had not been made with the Indigenous peoples?

Don't imagine that our journey was all work and no play. We managed to fit in visits to all sorts of amazing natural wonders: the giant redwood forests of California, where we walked among some of the world's tallest trees; the Grand Canyon, where the Colorado River has cut the deepest gorge into the layers of red rock over millennia; and many other great sights. Our favourite was the Canyon de Chelly in Navajo Country, a sort of mini Grand Canyon and a celebration of the history of Puebloan peoples. Up on the rim looking over at the perpendicular rock face to our left we saw, nestled halfway up on a precarious ridge, remains of the stone houses of the Anasazi, Ancestral Puebloans. How they built there is unimaginable. Then we heard a tinkling sound, and looking down to the floor of the canyon we saw the little white dots that were the sheep of the Navajo shepherds.

~

Another aspect of our research was visiting First Nations oral history programs based in universities, including the universities of Arizona, Utah in Salt Lake City, and South Dakota in Vermillion. These university-based programs offered an alternative source of historical information for students and researchers, bridging the gap between the established historical discipline and First Peoples' viewpoints. The training of Native American students in oral history methods was another benefit. We also learned that oral evidence stored in universities was being used by First Nations communities in their land claim cases.

A significant outcome of these university programs was the publication of books relating to the history of particular tribes, written and authorised by members of the tribal communities. We were able to bring home several of these books. Such projects would hopefully make the tribe an authority on its own history and culture rather than being written and defined by the colonisers. We were now raising other questions to be answered at home, like: Wouldn't it be progress if Australian universities followed suit, respecting Indigenous oral history as essential to a truthful retelling of the past, and promoting the employment of Indigenous academics to teach Indigenous Studies?

At Saskatchewan Indian Federated College (now the First Nations University of Canada), we experienced a fully-accredited Indian-controlled institution of the University of Regina, Canada. It offered a Bachelor of Arts in Indian Studies taught by First Nations peoples in art, education, management and social work, with legal studies in the pipeline. Students attended both general lectures at the various university departments and Indian Studies within the college.

My other takeaway from the North American study tour was a talk I was asked to give to Oglala students studying at the University of South Dakota in Vermillion. We had visited the Oglala Sioux reservation at Pine Ridge, South Dakota and shared stories of the impact of colonisation. When asked to give the talk, I was aware of the giant footsteps I was walking in as a visiting Yorta Yorta man. Names like Red Cloud, Crazy Horse, Sitting Bull and other resistance leaders were still uppermost in my mind from reading *Bury My Heart at Wounded Knee* and Mari Sandoz's *The Battle of the Little Bighorn* (1966). This battle is where General George Custer is said to have made his last stand on 25 June 1876, just two years after Maloga Mission was established in Australia for the survivors of the Yorta Yorta land struggle. Against this background, I made sure I stayed on course and trod very carefully on the subject matter. I was in the land of Wounded Knee and the place of many brave warriors watched over by Paha Sápa, the sacred Black Hills of the Sioux Nation. The Battle of the Little Big Horn was a memorable victory for the Sioux. Custer and more than 200 of his men died along Montana's Little Bighorn River. The battle is known to the Lakota and other Plains Indians as the Battle of the Greasy Grass. It was a violent clash over Lakota sovereign rights that resulted in the defeat of US forces, the most significant action of the Great Sioux War of 1876. It took place along the Little Bighorn River in the Crow Indian Reservation in south-eastern Montana Territory.

The fight was an overwhelming victory for the Lakota, Northern Cheyenne and Arapaho, who were led by several major war leaders, including Crazy Horse and Chief Gall, and who had been inspired by the visions of Sitting Bull (*Tȟatȟáŋka Íyotake*). The US 7th Cavalry, a force of 700 men commanded by Lieutenant Colonel George Armstrong Custer, a major general during the American Civil War, suffered a major defeat. Five of the 7th Cavalry's twelve companies were wiped out and Custer was killed, as were two of his brothers, his nephew and his brother-in-law. The total US casualty count included 268 dead and fifty-five severely wounded (six died later from their wounds), including four Crow scouts and at least two Arikara scouts.[4]

It was a profound experience to be in front of a group of sharp-eyed young Sioux students. Many were related to the leaders I have mentioned, and some even introduced themselves in that way before the lecture. So, here's me up front giving a talk on Yorta Yorta history and the impact of British colonisation and the reserve system. As I spoke, I felt uneasy and saw some students making funny gestures and laughing among themselves. I naturally interpreted this as a response to the way my talk was going down. Then suddenly, a couple of Sioux students stood up and said something like, 'Man, you're not goddamn talking about Australia. What you're saying is what goddamn happened here to us—we know that story so well.'

I was so relieved: an immediate connection and a sense of solidarity was forged. We were on common ground. The only difference was that it had happened much earlier and on a larger scale in the American frontier wars. But the origins of the conflict and how the crimes against humanity were committed were much the same. From a comparative historical analysis, we were on the same page about the way we as current generations saw and interpreted history. 'Thank you' was our response for what we were able to learn and bring back home to share with our own mob.

A major oral history contribution by the Sioux Nation was the book *The Great Sioux Nation*, compiled from oral evidence given to the Lincoln Treaty Hearing in 1974 at the Federal Court in Nebraska. The book contains testimony from every witness, edited and rearranged topically by historian and activist Roxanne Dunbar-Ortiz. It's a terrific resource on the culture and history of the Sioux Nation. This was years before the Yorta Yorta native title claim that produced a 12,000-page transcript of evidence, most of which was oral testimony from over sixty witnesses. The ideas from *The Great Sioux Nation* oral evidence are relevant to native title claims in Australia as a culture and history resource.

My search for the origin of the reserve system took us to the Newberry Library in Chicago. We had been told it would be well worth meeting Professor Henry Dobyns, a historian at the Center for the History of the American Indian. When I explained that I was searching for the origins of the reserve system, Dobyns pointed us to research showing the Irish link. 'Do you realise', he said, 'that the British had already practised their policies in Ireland by forcibly removing the Irish to the west of the country to clear the land for British colonists?' In 1649 Oliver Cromwell had invaded Ireland and tried to expel Catholic Irish to west of the Shannon to clear the land for British settlement. Here was another case of the policy of segregation and control. This insight motivated us to travel to Ireland and learn more of that history from Irish people.

~

Cathy's and my relationship had not only withstood the challenge of travel, but we had also gained experience for our unifying life goal: the quest for recognition and justice for Australia's First Peoples. Not only that, but we had also discovered a common love of travel when its focus was the discovery of histories and cultures.

We flew from New York to London. Cathy had spent over two years living there in the 1960s, but this was my first visit. Fresh off the plane we went into a small cafe and found ourselves right in tune with the nice, homely woman who welcomed us with 'What can I get you, love, a pot of tea? That's it, just make yourselves at home at that table over there.' This felt like coming home.

I was also at home with the iconic buildings—Westminster Abbey, the Tower, Piccadilly Circus, all names I had heard. I even visited the House of Lords Library to see for myself the Admiralty's secret instructions to Captain James Cook to take possession of any unoccupied lands he found on his first voyage to the Pacific.[5] I shared the lift with a real lord, a wizened old fellow complete with bowler hat and umbrella, asking me lots of questions before the lift dropped me off at the library and he toddled off to his parliamentary duties.

In those days it was cheaper to buy a round-the-world ticket than a return fare, so on we went to Paris. This was my first experience in a non-English-speaking country. We traversed France, Switzerland and Italy, reaching Brindisi and the ferry to take us to Greece. From Athens we flew home, happy to relax at last and full of inspiration for change.

Once we were home, we put pen to paper and laid out the findings from the study program. My report had the long-winded title *A Look at North American Indian History Programs: Some Ideas for Aboriginal Programs in Australia*. It outlined all the programs we visited and recommended models relevant to Australia. One recommendation was 'that the Commonwealth Departments of Education and Aboriginal Affairs recognise the importance of community and school-based oral history projects and establish oral history centres in each State'.[6] It was to our great satisfaction that this recommendation was taken up four years later when, in 1985, I was employed as a Koori historian by the Victorian Labor government to consult with the Koori community and relevant government agencies on the establishment of a Koori oral history program.

The final chapter of the report describes the cultural heritage centres we visited, particularly that of Yakima, which housed a museum, library, arts and crafts centre, media centre, restaurant and theatre. I used this example to advocate for Aboriginal people to establish their own cultural heritage centres and become the owners of and authorities on their culture. Such ideas were shared by many in the Koori community and over the next few years provided the inspiration for political action. The cultural revival of the 1980s saw cultural officers being employed to work in local communities. Aboriginal history programs were introduced into schools. The Dharnya Centre was built in the Barmah Forest as a live-in learning centre for elders to come and share their knowledge. All these positive events helped to instil pride in culture, identity, language and the value of our stories and contributed to the cultural revival, which grew stronger in the 1980s and has continued to be front and centre of the treaty process.

The North American study tour inspired me to be more informed, to learn our history so that we could empower ourselves to a position of strength and articulate the past from the Aboriginal viewpoint, keeping sovereignty and treaty upfront. Coming home, my mind was made up about further study. The next step was to choose which university would be best suited for me to continue my journey of learning to advance my knowledge. I chose the University of Melbourne because my brother Graham had studied there for his social work degree. He was one of the first Victorian Aboriginal graduates to come through, in the early 1970s, which made us all proud.

I wrote a letter to the Department of History expressing my interest in a degree. The head of the department at that time was Professor Geoffrey Blainey, a prominent historian who had written about Aboriginal history in Australia. He replied, and I still have his letter forty years later. He suggested I go elsewhere to pursue my interests in Aboriginal history. I was disappointed that the historian who had written *Triumph of the Nomads* in 1975 had failed to develop a course in

Aboriginal history at Melbourne University. At the time when he was teaching there, Aboriginal history was restricted to units within a second-year course: 'Aboriginal society and its characteristics' and 'The coming of the Europeans and their conflict with the Aborigines'. It was not until 1990 under Professor Greg Dening that a standalone Aboriginal history subject, 'Aboriginal and Koori histories', was introduced.[7]

Twenty years later, when I finished my PhD, things had come full circle and Melbourne University was seeking an Indigenous person to teach Indigenous Studies. To my advantage there were more progressive thinkers in universities by then who were supportive of Indigenous access and equity in education. At the time of my appointment as a lecturer I was fortunate to have senior historian Stuart Macintyre as dean of the Arts Faculty, where he promoted a greater role for Indigenous scholars and oral knowledge. Thankfully, that's where my employment at the University of Melbourne began, as an Indigenous lecturer within the Department of Political Science. All is history from there on.

I don't know what happened to Blainey's comment in his letter that he would follow up about me doing some tutoring. In any case, it quickly faded out of sight and out of mind for me. That we didn't actually get to meet and share knowledge was the end of the story. I would have liked to invite Professor Blainey to join me on the Oncountry Learning program that is taught in Yorta Yorta Country. He would have been able to meet Yorta Yorta people and learn about our rich culture and history. Dem's the breaks, as they say.

13
Land Rights and Cultural Heritage Reform

After being knocked back to do a degree at the University of Melbourne, I tried my luck at La Trobe University. They gave me two points of credit towards a degree from my associate diploma at SAIT. So, in 1982, I enrolled to do a major in History and Archaeology, and Aboriginal Studies as it was then called. With much enthusiasm from the overseas research, I started studying part time towards my degree.

La Trobe was one of the younger universities, building its reputation as an academic institution. It was competing with Melbourne and Monash universities and the Royal Melbourne Institute of Technology (RMIT), which had larger student populations. The History Department attained a good reputation for labour-oriented scholarship and some Aboriginal history subjects.

All the Aboriginal Studies programs then were taught by gubbahs. This was a huge backward step from those inspirational, fully integrated American Indian Studies programs I had visited. They were still fresh in mind, and I was hoping that such programs would start in Australian universities as recommended in our report. Unfortunately, my vision from the groundbreaking and enlightened overseas experience was way ahead of its time. Some advances have been made since then to include knowledge of the oldest surviving living culture in the world, but it's been a hard slog to gain parity and equality of Indigenous voices within the academy. Except for some conciliatory measures, we are still waiting to see the day when a fully integrated autonomous Indigenous Studies program is front and centre of an educational institution in Victoria.

Despite the lack of Indigenous teachers at the time, I was looking forward to studying history and archaeology. At that time, changing winds were blowing about cultural heritage management in Victoria. In 1982, cultural heritage reform and land rights legislation were key issues on the Cain Labor government's political agenda, but Koori people were excluded from the management and protection of Aboriginal cultural heritage. The *Archaeological and Aboriginal Relics Preservation Act 1972* was an antiquated law that was predominantly about the career interests of archaeologists. With the newly elected Labor government's reform agenda, our hopes were raised. Traditional owners were asserting their rights and lobbying the government for land rights and changes to heritage laws. We pushed for ownership, management and control of our heritage as a fundamental human right.

My previous experience of archaeology had been in 1979. When I returned from the Task Force, I volunteered to join a dig in the Nyah Forest, down the Murray Valley from Itchica. The head archaeologist organised a group of students and members of the local Aboriginal community to help excavate a mound in the forest. A huge upheaval broke out only days into the dig because the head archaeologist was impatient with the slow progress. He wanted to get to the bottom levels to get charcoal to radiocarbon-date the timeline of the mound. To speed things up, he brought in a front-end loader that recklessly uncovered skeletal remains in the mound. This sent shock waves through the community and offended the Aboriginal volunteers working on the site. In protest, we downed tools and walked off. This was just one example of arrogant archaeologists assuming control of our heritage. It remained uppermost in my mind when I chose to study archaeology at La Trobe. Combining the disciplines of history and archaeology was strategic. I knew it would be empowering to be able to validate evidence of Indigenous occupation and use of ancestral lands. I wanted to use the degree to build on my previous studies. The longer-term plan was to use my knowledge and skills for my own community and First Peoples of Victoria.

After I completed first year, the head of the Department of Archaeology offered me a part-time research position that allowed me to do my own research into Aboriginal sites in Yorta Yorta Country, and to continue with the oral history work I had started before our overseas trip. The research coincided with the reform measures happening under the new Labor government. The antiquated heritage laws were on its hit list. I took up many of the reform issues with archaeology lecturers and students, and some of the postgrad students also came on board for support. We set up a working group called ABARCH (Aborigines and Archaeologists) to discuss issues relating to research, management and protection of Aboriginal sites.

Consultation with Aboriginal communities on sites and the use of materials from site excavations was rather controversial. It was a Pandora's box that had not really been dealt with. There were no codes of conduct or duty of care for dealing with community consultation. I challenged the assumptions of archaeological practices and Western schools of thought and raised questions about the ethics of archaeological research and the importance of the principles of Indigenous cultural and intellectual property rights.

At that time there were few guidelines on appropriate cultural protocols for fieldwork. It was very much a 'We know what's best' approach. There was little if any accountability to Koori communities for archaeological research. There should have been a relationship between the academic researcher and the community, but instead Koori interests were represented by outsiders. There were some willing archaeologists, however, who wanted to transcend past approaches and develop a more collaborative relationship with Kooris.

It was a rapidly changing political environment. Koori assertions of heritage rights provided two options: one was to continue in conflict; the other was to work together in a reciprocal relationship. The seeds of reconciliation were being sown but whether this would bring about the desired changes was a key sticking point. This is why we formed ABARCH, to assist with reconciliation.

Unfortunately, ABARCH and its attempts at reconciliation were short-lived. We tried to be a forum for Aboriginal people and archaeologists to come together and discuss heritage issues, but some archaeologists couldn't accept change or that Koori rights were an integral part of their work. Many, particularly those with a colonial mindset, seemed more concerned about maintaining the status quo than about developing a dialogue with Kooris. The message on our posters, 'Our Heritage, Your Playground', described the attitude of many archaeologists.

The changing political environment created better relationships and understanding, but in some ways it had a polarising effect on those who found the bridge too difficult to cross. From my perspective it was a valuable exercise because we raised the awareness of many archaeologists. Up to that point, they'd had very limited, if any, contact with Kooris except for what they read in books. As a result of our work, many bridged the gap and recognised the value of working together. It was a steep learning curve for all parties and one that put Koori rights on a more equal footing. My role as researcher and political campaigner for change within the Department of Archaeology was a rather contentious one; nevertheless, I was fortunate to see positive outcomes.

In 1983 I got to work on a joint project with a postgraduate student to report on Aboriginal associations with the Murray Valley region for the Victorian Land Conservation Council (VLCC; now the Victorian Environment Assessment Council), the government authority on the environmental health of the 10 per cent of public Crown land that remained in Victoria. It was through the inclusion of Aboriginal people in projects like this that seeds were being sown for greater recognition and awareness within government. The VLCC was seeking submissions on the Murray Valley study area.

The Yorta Yorta submission combined source materials from archaeology, anthropology, historical records and oral history. The materials were used to demonstrate sustained Yorta Yorta connections to Country from time immemorial to the present, and the submission pushed for this connection to be formally acknowledged by the Victorian Government. This would allow for the continuity of Yorta Yorta connections and enable the preservation of the natural and cultural values of the Crown lands. I included an account of the Yorta Yorta history and contribution to environmental management, and archaeological dates for the area. I showed how the Yorta Yorta had adapted and continued to practise their culture and to maintain their sacred relationship with the land. The report was the first of its kind to be inclusive of Aboriginal connections with Crown lands in Victoria.

After that report, my study plans changed direction. There was so much happening at the community level. With the changes in Aboriginal Affairs policy, communities were ready for action. The Yorta Yorta Tribal Council was formalised in 1983. A leading figure in it was Elizabeth Hoffman, who had retired from the position of director of the Aborigines Advancement League in Melbourne to work back home. A new generation was rising to re-establish Cummeragunja community. Key objectives were building back a community that had been affected by the walk-off, and regaining our traditional lands. We had a vision of Cummeragunja and Yorta Yorta lands as the backbone of a proud Yorta Yorta community.

At the same time, the Victorian Labor government presented the 1983 Aboriginal Land Claims Bill to parliament. The bill acknowledged prior ownership of land and established a framework for the granting of Crown land to Aboriginal people in Victoria, subject to certain limitations relating to the public interest.

As a member of the Yorta Yorta Nation, I was asked to help in our struggle for land justice under the government's reform agenda. Assisting with the land claim meant putting my studies at La Trobe on hold. The pull of ancestral lands and the call for justice was too strong. I was back on Country with the Yorta Yorta claim for the Barmah Forest. My cousin Sandra Bailey Cooper was also asked to work on preparing the land claim. She had completed a law degree at the University of Melbourne. I was engaged to do the cultural and historic research for the claim and Sandra agreed to do the legal work. We worked hard to finish it, anticipating that the bill would be passed, and in 1983 lodged the Yorta Yorta claim for the Barmah Forest.

In preparing the claim, we witnessed the divisive hostility surrounding land rights. The lodgement of the claim was a mindboggling experience, especially when our intentions hit the media. Opposition to the claim by local media was unprecedented. Corporate and vested interest groups, local government, farmers, councillors, the National Party and the Australian League of Rights all combined to run a hostile scare campaign against the Land Claims Bill. They came out in force to undermine the Victorian Government's land rights proposal.

The extent of misinformation and antagonism was particularly evident at a public meeting in Nathalia in 1984 organised by local councillors, farmers and politicians to discuss the government's land rights proposals. Some 700 people attended, mostly from the local area and within traditional Yorta Yorta land. Anti-Aboriginal sentiment had already been created through the unbridled media misinformation campaign. The chair of the meeting described Aboriginal people as a 'conquered race'.[1] Speakers on land rights were all non-Indigenous. The National Party spoke for local land interests, while Dr Ken Coghill, the Aboriginal Affairs assistant to the Victorian premier, represented the newly elected Labor Party's position. The party wanted to get some scores on the board in Aboriginal Affairs, particularly considering the government's shameful track record on land justice. They were hoping to pass the Land Claims Bill, but to become law it needed the support of the Upper House, the Legislative Council, which was dominated by the Liberal and National parties. The National Party speaker was quick to jump on negative stereotypes of Indigenous society, inflaming the meeting and stirring up old prejudices. He mounted an irrelevant attack on Aboriginal people at Lake Tyers, claiming they were 'behind in their rent'.[2] He then attacked Aboriginal people generally for claiming land that, he argued, they were not entitled to. He used government definitions of Aboriginality to create division and discord at the meeting.

After the speakers presented their views, the forum was opened for general discussion. Local farmers were quick to roll out old prejudices that the Yorta Yorta had heard for so long: the land was going to be 'locked up' and made inaccessible to others; the return of land meant the land was not going to be looked after. When Yorta Yorta people in the audience tried to take part in the debate, they faced hostility.

The Nathalia meeting shows the heat in land rights conflicts of the 1980s. It was the most hostile meeting I have ever attended. On reflection, it was the first time I ever felt like an alien in my own land. It exposed a mindset that was driven by systemic racist attitudes and an underlying fear and insecurity regarding the theft of Indigenous land. It brought home the barriers that our ancestors had been up against when they challenged the Anglo systems. This racism was championed by far right and antisemitic groups like the League of Rights, which had a stranglehold in parts of rural Australia for many years. They attacked Indigenous rights and undermined any policies aimed at addressing injustice and inequality.

Regional newspapers, led by the *Numurkah Leader*, ran racist comments and articles. In one news item, under the provocative headline 'Land War: the Battle for the Barmah Forest', a senior local councillor equated Yorta Yorta people with the 'purity of his cattle'.[3] Another councillor, a schoolteacher in Nathalia, expressed his racial superiority over the Yorta Yorta by saying that 'Aborigines were a conquered race' whose 'rights depended on the humanness of the conqueror'.[4] The extremist League of Rights supported these views, painting a sinister image of land rights being a threat to Australia's sovereignty inspired by communist manipulations.[5]

Yorta Yorta elders responded to the vicious press. Speaking on our struggle for justice, Aunty Frances Mathyssen said, 'Nothing will ever stop us! It's our life we are talking about.'[6] Margaret Wirrpanda, chair of the Yorta Yorta Tribal Council, explained our position, which was recorded in the *Herald-Sun* under the headline 'A nation fights for its heritage': 'The Yorta Yorta people, she said, have [been instrumental] in the land rights fight that has continued since the land was taken.'[7] As Yorta Yorta elder Elizabeth Hoffman explains, here we go again: 'We are fighting from our old position of nowhere.'[8] There was no adequate empowerment or support for a positive, anti-racist public awareness campaign. The power dynamic showed the inequality for claimants. The extent to which the Yorta Yorta had to continually justify their very sense of being confronted us again in the Yorta Yorta native title claim a decade later (see Chapter 16).

The result of the 1984 claim was just another example of divide-and-rule politics. The claim didn't get up because the Labor government lacked the power to create a legitimate land claims process. They did not have the numbers in the upper house to pass the legislation. Our work, however, was not lost as in 1992 it formed the basis of the Yorta Yorta native title claim.

The struggle for justice is daunting and the barriers to our fight for justice are never-ending. The question I'm often asked when confronted with such a task is 'How does one deal with it?' I choose to deal with it by retreating to my own cultural space. I draw on our past to empathise with those who carried the flag before us. Our history teaches us that there is no magic wand to wave that will light up a new day. Returning to the fold to keep chipping away is not a cure-all, but it helps to soothe the restless soul. Justice is ever elusive but never out of sight or mind.

After that leg of the land rights journey, there were bigger fish to fry on the heritage front. My studies at La Trobe were on and off. In a simple twist of fate, I became president of the Victorian Koori Heritage Working Group in 1984. The struggle continued.

14

Bringing Koori Culture Centre Stage

In 1984, the Koori Heritage Working Group (KHWG) emerged from a Victoria-wide heritage seminar at the Aborigines Advancement League. Its members were chosen to represent community interests in the changes to the heritage laws. The KHWG brought together members and representatives from local community organisations across the state. Its mandate was to develop a charter that reflected how Koori people could regain control of their heritage. To achieve this, it ran a series of consultations at different culturally significant locations in Victoria. My experience of the NAC elections in 1979 served me well in these statewide consultations.

The drive to establish the KHWG had actually started in the late 1970s. 'Putting Culture Back Up Front', 'Cultural Revival Is Survival', and 'Koori Heritage, Koori Control' were messages that drove the Koori heritage revival. We needed to get back to a holistic view of our heritage and its inseparable relationship with land, identity and community. Local community organisations needed to have powers to protect heritage property at the local level.

Community-based organisations in Melbourne were centred round Fitzroy. Initially this had been a place of refuge and cheap housing for people coming in from reserves, including Cummera. Fitzroy in the 1970s became the home of the Victorian Aboriginal Legal Service and the Victorian Aboriginal Health Service, as well as childcare, housing and youth services. Mainstream social services had proved unable to meet the needs of our communities, and these Aboriginal organisations filled the gap, providing spaces where Kooris felt safe and their life experiences were understood. As momentum grew in the 1970s for Indigenous affairs generally, much effort was directed towards the establishment and control of these vibrant service delivery organisations.

The KHWG took the initiative to focus on fundamental rights-based issues, which included reclaiming our cultural heritage. The call for land rights ran concurrently with the heritage political struggle. Indeed, it was an opportune time for reform, with the newly elected state Labor government committed to land rights and self-determination, and a minister for Aboriginal affairs who was also the attorney-general, Jim Kennan. This certainly provided the impetus to put culture and land rights back up front and to empower organisations to have control over their social, economic and cultural affairs.

Looking back, one can say this was the impetus for an emerging cultural revival, a cultural renaissance, expressing itself through our unique ways of being and seeing the world through Koori eyes. It was through art, literature, dance, theatre and music that First Peoples culture in Australia regained its rightful place as the embodiment of Indigenous identity and connections with Country. Culture was viewed not as frozen in time, but as steeped in tradition that had continually adapted to changing circumstances. The timeline of 60,000 years grounded us in our Aboriginality and gave us power to advocate for rights that were inherently ours.

In the early 1980s the Koori Information Centre (KIC) opened its doors on Gertrude Street. It was at KIC that the KHWG found a working space to campaign from. We benefited from KIC's publication *The Koorier* to get information out to communities. It helped us to promote KHWG cultural aspirations and to engage in the community consultations that were happening across Victoria. I was now in the centre of Koori political activity, enjoying the chance to broaden relationships to include those from other communities around Victoria. Popular gathering places for us in Fitzroy outside work were the Builders Arms Hotel in Gertrude Street and the Eastern Hill pub in Victoria Street. This is where we used to catch up at the end of the week to yarn about issues. It was a great place to bump into relatives and meet other groups. 'Who's your mob?' was our way of identifying as community members.

One of the influential people I met at that time was Uncle Albert Mullet, a Gunai man from Gippsland. He was senior elder of the KHWG and a strong leader and mentor for us younger members. The KHWG wanted to bring people together to make policies based on Koori perceptions of their own heritage. We developed the Koori Heritage Charter to guide our negotiations with government on the reforms required. One of our priorities was to repeal the racist *Archaeological and Aboriginal Relics Preservation Act 1972*. That Act gave ownership of Indigenous heritage to the Crown, with some token representation—there was only one Koori person on an advisory committee of ten members.

We heard in our community consultations that 'ownership and control' should be returned to Kooris and the definition of heritage should reflect Koori values. The Koori ideology that underwrote the principles of the charter was about not locking heritage in a time warp, and recognising the links between contemporary and traditional connections. The working definition of heritage that emerged from the KHWG consultations included:

> Those distinctive spiritual, material, intellectual and emotional features that together make up our present and past identity as Koori people. It is not just the arts, monuments, and written works, but our way of life, our basic rights as human beings and our values, beliefs, and traditions. This encompasses both physical and non-physical things like our tribal lands, sites sacred, significant, and historic, burials, skeletal remains, artefacts, art, oral knowledge, language (verbal and non-verbal), ceremonies, documentary evidence and archival materials including genealogical information.[1]

Fundamental human rights of self-determination, sovereignty and equality were the substance of the charter, and they became the guiding framework for all negotiations on heritage reforms. The working definition from the KHWG consultations was consistent with the subsequent report, *Our Culture Our Future*, prepared in 1998 by Indigenous lawyer Terri Janke with AIATSIS and ATSIC.[2] Indeed, when looking at the resilience of our heritage, we need to recognise our survival through the devastating impacts of invasion and colonisation. Both wrought havoc on Indigenous culture and lives across the nation. The legacy of colonisation is still being dealt with in 21st-century Australia. At the time of writing, we are hoping the truth justice process can find answers to the magnitude of the impact of colonisation through the Yoorrook Justice Royal Commission.

The relationship between cultural heritage and self-determination was also defined by the KHWG. Self-determination was the key driver of the reform measures and extended the debate beyond domestic politics into the international arena. We wanted to draw on those international conventions to give substance, jurisdiction and power to the Koori voice.

The definitions of self-determination bandied about by governments are inconsistent with Indigenous worldviews. Aboriginal communities in Victoria need to define what self-determination means to them, rather than having a definition imposed by government bureaucrats. These days the framework of self-determination under international law is articulated in the United Nations Declaration on the Rights of Indigenous Peoples (UNDRIP), which was created by the Working Group on Indigenous Peoples of the UN Economic and Social Council and passed by the UN in 2007.

The right to self-determination as defined by UNDRIP is about freedom and human dignity. It states that 'all Indigenous peoples have the right to self-determination and by virtue of that right' are free to 'determine their political status' and to 'pursue their economic, social, and cultural development'.[3] The equivalent Aboriginal view of self-determination is community control, which includes the transfer of power and resources. We want people to determine their own destiny and have control over their own affairs. Real self-determination requires that governments give access to and ensure representation of such groups in the democratic process, particularly in relation to decision-making on issues affecting traditional land, economic development and cultural responsibilities.

When we talk about cultural heritage and the right to self-determination, we need to remember that Aboriginal people before colonisation enjoyed and practised political autonomy under their sovereign status. Prior to invasion and the appropriation of our cultural heritage, our traditional lore recognised and protected our political, cultural, social and economic rights. It has only been since colonisation that these longstanding rights have been denied.

In the struggle to retain our cultural rights, the KHWG acted as a voice between the Koori community and federal and state governments. We also worked as a mediator between archaeologists and those institutions involved in heritage management. Our first political act was to reject the Victorian Government's *Aboriginal Cultural Heritage: Victoria* discussion paper in 1985,[4] which was one of its policy commitments when it took office. We rejected it because it did not address the fundamental issues of ownership and control and had been written without consultation with Traditional Owners. Its direction was largely driven by vested interests who wanted to maintain the status quo.

At this time, other Indigenous and non-Indigenous people were also looking at the extent to which heritage laws excluded Indigenous rights. Law professor Greta Bird criticised the Anglocentric nature of the Victorian *Archaeological and Aboriginal Relics Preservation Act 1972*, arguing that it served the interests of scholars trained in the European tradition rather than Kooris.[5] Justice Kenneth Jenkinson pointed out that the provisions of the Act gave no guidance on the legal recognition of Koori rights; instead, they were directed to 'facilitating the scholastic and educational activities of a Western European Community planted on alien soil'.[6]

Politicians were also questioning the inadequacies of heritage laws and Koori rights. Shadow Minister for the Arts Race Mathews hit the nail on the head when he said, 'It must be extraordinary to our Aborigines that the history, culture and art of this race should automatically be entrusted to the care of people from a completely different background.'[7] Giovanni 'Johnny' Sgro MLC went much further, saying, 'it is the black people's heritage, not ours' and claiming that 'white people cannot be trusted anymore'.[8]

~

While we achieved significant reforms in the 1980s, including the enactment in 1987 of Part IIA of the federal government's *Aboriginal and Torres Strait Islander Heritage Protection Amendment Act 1984*, which gave

Victorian Aboriginal peoples a greater role in protecting their cultural heritage, many changes have taken place since. Part IIA decolonised the Anglocentric Aboriginal relics laws of the 1970s and empowered the First Peoples of Victoria to have ownership and control over their heritage—a watershed achievement in Indigenous heritage reforms in Australia. The generational shift in the power dynamics of Victorian heritage management, control and policy direction was groundbreaking. But did the 1987 reforms remain intact?

Part IIA stated that the Government of Victoria acknowledged 'the occupation of Victoria by Aboriginal people before the arrival of Europeans' and that 'the Aboriginal people of Victoria are the rightful owners of their heritage and should be given responsibility for its future control and management'.[9] These hard-fought reforms were achieved by the KHWG. Another major change included oral knowledge in the definition of cultural heritage. Under the reforms, the definition was broadened to embrace non-physical aspects of culture, including Aboriginal folklore and oral histories, which are an integral part of our cultural life. Songs, rituals, ceremonies, dances, art, customs and spiritual beliefs are significant to Koori people under our traditional laws and customs.

While local communities were afforded some control through the Act, heritage campaigner Henrietta Marrie (nee Fourmile) reminded us that 'ultimate authority for the ownership and control of Cultural Heritage stayed with the Minister'.[10] This was clearly identified in Chief Justice Elizabeth Evatt's 1996 review of the Act. Evatt found that while some authority was given to local communities and traditional custodians under heritage laws, in all jurisdictions the minister retained veto powers. In most cases where there has been a conflict between Indigenous heritage and economic interests, it is Indigenous rights that have been walked over. We have witnessed many examples in Victoria and Australia, including with Alcoa on Gunditjmara land (1980), Noonkanbah pastoral station in the Kimberley (1980), the Old Swan Brewery on Perth's foreshore (1989), women's business on Hindmarsh Island (1995), Djab Wurrung sacred birthing trees (2018–20) and Rio Tinto's destruction of Juukan Gorge in the Pilbara (2020).[11]

However, looking back, Part IIA in 1987 was a revolutionary shift in thinking and bold action. It changed the power imbalance between government control and Koori heritage entitlements and marked a recognition of Indigenous cultural values and beliefs that have been practised and enjoyed since time immemorial. Most significantly, it decolonised the Anglocentric definition of Aboriginality that drove the antiquated thinking behind Aboriginal heritage ownership and protection laws.

Decades later, the Victorian *Aboriginal Heritage Act 2006* and subsequent amendments in 2011 and 2016 whittled away many of our reforms and gave more control back to government. From changes to the Aboriginal heritage laws in Victoria in 2023, we can see clearly that the minister retains overarching powers in all aspects of the heritage program.[12] The minister controls the process by which people are chosen to represent Traditional Owners, by selectively appointing members of the Aboriginal Heritage Council. The ultimate power of veto is vested in the Crown. Restrictive legal systems within government structures maintain the power imbalance between Koori rights and political agendas. Our experience of the government power dynamic justifies this proposition.

The other huge Pandora's box of cultural conflict is the moral issue of Aboriginal ancestral remains, which came to a head in 1983 when Koori museum workers discovered that there were large collections of Aboriginal remains stored by Museums Victoria (MV) that could be loaned out to universities for scientific studies. In 2024 Aboriginal writer Celeste Liddle wrote about the immorality of the grave-robbing:

> In cultural institutions across the UK and Europe are many Aboriginal human remains, stolen from this country. In many instances, these remains were used by scientists, anthropologists and eugenicists to 'prove' Aboriginal inferiority and justify colonisation. Some concerted community efforts have seen the repatriation of remains, but there were so many taken and there is so far to go.[13]

As recently as the 1980s, MV held over 1600 ancestral remains, some as old as 14,000 years, in its Murray Black and Berry collections at the University of Melbourne.[14] The collection included skulls that were dug up and stolen from Yorta Yorta Country in the early nineteenth century. The KHWG and MV's Koori liaison officer were instrumental in restricting the use of skeletal remains for scientific studies and public displays, including those held by the University of Melbourne. This became the catalyst for Jim Berg's legal actions against MV and the university in 1984.[15] Since then, many Koori communities have been successful in regaining control of ancestral remains and reburying them on ancestral lands. There are still many more, however, that have not been repatriated to their proper resting places.

15

Koori Oral History Program

At the age of forty-three, with some good timing, I was employed by the Cain Labor government to set up the Koori Oral History Program and to work on other cultural matters. The KHWG reform measures had put oral history back on the cultural agenda, and my work on cultural heritage reform led to me being employed by the state government. I was an adviser to the minister for Aboriginal affairs on cultural matters, including the establishment of the Koori Oral History Program (KOHP). My studies at La Trobe had to take a back seat again.

For the next eight years I was a public servant, an insider in the busy world of the Office of Aboriginal Affairs Victoria (OAAV), on the frontline of the consultations and debates happening with government and key stakeholders. I was lucky to have a top group of Koori people supporting me from the old guard of the reform movement. We worked together and achieved some significant changes.

Being employed as a Koori historian was a quantum shift. I was constantly in touch with the attorney-general and minister for Aboriginal affairs, Jim Kennan. Surprisingly, he was approachable and supportive and made a commitment to Koori ownership and control of their heritage. This was a major change in cultural heritage administration and policy direction. These principles formed the basis of the subsequent *Aboriginal Heritage Act 2006* and its amendments of 2021.

One way of having a more coordinated approach to the heritage program was to bring it all together under what we called the One Roof option, which was not adopted at that time. Achieving an overarching cultural institute was the longer-term objective. It wouldn't happen with a stroke of the minister's pen: it would be an incremental process. Whether it will be included in treaty negotiations is now being considered.

Part of my job was to do the consultations for the establishment of the KOHP. I had a lot of work to do gathering information, talking to communities about the program, and presenting a report on the way forward. Choosing the most appropriate place for the program was a big job. Finding a location that could house it and be a safe place to store the materials collected was essential. After many consultations with relevant groups, it was decided that the appropriate place to house the project was the Victorian State Library. The library agreed to accommodate the program, providing resources and access to its collection of documentary materials on Aboriginal history. The location was suitable, and the library environment was compatible with the oral history work plan.

After two years of consultations the KOHP was formally launched in the State Library in 1987. It was a grand occasion attended by many people, including the director of the State Library Jane La Scala, Minister for Aboriginal Affairs Jim Kennan, and the governor of Victoria, Davis McCaughey, as well as Aboriginal elders. The governor was well versed in the concept of oral history and spoke of its value as an Indigenous knowledge source. Speaking to the poster we launched for the opening of the program, 'Keeping It for the Future: I Share This Story with You', Uncle Albert Mullet of the KHWG gave a wonderful talk from a Koori perspective on the importance of oral history and the cultural revival. My brother Clive, an accomplished artist and graphic designer, designed the logo for the program poster.

After the launch, it was time for work. It was a long way from my studies in Adelaide, but the encouragement I had received for oral history from dear Rosemary Ingoldby paid off. I was also applying the knowledge I'd gained from the inspirational Native American history programs we had visited. Here I was, working in a traditional Western institution of knowledge keeping. I felt I was in a world of mystery and intrigue. The library's marble staircase leading to our office was steeped in European tradition, and Roman-like columns held up the ornate domed ceiling. I was working from within a traditional library of written works, with all their glory and accumulated fortune. I felt empowered that our people's knowledge, which preceded these Western institutions by thousands of years, was finally being accepted. Had we really had to wait so long to justify our knowledge as a valid source of history? At the time I also pondered whether our knowledge would find its rightful place at the front and centre of a Western library system.

~

The first job for the KOHP was to source the technical equipment we needed to record and document information. With a limited budget for operational costs, I also had to find people to work on the program. I employed two assistants to help me with the management and recording of information, and we got a vehicle for the fieldwork component. I was extra-cautious in making sure to get the best-quality equipment for audio and video recording. We were working in the pre-digital-technology era; the transition to digital technology did not take place until the mid-1990s.

The fieldwork component was an intense period. We travelled to various communities throughout Victoria to consult with elders who agreed to have their stories recorded. There was a sense of urgency as stories were being lost with elders passing on. My first task was to develop a conditions agreement on the ownership and protection of their oral knowledge. The agreement declared that Aboriginal knowledge was owned by the providers of the knowledge, the Koori people. It drew on the UN Indigenous cultural and intellectual property principles. We had to get an individual's permission before using any of their materials; the materials were lodged under the agreement and treated as totally confidential; and it was illegal to access any data without written permission from the individual themself. Over time, ownership conditions of oral knowledge have evolved to embrace the concept of data sovereignty. This is an Indigenous-rights-based construct that recognises and protects Indigenous ownership of data, including oral knowledge.

We had a full consultation process with all the local community-based organisations to get the conditions agreement up and running. This was the third time I had been engaged in a statewide consultation process, but this time I was combining it with managing the operations of the KOHP. It was a big job, and I was very relieved when the agreement was finally signed off by the Crown solicitor. Getting people's knowledge protected was a groundbreaking achievement.

The KOHP was like a travelling outdoor studio. We had so much recording equipment on board. It was very much an on-the-run program. We were travelling, contacting people and arranging times to visit and record their stories. The recording and interview skills I had up my sleeve from previous oral history work was a big advantage. I was able to train my staff in methods and techniques as well as research skills in library work.

A highlight of our work was creating a video recording of the 1998 Bicentenary event in Sydney. We drove there and joined thousands of Aboriginal people from all over Australia. Big mobs came together, determined that this national event would not just be a tribute to Captain Cook and British colonisation. We were aware of the previous protest at the Sesquicentenary, which had been called a Day of Mourning. Leaders of that campaign were fresh in the memory of the Bicentenary participants. Over 50,000 people came together and marched in an act of reconciliation. I believe this event helped to put reconciliation on the map.

We recorded many interviews at the march. We also recorded the keynote addresses given in Hyde Park, where the march ended. We brought all the materials back and catalogued them for the KOHP. Most of the transcription of recorded materials was done by computer in DOS—it took a lot of time and energy. We then labelled and catalogued the material according to different subject categories. Audio transcription technology advanced in the 1990s, but before that most oral history transcription was done by hand—and don't I know it! My daughter Yolanda knows it too: she helped with the transcription for *A Picture from the Other Side* in 1981.

A lot of the materials we collected were from individual interviews with elders who lived on reserves. The main ones we visited were Lake Condah and Framlingham in western Victoria, Lake Tyers in East Gippsland, Ebenezer in the Wimmera, Cummeragunja in northern Victoria and Coranderrk in the Yarra Valley. We also kept an ear to the ground on other community happenings. We recorded many cultural exchanges that took place at Camp Jungai in Taungurung Country and at events hosted by the Aborigines Advancement League. The area we covered over such a short period produced a substantial amount of material.

On reflection, including oral history in the definition of cultural heritage was groundbreaking. We had to fight hard for its inclusion and it had to compete with other programs for its share of heritage resources. Unfortunately, support through government Aboriginal Affairs administration was ad hoc and lacked long-term commitment. Indeed, it was a piecemeal arrangement—like other programs, Aboriginal culture was broken into separate categories. It was like dissecting our holistic culture and putting the pieces in separate boxes. This created a competitive funding environment where each program had to fight to maintain its existence. In that light, I think the One Roof idea would have been a more compatible option.

~

After serving eight years in the government system advising and managing the program, it was time for me to hand over the reins. The KOHP stayed in the State Library until it transitioned to the Koorie Heritage Trust in the late 1990s. The trust also grew out of the cultural renaissance. Under the direction of Jim Berg, it provided a Koori heritage space to house cultural materials, as well as curating and managing cultural property collected from museums, private collectors and the community. The KOHP collections were transferred to the trust's care and management, and the program continued as a functioning unit there until being wound up in 2010. The equipment, materials and transcripts are stored by the trust for safekeeping, and remain accessible to those seeking to use them under the terms of the conditions agreement.

Having an overarching One Roof cultural heritage centre in Melbourne was a pipe dream of our reform agenda. In the 1980s, the idea of a cultural institute was a cornerstone of the Labor government's commitments to Koori heritage rights. Attorney-General Kennan was the minister for Aboriginal affairs during the Cain and Kirner governments and to his credit he provided strong support for the concept of a Victorian Aboriginal cultural affairs institute.

Seeing the huge shifts that have taken place in heritage diplomacy since that time is rewarding—now, there is talk of a cultural institute in discussions on treaty matters. An institute of cultural learning would bring cultural heritage management and technological development into the modern era. It would allow for multidisciplinary learning, innovation, and the development of career opportunities for Kooris in the administration and management of their heritage. It is a culturally appropriate model for the future management of all aspects of Aboriginal heritage and its specialist functions.

After my time working on heritage campaigns and setting up the KOHP, I felt the call back to study and in 1992, at the age of fifty-one, returned to complete my degree in history and archaeology at La Trobe. With renewed energy I wanted to finish my degree and continue to the postgraduate level. The storyline now takes us to La Trobe University and from there to the land rights struggle, which culminated in the Yorta Yorta native title case.

PART IV

Land Rights

16

Native Title or What?

In 1992 I returned to study at La Trobe after fifteen years of land activism, cultural heritage reform and oral history projects. I was hungry for new knowledge. Concentrating on the road map I had set for myself, an arts degree in archaeology and history was within my reach. I had no problems returning to academic learning. With overseas study up my sleeve, I wanted to learn more about politics, legal studies and human rights.

I had a particular interest in land and heritage justice. With my experience and knowledge of Traditional Owner groups in Victoria, I could walk tall and proud in the Koori and mainstream worlds. My ancestors taught me to value the power of education, and I was encouraged by Sioux scholar Vine Deloria's advice to be better than your opponents. Being as good as you can be and being treated equally for your efforts were good enough incentives for me.

I joined La Trobe's vibrant Koori/Gubbah Club with students from different cultural backgrounds. These were students who supported Koori issues, having learned about human rights violations in the Indigenous Studies courses and from the 1991 deaths in custody royal commission. The club was organised by my cousin Julie Andrews, who was then doing her undergraduate studies at La Trobe. We produced a magazine and had social and cultural events on campus with guest speakers and musicians. My old band The Shades from Itchica even played for a couple of social gigs. The club visited Koori communities for cultural exchanges and I enjoyed sharing some of my own music around the campfires at our on-Country gatherings. Support units for

First Peoples were emerging in universities. They were federally funded and provided a base for younger students coming from remote areas. It was great to be on campus with some of your own mob.

University life was a relief after the rough-and-tumble of Aboriginal politics. I completed an honours thesis about the reforms we had achieved with the Koori Heritage Working Group in which I critically assessed the interface between Indigenous rights and the practice of archaeology, and the important issue of ownership and control. The thesis focused on Victoria as a case study in cultural heritage rights and management. I studied the United Nations legal agreements on racial discrimination, self-determination and Indigenous rights and used these to support our claims for the return of cultural knowledge and property. Later, these international agreements became the legal framework for the Yoorrook Justice Commission inquiry. My thesis argued that Indigenous ownership and control of cultural property was excluded by British heritage laws and should be returned to the Traditional Owners under international and domestic law.

On completion of my degree in 1993, I was awarded first-class honours. This got me into the PhD program and I was chosen as Indigenous Scholar of the Year. I shared that title with another member of the KHWG, Ricky Mullet of the Gunai Nation of East Gippsland, who had graduated with honours from the Australian National University. The other Victorian Indigenous person to complete honours along with Ricky and me was Mark Grist of the Wergaia, Wamba Wamba and Nyeri Nyeri of north-west Victoria. This made three First Peoples honours graduates in archaeology in the same year—a proud achievement for us and our families.

~

While I was working on my honours thesis, a key legal decision had a profound impact on my life and my community. In 1992 the High Court of Australia found that a group of Torres Strait Islanders led by Eddie Mabo held ownership of Mer, their land. It had been a ten-year legal battle. The Mabo case established a framework for claiming native title. The same principles could apply where other Indigenous claimants showed they maintained their connections with ancestral lands. The landmark decision gave rise to the important Commonwealth *Native Title Act* (1993). The High Court's removal of terra nullius as a legal barrier to land justice in Australia was an added incentive.

Following the Mabo case, there was a level of optimism for Aboriginal and Torres Strait Islander claimants. Yorta Yorta were the first cab off the rank on mainland Australia to test the decision. If any Traditional Owner group in the more populated areas was willing to step up to the plate and establish that they had survived colonisation and held on to their connections to their ancestral land, it was the Yorta Yorta.

I need to qualify that our claim did not fall out of the sky after Mabo. The history we had put together of previous attempts to claim land squashed any such notion. Our timeline of land struggle stretched back more than a century before Mabo. In fact, this claim would be our eighteenth attempt to settle the long-standing injustice of land theft and dispossession.

This didn't distract me from my studies and in fact put me in the box seat for my PhD. My thesis title was *'Not One Iota': The Yorta Yorta Struggle for Land Justice.* I borrowed the first part of the title from Uncle William Cooper. In 1938, in a letter to Prime Minister Joseph Lyons, he asked how much land had been returned to his people's call for land rights and answered his own question in just three words: 'Not one iota.'[1] You couldn't get a clearer or more straightforward answer than that. It put fire in the belly of my generation of activists.

I was now balancing my PhD with my commitments and cultural obligations. I was also one of the sixteen principal claimants, as a representative of my extended family group. To work on the claim, I was employed by the Yorta Yorta Nation as senior research officer. I was privileged to help collect most of the oral material for our claim—the largest oral history project ever conducted on Yorta Yorta land. The body of material made up nearly 60 per cent of the 12,000-page transcript of evidence. It is an overwhelming repository of Yorta Yorta oral knowledge and is used today in education, language, books, music, media, land management and cultural awareness programs.

~

A lot happened in 1994. I started my PhD, the Yorta Yorta put in a native title claim, and to top it all off I was diagnosed with bowel cancer. This was a big shock. Suddenly, my mortality confronted me head-on and put me in fear of the unknown. The big C shook the daylights out of my social and emotional wellbeing. After surgery I had chemo for six months.

To keep my mind occupied, I continued working on my PhD under my soulmate's tender loving care. I did a lot of research and intensive reading on land law, human rights, and case studies of land rights in Australia and overseas. Going back to the river and the bush to seek solitude with Cathy and our beloved dog Dhulla really helped my healing. At the end of the six months of treatment, I was given the all-clear—thank you, Biami.

The psychology of facing death is powerful. While the physical recovery of your body runs its course, the psychological recovery takes much longer. I was lucky to have Cathy, family and students around me, and the bush, to fully recover. The PhD research, writing, music and my guitar helped to pull me through. The biggest thing I learned was the correlation between continued stress and ill health. On reflection, there were signs that something was not right with my body. The preoccupation and energy I had put into making sure the oral history program succeeded had taken its toll.

My renewed awareness of health and the quality health care I received had positive outcomes. In my favour I had a brilliant surgeon, who has since passed. His name is Tony Reid and he is honoured for his quality of care and excellent surgery skills in a plaque at the Heidelberg Repatriation Hospital. He was a very tall, gentle man and through the care of his skilled hands he saved my life. He was also well versed in Indigenous art and we had many discussions on the rich diversity of traditional and contemporary art in Australia. When I came through the ordeal, I called him the 'gentle giant'. The significant takeaway from this profound experience is that it made me humbler to those whose life chances were less fortunate. Thank you, Tony.

~

The native title process relied on the courts to make land justice decisions rather than the state land claim processes. From our previous claims, only part of the Cummera lands on the NSW side had been returned to the Yorta Yorta, in 1983. This was through the NSW *Aboriginal Land Rights Act 1983*. Most of our traditional lands were off limits as far as the federal *Native Title Act 1993* was concerned, which restricted claims to Crown land—the leftovers. While the traditional boundaries of Yorta Yorta cover a large area, the public (or Crown) land where we could claim was less than 10 per cent of the original Yorta Yorta land that our ancestors had occupied since time immemorial. The public land for the claim included both sides of Dungula, including the Barmah and Moira (Millewa) forests and other Crown lands within the claim area. These lands were administered by the Victorian and NSW governments.

Being restricted to Crown land was a huge compromise forced on Traditional Owners. Most of the land had already been granted by the Crown to private landholders without application of fair and just principles of compensation to the Traditional Owners. These are matters that have since been revived by the High Court in the landmark decision of the Commonwealth v. Yunupingu (On Behalf of the Gumatj Clan or Estate Group) & Ors (2025).[2]

We were wary of the approach of state governments towards land justice. Our claim was likely to be a step too far for the NSW and Victorian governments because it wasn't about a remote area, like many of the claims in northern Australia. On the contrary, the Yorta Yorta claim was in a busy non-Indigenous rural farming district. We clearly established that we maintained connections with Country in the claim area. This was formally recognised in Victorian Government Crown land management reports. If we were successful, it would obliterate the underlying myth that only remote Indigenous groups untainted by the impact of colonisation had connections with their traditional land.

Once notice of the claim was lodged, we had the job of organising the logistics of the legal process. To prepare our claim, we secured the services of the lawyers who had represented Eddie Mabo, Bryan Keon-Cohen and Ron Castan. Ross Howie, who had represented Traditional Owners in land claims in Central Australia, came on board and the legal counsel was the firm Arnold Bloch Leibler. The solicitor representing the legal counsel was Peter Seidel. They were confident that the Yorta Yorta case was strong and capable of succeeding. After consultations between the Yorta Yorta Nation and legal counsel, the Yorta Yorta Nations decided to lodge an additional land claim to those previously mentioned. The preparation and lodgement of the claim began in 1994. We hired not only lawyers but also experts in anthropology, history, archaeology, linguistics and genealogy. From this entourage we saw the native title industry emerge big time and assume authority for interpreting and representing our knowledge.

Following the success of Mabo, going straight to the Federal Court to deal with the matter was tempting. On the advice of our lawyers, however, we chose to go to the National Native Title Tribunal. The *Native Title Act* provided the option of a claim being heard before the tribunal if consensus could be reached. It's a confidential process that allows parties to reach agreement on some or all of the matters that must be agreed on. If successful, it allows the Federal Court to make a consent determination as an alternative to the formal adversarial legal processes faced in courts. A favourable outcome would result in a consent agreement ratified by the Federal Court. The tribunal was a new system under the spotlight in Australian land justice adjudication. We were nervous but hopeful about getting a good outcome. It was on that basis that we agreed to place some faith in the process.

Our mediation process began in Shepparton in September 1994. Being the first to go before the newly formed tribunal, we felt as if we were 'guinea pigs to the system'—a system that was 'still in its experimental stages'. Those were the words of Mick Dodson, the Aboriginal and Torres Strait Islander human rights social justice commissioner at the time.[3] There was pressure for the tribunal to account for itself, but in my opinion its inability to deliver a mediated outcome as an alternative to fighting it out in the courts was a foregone conclusion.

On the first day of the hearings, the lawyer for the Yorta Yorta was invited by the judge to set out the claim. For a moment in history we were given an opportunity, space, time, a silent audience and a respectful judge to say who we were and what we wanted. We had time to define in our own words our identity and our aspirations for our land and our community's future. The Yorta Yorta presentations went to the heart of what it is to be Yorta Yorta. We raised the important issues about land care and management. We spoke of the degrading treatment of the waterways and the loss of plant and animal life. It felt as though the tide of history was at last turning in our favour. It felt as if we were on the edge of a new start. We spoke with the same air of conviction and compassion as our ancestors: pride, dignity, diplomacy, forbearance and passion for the land. To most of the audience this was a new story, an unknown aspect of the Aboriginal community beside whom they had lived for generations without really knowing them. Our pride and passion challenged their assumptions and understanding.

When the issues were brought out in the open, familiar tensions and hostilities arose. Old statements such as 'We've never seen an Aborigine around here' re-emerged. Ironically, some of these came from tour operators who often used Yorta Yorta heritage to promote their tours. My cousin Neville Atkinson responded to these prejudices by saying, 'We are still not at the stage where we can say who we are and not be insulted.'[4]

While the tribunal had some control over evidence and the content of any documents produced, it failed to control the media leaks and politicians' misuse of reports of the confidential mediation sessions. Prominent among these was the McPherson-owned network of regional newspapers, including *Shepparton News*. Its proprietor, Ross McPherson, was against the claim, and native title generally. One news article was entitled 'Native Title Fears' and presented ludicrous and biased accounts of the mediation sessions, reporting inaccurate descriptions of the claimant's policy document.[5] Someone from the mediation meetings had leaked our document to the media. The Aboriginal community had to counter the tide of regional racism that these articles promoted. Prior to and throughout the extended legal proceedings, conservative politicians challenged our Yorta Yorta identity and heritage in regional newspapers.

The tribunal's inability to prevent damaging public statements was a flaw in the Act. A climate of fear and racial hostility was fostered. Dairy, timber, tourist and recreational interests were portrayed as under attack. Forests and rivers would be taken over. Aboriginal people might even claim the main street or an average person's backyard and their children's school grounds, according to the more extreme voices. This antagonistic climate may have influenced the process of the law. It certainly had seismic effects in the region. There was a rising tide of racism towards Aboriginal people, and our chances of negotiation and mediation faded with the impact of this hostility. How could we reach a regional agreement between Indigenous and non-Indigenous land users with this against us? Many of us, including supporters of our claim who witnessed the regional racism, had every right to say, 'Oh no, here we go again.'

Organising the community and attending the meditation sessions fell on the shoulders of individuals, some of whom had to pay out of their own pockets to get to sessions. Because of their commitment to the claim, many of the Yorta Yorta worked on a voluntary basis. Sadly, most of the money invested in a native title claim goes to the industry while the Traditional Owners do a lot of unpaid work in the background.

Many Yorta Yorta felt excluded and under-informed through the mediation process. Commissioner Dodson's December 1995 report[6] highlighted these issues, addressing the flawed elements of the native title process. He described how public ignorance fuelled hostility and racism, which undermined claimants' negotiating positions and wore down their stamina. Lack of understanding about native title definitions and processes also directly slowed down mediation meetings. Instead of finding ways to reach agreement, parties needed time to learn the legal principles and implications.

In Canada, there have been comprehensive regional settlements after decades of negotiation and hard work. They have used adapted processes to take the time to include community and reach decisions. Unfortunately, there were hardly any discussions between the Yorta Yorta and the tribunal to prepare for our mediation process. Our experience showed how hard it was to steer a course through a minefield of bias, bigotry and the conservative rural elite. Powerful opposing interests damaged the chance of reaching a regional agreement through mediation.

Commissioner Dodson urged governments to take a more constructive role. He recommended community education about native title, pinpointing that 'ignorance produces and fuels hostility and racism'.

He also recommended the *Native Title Act* be changed so that people would be punished if they breached the confidentiality of mediation.[7]

We had got our hopes up with Mabo, so it was a huge disappointment when mediation failed for our Yorta Yorta case. After many months of negotiation, we achieved nothing. We were still fighting from our old position of nowhere.

Mediation made many non-Indigenous stakeholders richer, including lawyers; they were profiting from the growing native title industry. This issue crops up again and again. That is, when the government sets up a structure to deal with an issue in the Aboriginal community, the structure soon becomes an industry in itself. It mainly benefits the non-Indigenous experts who are employed to fix the issue. The pretext of consulting and including Indigenous people actually masks and legitimises power relations. The outcome mostly results in the status quo being maintained.

With the benefit of hindsight, a more pragmatic approach was required. The Federal Court would have been a better option for us than being used as guinea pigs for the new tribunal. Our advice from the lawyers to enter mediation against so many obstacles was a big mistake. In my view the tribunal lost control of the process in the early stages and should have pulled the plug to allow us to concentrate on going to the Federal Court. But that is all history now. After twelve months of meetings with many parties, the mediation failed.

At the end of the day, a key question remained for me and many other kinsfolk: would our voices ever be heard and listened to?

17

Nineteen-Second Judgment

In 1996 we went back to the Federal Court to settle the matter. Now we were faced with presenting our claim to the Federal Court. Proceedings before Judge Howard Olney commenced on 8 October 1996. Some sixty Yorta Yorta witnesses gave evidence, including representatives of the neighbouring Kulin Nation and river-based groups of the lower and upper Dungula region. There was general support for the overarching Yorta Yorta linguistic and territorial boundaries, but more than 400 parties opposed our claim.

Going before the Federal Court to seek rights to our land was a harrowing experience. I was fully involved in the process until the final decision was handed down in 2002. Just the work of preparing for the hearings was overwhelming. The eight years of litigation was less than Mabo, but long enough. The emotional energy, time and money needed to make a claim under native title is extraordinary. Many of these experiences were shared by other senior elders who have since returned to the eternal Dreamtime. I pay my deepest respect to them and their families.

The work in mobilising and catering for the witnesses and the numerous opposing parties was done by the Yorta Yorta Nation, without adequate resources. Coordinating the on-site evidence for the claim area was a mammoth task for the Yorta Yorta Nation. A multitude of hearings were held at cultural sites on Country where evidence was taken from Yorta Yorta witnesses for the judge to examine under the native title framework.

The number of people involved in the hearing on both sides was formidable, including court representatives, Yorta Yorta witnesses, family members, community organisations, media, lawyers, government representatives and many others. It was like a travelling circus. Marquees were put up on site and nearly everyone, including the judge, transformed from white-collar workers to bushies wearing different types of Akubra hats.

We were conscious that this circus would have turned the spirits of the ancestors in their eternal resting places. Indeed, we often wished they were with us to guide us through the process. The oldest law of the land, which had sustained our people and Country since time immemorial, had been given short shrift by imported British law. Whether the new law could deliver the justice our ancestors had been denied was the real question.

~

In 1998, after two years of interrogation before Justice Olney, we sat in the courtroom in William Street, Melbourne waiting patiently for the judge to deliver his verdict. After the formidable judge's knock that we were so familiar with, he appeared in his wig and gown, noticeably anxious, and read a nineteen-second statement telling the Court that the Yorta Yorta case had failed. He left quickly, giving no reasons or summary of his judgment.

What an insult! What a travesty of justice! We had been through so much. We sat in court, absolutely stunned.

The essence of the full judgment came down to an ill-fated phrase: that 'the tide of history' had 'washed away' our use of traditional laws and customs.[1] Olney's interpretation was that because we asked to have land so it could be farmed, this meant we were no longer observing traditional laws and customs. Being prepared to adapt our ancestors' ways to modern conditions was taken to mean we were no longer entitled to our land, nor were we owed restitution for the theft of our land by the Crown.

~

It didn't take us long to decide to appeal the shocking decision. While the arrival of Europeans amplified the extent of change, the Yorta Yorta had always adapted and continued to flourish. 'Always was and always will be Yorta Yorta land' succinctly sums up the fact that no tide will ever wash away what was created and ordained by the creator. We appealed to the full bench of the Federal Court on the grounds that 'the trial judge erroneously adopted a "frozen in time" approach' and 'failed to give sufficient recognition to the capacity of traditional laws and customs to adapt to changed circumstances'.[2]

In August 1999, as our appeal was about to begin, Justice Ron Merkel agreed to stand down from the hearing due to allegations of bias. He had been due to sit alongside Chief Justice Michael Black and Justice Catherine Branson in the hearing, but until two months earlier he had been a trustee of the Koorie Heritage Trust. He was replaced by Justice Leslie Katz. It was never clear why the same scrutiny of perceived bias was not considered for other people involved in all sides of the case, or why his perceived bias only mattered for this case. Moreover, just five years later he rejected Olney's use of 'the tide of history' in the Yorta Yorta case. This was in the Wotjobaluk native title case that he presided over in the Wimmera region in 2005.

Justice Merkel has an enlightened view of Indigenous history and culture and the law of native title, but that should not have been a barrier to his ability to administer the law in accordance with the *Native Title Act 1993*. As it was, Branson and Katz ruled against our appeal two to one. The dissenting judge, Black, agreed with Merkel's opinion that Olney had undermined the Act. I will leave it for readers to draw their own conclusions on the anomalies posed in the way the native title law was interpreted and applied in our case.

After the Yorta Yorta appeal to the full bench of the Federal Court was unsuccessful, we took the matter on appeal to the High Court. Our hopes were raised knowing that we were going to Canberra, where the landmark Mabo decision had been celebrated. But in December 2002 the High Court ruled that the Yorta Yorta did not have native title. Some of my students sat with me in the High Court to watch the seven judges who presided over our final appeal. A number of judges had moved on after the Mabo judgment and been replaced before our case came before the court.

In two decades of teaching the Yorta Yorta claim as a case study in native title, I did not find one student who agreed with Olney's judgment. I think that also applied to the general analysis of the judgment in the political and legal community. For my people, it was rewarding to know that students in one of the top law schools of Australia—that of the University of Melbourne—were well versed in the Yorta Yorta native title case. This was enough to turn the tide on the assessment of how the law was applied. I'm pleased it remains embedded in student thinking and analysis of our iconic case.

This was the end of our legal path, but the political journey was still ahead. That judgment didn't end our struggle for land justice—how could it? It had begun in 1881 when our great-great-grandfathers and uncles petitioned for land on the grounds of their prior occupation. Puppa Henry and others had been granted farm blocks at Cummera in 1898 that were later taken back. These and other claims remain unresolved.

~

While our struggle for land justice continued, I completed my PhD in 2000. I had fulfilled the aim I set myself and I acknowledged how many people contributed to the final product. In the opening pages of my thesis I thanked Uncle William Cooper, Granpa James, my parents, Cathy, my supervisor Professor Margaret Thornton, fellow researcher Rod Hagen, and solicitors Arnold Bloch Leibler for access to the evidence presented in the Yorta Yorta case. Most especially I thanked the Yorta Yorta Nations Inc. for sharing so much important knowledge and material.

My PhD provides rigorous evidence in support of Yorta Yorta land justice. I have mentioned some in this book, but in my thesis, there is more detail about the timeline of Yorta Yorta occupation, our survival in the face of European invasion, the 150 years we spent trying to get land rights recognition, the Mabo case and the mediation attempts, our claim in the Federal Court and the errors in the Court's decision.

I now felt empowered as a Yorta Yorta man backed by high-level academic qualifications. It was not a gift, but a reward for hard work over many decades. I now had more knowledge and skills to share with my community, and to stand up for inequality. With a PhD I could sit at the table in my own right.

~

Less than a year later, the Yorta Yorta struck back with renewed vigour when the Melbourne Workers Theatre and Playbox produced *Yanagai! Yanagai!* at the Malthouse Theatre in Melbourne. This wonderful play, written by my cousin and Yorta Yorta playwright Andrea James, exposed the lie at the heart of the Yorta Yorta native title claim.[3] The audience were treated to the drama and humour of the Yorta Yorta confrontation with the native title saga. Our creation story, language and love of Country make a mockery of the idea of being 'washed away' by the 'tide of history'. 'We are here. We are here. We are here' is the opening declaration in the play. The actors defiantly use Yorta Yorta language, demonstrating our ongoing culture. 'When we speak—This beautiful language! Like honey. This language tastes good. It is ours!!!' The Yorta Yorta meet Edward Curr and immediately assert their sovereign rights by telling him to go away: 'Yanagai, Yanagai.' Then as old men they are Curr's servants. In good English tradition they serve him cups of tea, which he delights over. We in the audience know that it was Curr's book *Squatting in Victoria* that Justice Olney used as his definitive source in our native title case. But at that time we did not know that Curr's father had been responsible for massacres of Tasmanian Aboriginal people at Cape Grim and other locations in north-west Tasmania.[4] That was where Curr was born and where he lived before coming to Yorta Yorta Country.

The final scene of the play opens in darkness. Thunder and the loud ticking of a clock are heard. The four characters who opened the play reappear on stage. One of them announces 'Nineteen seconds' and looks at his watch. The others make fun of what a person can do in that time. As one is reciting the nursery rhyme 'Baa Baa Black Sheep', they are interrupted by three loud knocks. The character Olney enters and mutters incoherently: 'The court determines that native title does not exist in relation to the areas of land identified to Schedule D to Native Title Application FVN 94/1 accepted by the Registrar on 26 May 1994.' He bangs his gavel and leaves, while all recite, 'Nineteen seconds for that.'

It was thrilling to share the Yorta Yorta spirit with the black and white audience—such a proud and moving moment. 'Nineteen seconds' became a catch-cry in the analysis of the judgment. To me, the decision was a big shock when it was so quickly handed down. I used its absurdity to write an article called '19 Seconds of *Dungudja Wala*' (the Yorta Yorta words for 'big flood').[5]

~

Being the first Indigenous group to choose the native title process on mainland Australia was a monumental call. It seemed commendable that Australia was trying to bring in laws on recognition of Indigenous title and rejecting actions that justified the theft of Indigenous land. It seemed like barriers to land rights had been dismantled and there was a more level playing field for Indigenous justice. While the removal of old barriers was encouraging, the construction of new ones was disheartening. Through our Yorta Yorta claim, the barriers for land justice in highly populated areas took us back to the pre-Mabo era. The ideals of equality and justice before the law remained elusive. By setting the ground rules for claiming land justice and respect for native title, the High Court actually created major barriers to achieving land justice. The property interests of settlers and their descendants were given priority by the High Court in Mabo when it refused to uphold fair and just principles of compensation for Traditional Owners. The rules say that native title holders can only get compensation for things the government has done since 1975. The High Court judgment does not support Traditional Owners' rights to compensation for the theft of their land.

In the Mabo case, Justice Brennan's notion of the 'tide of history'[6] was presented as an extreme-case scenario of native title loss. Its application to the Yorta Yorta in its absolute sense, however, left negative implications for other claimants. That phrase haunted us, and we would make sure that it came back to haunt Justice Olney. Given that it was an idea raised in Mabo rather than a legal doctrine, it has remained the subject of legal conjecture ever since. Underpinning the events on which this 'tide' rests is a history of land injustice and flagrant human rights violations. They are sourced in violence and bloodshed over the ownership and control of land: massacres, wars, killings and genocide, and systemic injustices of similar gravity. It is ironic in the extreme, and obscene, that the crimes against humanity that constitute this 'tide' can be invoked by those seeking to deny Indigenous groups their rights to land.

Following Justice Olney's judgment, the fiction of terra nullius, rejected by Mabo as having no place as a barrier to Indigenous land justice in contemporary law,[7] was replaced by the 'tide' metaphor. Indeed, the Olney decision is a graphic illustration of how the 'tide' language was construed to justify land theft, to maintain the status quo, and to support the continued dispossession of Indigenous people. In this context, the tide of history is gammin words dressed in disguise and used as a trope for dispossession. By basing his ruling on non-Aboriginal sources, Olney showed ignorance of accepted standards. It is universal practice to look at the context in which something was written in order to understand the prevailing cultural biases of the time. Early white observers were notorious for interpreting traditional culture through their own blinkers. Privileging European sources over Indigenous knowledge is an Anglocentric approach. The British legal system already carries historical bias and inequality towards Indigenous people by the exclusion of their oral testimony. Olney's exclusion of Yorta Yorta knowledge was a reversion to antiquated practices.

The issue of who is being empowered under the native title process needs to be exposed. Most of the resources went to the native title industry, while Traditional Owners benefited the least. The irony is that if you take native title claimants out of the equation, the industry has nothing to represent. I often wonder why the industry is needed when native title holders should be able to represent themselves. After all, isn't this our inherent right?

The expenditure of those opposing the Yorta Yorta claim has not been made public, but the following approximations give some indication of exactly whom the Native Title process empowers. Costs for a case of this magnitude would have been at least $50,000 per day in 1996 CPI figures. We are looking at a multimillion-dollar enterprise. The Kennett Liberal government in Victoria alone is said to have spent $4 million.[8] Local governments, the NSW Government, and land and water authorities all had high levels of expenditure in opposing our claim.[9] The large cohort of lawyers and non-Indigenous experts stood to gain more from prolonging the process than from seeking a resolution. Indigenous people were further disempowered by these litigious and protracted proceedings. Unless called on to give advice or evidence, we had to be content with being represented by others.

This may be a sign of how deep the psychosis of white domination and racism still runs, particularly within government and in parts of regional Australia. Important questions like these confront truth justice and reconciliation processes. This is not to deny that Indigenous and non-Indigenous Australians are trying to achieve high ideals. But the first historic task for truth justice and reconciliation surely must be a fair and just settlement of land for Indigenous people as a basis for achieving substantive equality and autonomy.

~

It is useful to reflect on the thoughts of Uncle Kenny Briggs, one of our most senior Yorta Yorta claimants, who sat patiently through the gruelling court processes waiting for justice to be delivered. After we watched the process unfold each day, we would retreat to have our own debriefing session and regroup after the draining cross-examination from the opposing lawyers. We supported each other, often asking whose turn it was to be gutted that day.

Uncle Kenny had a clear mind on our many failed attempts to get land justice and was as sharp as an axe when it came to watching the drama unfolding. About halfway through the process, we were closely observing the body language and growing impatience of Justice Olney. Uncle Kenny leaned over, tapped me on the shoulder and said, 'We're not gonna get anything from this judge. I don't trust him.' Yes, and it seemed to me at that point in the case that the judge had already made up his mind and we were just going through the motions.

The power of vested interests, status quo politics and racism had as much sway in this outcome as they'd had in the past. I agreed with Uncle Kenny. I still think a lot about all those relatives who suffered from this terrible judgment, and those who are no longer with us and did not see the justice they rightly deserved.

This was not the end of our struggle for land justice. We returned to the old position of base-camp politics and next pushed for land justice on the political front through the Barmah–Millewa National Park campaign.

18

Refusing to Yield

Yorta Yorta people are renowned for their resilience, but after the shocking High Court decision many of us took a step back for a while to heal ourselves from the emotional drain. We drew on support from our families, friends, students and others who were equally outraged at the injustice dealt.

Returning to base camp to muster support after the grief of the High Court decision was naturally a slow process. Some went bush and camped on the river and didn't want to come back until they felt they had recovered enough in their own way of healing. Others kept the campfire burning at the base camp, which allowed them to churn over the issues outwardly and focus on what our next steps would be. The elders who had carried a lot of heavy loads throughout the process spent time recovering at their own pace and seeking solitude within their own family group.

I retreated with Cathy and spent time with her family in Wentworth Falls in the Blue Mountains. Like others, I felt exhausted and spent time sharing the experience with both our families. It gave me time to think, and there was much goopna ngarwu (deep thinking) time. At one stage I went bush with my cousin/brother Gary Nelson. We tried to console ourselves with goopri for a while. One of my favourite songs, 'From Clare to Here', which has become an iconic song for Irish people, came home to me with its lyrics about drink easing the pain of it and helping to level out one's thinking, for a while at least. But it is not the remedy for a restless soul. The fire for justice kept burning in my gut and needed to be released. I confronted the reality of human existence and went deeper into the soul, asking questions about myself and what the next course of action might be. I tried to visualise how those uncles and aunties had dealt with similar setbacks during the struggle for rights on reserves and in the towns. I remembered those who led the protests in the streets seeking citizenship rights. I paid tribute to those who led the Day of Mourning protest on the 150th anniversary of British invasion.

In recovery, I reflected on Uncle William Cooper's story and was consoled by his gentle words. He described the setbacks he experienced, and I gained inspiration from what he achieved. Uncle William said that 'our pen is our spear' and told us to 'have the courage to use it', for resistance 'is refusal to yield to silence'.[1] Courage, resistance, and the refusal to yield to silence were messages that lingered in my mind. Our ancestors didn't just sit back, they bounced back with renewed vigour and determination.

In 2002 Cathy and I returned home from overseas to news that the newly re-elected Victorian Labor government, who had blatantly joined parties opposing our land claim, wanted to meet with us to discuss land matters. They apparently wanted to rectify the damage done to their relationship with the Yorta Yorta. Some of the ministers, like Attorney-General Rob Hulls, seemed to have had a morality check on their betrayal of our native title claim. He later expressed what seemed repentance for his party, calling on 'the legacies of dispossession and assimilation, of racism and disadvantage' to be 'dismantled on every front' and that the 'possibility of genuine land justice is one such front'.[2] 'Bring it on!' was my kneejerk response. It was a big turnaround for the Labor government on the land rights question at that point.

In hindsight, they could have resolved the legacy of dispossession by granting genuine land justice to the Yorta Yorta then and there. It could have been done by returning all Crown land within the claim area in Victoria to the Yorta Yorta as the Traditional Owners. This could have been done by granting freehold title rather than the diminished form of native title, which reduced the original and absolute Traditional Ownership rights to a much lesser and weakened form of ownership.

Being renowned fighters, the Yorta Yorta bounced back onto the front foot. Our achievement in negotiating a land management agreement covering the heartland of Yorta Yorta traditional territories is a remarkable story. It was achieved through an effective political campaign for Barmah–Millewa National Park organised by the Yorta Yorta with the support of a range of local and state non-government organisations:

- Yorta Yorta Nation Aboriginal Corporation
- Friends of the Earth, Victoria
- Victorian National Parks Association
- The Wilderness Society Victoria
- Environment Victoria
- Goulburn Valley Environment Group, Shepparton
- Australians for Native Title and Reconciliation (ANTaR)
- Shepparton Region Reconciliation Group
- Australian Conservation Foundation
- Murray Lower Darling Rivers Indigenous Nations.

In all, it was a pretty formidable collective of committed people who came on board to support the Yorta Yorta Nation in its campaign for a national park. From this the Barmah–Millewa Collective was formed. We had some outstanding leaders up front in Jonathan La Nauze from Friends of the Earth, Nick Roberts from the Victorian National Parks Association, and Lou Costa from the Goulburn Valley Environment Group. They worked in close consultation with the Yorta Yorta Nation and the Barmah-Millewa Collective.

It was a powerful eight-year campaign that reached out to a broad spectrum of communities, including NSW organisations. Information was disseminated through a range of local and state media outlets. A lot of meetings were held on Country in the Barmah–Millewa Forest to discuss issues and develop strategies. We organised a major summit in 2007 that drew all the key players together at the Yenbena Training Centre in Barmah. It also included the Wreck Bay Aboriginal Community, who were the Traditional Owners of Booderee National Park in the Jervis Bay Territory; they shared knowledge and experience of their joint management program. The solidarity forged between environmental campaigners and Indigenous people and the ongoing support of students proved to be a significantly powerful winning force.

Our national park campaign was opposed by local cattle graziers and loggers, who were set to lose the privileges they had enjoyed for so long. They had been able to exploit the use of the Barmah State

Park for cattle agistment and logging on Crown lands for personal gain. The Yorta Yorta people were again faced with constant demands in the local media to defend their rights as Traditional Owners. With environmental allies and the support of the Labor government in Victoria, however, this time we won the day.

At last, the tide was turning in our favour. On 30 December 2008, Premier John Brumby announced that the Barmah Forest would become one of the first national parks in Victoria to be jointly managed with the Traditional Owners. In 2010, the Yorta Yorta Nation Aboriginal Corporation and the State of Victoria came together and agreed to develop a joint management plan for Barmah National Park. The park covers 28,505 hectares of floodplain forests and wetlands along the southern bank of Dungula between the towns of Barmah and Tocumwal, approximately 220 kilometres north of Melbourne. It would now be managed for the community as a whole, and Yorta Yorta cultural heritage and the natural values of the park would be protected. This was not just a win for the Yorta Yorta Nation, it was a win for future generations and recreational users of the newly created national park. The national park status eliminated the hard-use activities impacting on the forest wetlands, including hoofed animals and logging. These activities were considered incompatible with keeping the natural and cultural values of a national park for the enjoyment of future generations.

The positive outcome empowered the Yorta Yorta to pursue their interests through the joint management agreement. This was to be negotiated with the state government through its land management authority, Parks Victoria. A hand-back leaseback agreement that can deliver inalienable freehold title is still to be fully negotiated. Much research has been done on the diversity of national park models in Australia, and this forms the database on adapting relevant models to the Yorta Yorta context. The joint agreement will begin as a co-management scheme. It is intended that a hand-back leaseback agreement will happen in the next five years. This means that the land is handed back to Traditional Owners on the condition that it is then leased back to the government. The first five-year management plan, which began in 2023, will take us up to that point.

In the final analysis, it seems that the path to land justice through the political process was more productive and arguably delivered much more than the failed legal process. By comparison with native title, the national park agreements for the Barmah Forest and the adjoining Millewa (Moira) Forest wetlands have much more provision for delivering environmental and cultural protection. They will also contribute to economic and educational advantages and longer-term outcomes.

The joint agreement provides for a majority of Yorta Yorta people on the board of management. It includes rights to occupy and use the land and to make decisions on the resources provided by the state for the management plan. This means that holistic views and traditional knowledge can be applied to environmental preservation, regeneration and sustainability. Moreover, it presents the potential for 'cultural flows' to be required in the allocation of water usage. Cultural flows signify allocations of water for the purpose of cultural practices and traditions and are associated with Yorta Yorta rights in relation to water resource management. Yorta Yorta cultural practices and the environmental health of this region are so closely interwoven that a benefit for one necessarily produces a benefit for the other.

The current agreement allows for the re-establishment of the magnificent Dharnya Centre as a live-in educational facility under Yorta Yorta management. This will provide opportunities for cultural tourism and also benefit the rising interest in the concept of Oncountry learning programs. These will add to the economic and employment opportunities generated.

~

Remarkably, when combined with the native title claim, the work to achieve the national park amounted to nearly twenty years of dedicated commitment and perseverance. The return to base-camp politics had been the last strategic option available after the failure of the native title legal process. Full recognition goes to the Yorta Yorta Nation and its broad-based network of support groups. Indeed, it was Uncle William Cooper's brilliant political strategy of 'the power of the voice, the spear of the pen' that pulled it all together in solidarity with the Yorta Yorta Nation.

One can step back and reflect on the scenario of what all those years of struggle may have delivered if we had been successful in our native title claim in contrast to what we achieved though the political process. What might have been the outcome if the course of justice had not been perverted in the Yorta Yorta case, and if Justice Olney had found that native title existed?

The most obvious question that the judge would have had to address, in accordance with the native title requirements, is the extent to which native title existed in the Crown lands being claimed. The failure of the mediation process to reach a consensual agreement exposed the demands by graziers, loggers and other vested interests to have their interests protected. The most likely outcome for the Yorta Yorta if they had won native title would have been a patchwork of use rights that accommodated all these other interests. These are the limited rights that can now be achieved under native title.

The other key issue that can now be revisited is that if native title had been found to exist and a co-existive arrangement had been the outcome, a huge burden would have been placed on the Traditional Owners' management practices. Dealing with the multitude of interests in the future management of the forest wetlands, such as cattle grazing and timber cutting, would have led to many difficulties. The recommendations to remove those impacts on the value of national park preservation cleared the way for the Yorta Yorta to advance their interests through the pathway of the national park management agreement.

That is where the ongoing Yorta Yorta campaign sits. Altogether, we have tried seventeen times to claim back our land. We owe it to our ancestors to keep fighting the injustice of land theft. We owe it to our children to build a more secure economic base for the future. Whatever eventuates will come from the elected body that represents family group interests in the future management and care of the ancestral lands. The hand-back leaseback of the Barmah National Park and return of other Crown lands as compensation for dispossession is in the hands of the Yorta Yorta Nation.

I completed my role as senior researcher with the Yorta Yorta Nation in 2010 and returned to my job as senior lecturer in the School of Social and Political Sciences at the University of Melbourne. The continuity of my commitment to Yorta Yorta land justice, self-determination and sovereignty remained the same.

PART V

Teaching and Travels

19

Oncountry Learning

After I finished my PhD, I couldn't get a job teaching at La Trobe, even though the Indigenous Studies lecturers were all non-Indigenous people. Meanwhile, in around 2000 the University of Melbourne created a position for an Indigenous lecturer in what was then the Department of Political Science. I applied and started there as a lecturer in 2001 while the Yorta Yorta native title claim was still active in the courts. Being at the University of Melbourne, I was proud to be walking in Granpa James' footsteps and those of his son Uncle Shady. Granpa studied medicine and Uncle studied law.

It was gratifying to include lectures about native title and our Yorta Yorta case. Two courses I taught to undergraduate and postgraduate students were 'Rights: Land and Heritage' and 'Indigenous People and the State'. The details of the claim were fresh in my mind, so I had my own experiences to draw on.

In my role as Indigenous Studies lecturer, I created a learning module that I could teach on Yorta Yorta Country. It is a week-long field-based program using principles of experiential and transformative learning. I called the course Oncountry Learning and as an act of self-determination I 'Yorta Yortarised' the teaching team. It is an accredited degree subject in the School of Social and Political Sciences and grew out of a voluntary community-based education program that was mostly conducted at the Dharnya Centre in the Barmah Forest. As discussed in Chapter 18, the Barmah Forest is now a national park under the

Yorta Yorta Traditional Owner Land Management Board. Being a national park on Crown land, it is the keeping place of much of our cultural heritage history, protected under the heritage laws.

The course began a year after our native title case was heard and is run and taught by Yorta Yorta people using the storyline way of teaching, a pedagogy unique to Indigenous knowledge systems and ways of knowing. The storyline teaching method picks up the diversity of storylines that run through Country like branches on a tree and then locates the storylines in time and place. Time is the history that precedes the more recent colonial overlay, while place is the sites and locations that represent the tangible evidence of Yorta Yorta occupation and use of the land and waterways. It allows us to examine the tangible evidence and appreciate the enormous timeline and antiquity of Yorta Yorta occupation.

I designed the course to give students a deeper understanding of learning through storyline teaching. The best way to do this is through the cultural concept of goopna ngarwu (deep listening) and spending time on ancestral lands. The feedback from students learning through this method is very powerful. The quality of teaching feedback is consistently high, and the students' reflective essays are rewarding to read.

Before students come on Country and in preparation for the course, they have an introductory briefing session at the university. This is followed by a Welcome to Country ceremony and an invitation to learn from our worldview and teaching pedagogy. The students are taken to the site of the 6000-year-old cultural mounds in the Barmah National Park and examine the way the Yorta Yorta sustained themselves with the rich wetland resources and how they kept things going at the hunting-fishing level. This was long before the first stages of irrigation agriculture happened in the Indus Valley of South Asia.

The teachers then use the storyline approach to connect with the more recent history of Maloga and Cummera. The students hear stories of reserve life and Stolen Generations experiences through the 1983 documentary *Lousy Little Sixpence*.[1] The storyline then takes students to the full story of our native title claim, which they hear from elders and others who were involved. They also visit the places where we recorded the evidence for the transcript of the case, most of which is oral testimony. From there they follow the storyline to more recent events in the Yorta Yorta calendar. Students visit the Academy of Sport Health and Education (ASHE) in Shepparton, which runs a vibrant program in partnership with the University of Melbourne and Rumbalara Football Netball Club. They visit key local community-managed organisations that deliver education, health, sport and community-based programs and get to see the extent to which organisations and communities have achieved greater control of their affairs. Teachers and students discuss systemic barriers that prevent Indigenous Australians achieving land justice and equality and then look at UNDRIP, which becomes a framework for evaluating the principle of self-determination, or Koori control as it is translated in the community.

During one of my informal teaching sessions in the forest, a ten-year-old kid gave the best definition I've ever heard of Mabo and native title. He was at the camp with his dad, a lecturer in property law at the University of Melbourne. On the first morning, we gathered in a circle around the campfire for the Welcome to Country session. I started with 'You've all come here with an interest in learning about our claim, so first please tell me, what do you know about native title?' There was dead silence—but you wouldn't have heard a pin drop because we were on the dirt. I watched everyone around the circle, waiting for a response. Nothing. Then this shy young kid nervously put his hand up and said, 'Yes, well, err, um, I think it's something that the Aborigines want but the government won't give it to 'em.'

His profound statement sent waves of laughter like kookaburras through the whole group. I said, 'Well, young man, I think you hit the nail on the head. Thank you!' That is the simplest and best definition I've ever heard, and it belongs to that young man. I assured him that I would always acknowledge his intellectual property when quoting his precise definition in my native title teachings. He was very pleased and thanked me. 'Never underestimate the ability of our younger generation to think for themselves' was my takeaway. Indeed, that young man threw more light on the question of native title than many of the people I have listened to over the duration of the enigma.

~

Oncountry learning has had a profound effect on student thinking, and the students have given us great feedback. Overall, there have been positive outcomes for students, teachers, the University of Melbourne, and the Yorta Yorta Nation as a whole. Some of those outcomes are:

- students forming strong connections with Aboriginal communities along Dungula, and going on to contribute to the Yorta Yorta fight-back campaign for the national park
- students going on to work on research projects with Indigenous organisations
- one student writing the outstanding *1938: An Opera* about the Aboriginal Day of Mourning and Uncle William Cooper.
- many students becoming tutors in the university's tutorial assistance program for Indigenous students
- law students going on to promote Indigenous and human rights, including one who now works for the United Nations Human Rights Council
- three engineering students going on to work with Engineers Without Borders in Indigenous communities in Australia and South-East Asia
- some students becoming journalists and contributing articles on Indigenous issues to major newspapers
- four students being involved in Indigenous radio and ANTaR
- one student who studied law being instrumental in getting the support of the lawyers who helped us in the Bolt case in 2011 (see Chapter 20).

I enjoyed mentoring Indigenous students. Some are now on overseas scholarships; one is doing a PhD on the repatriation of cultural materials to the Bininj community in north-east Arnhem Land; an honours student went on to work with the Gagudju Association in Kakadu; and another produced a video on the Dharnya Centre. We now have a vast and treasured network of students in different parts of the world, many of whom I keep in touch with through social media. Indeed, my travels have included catch-ups with former students.

The concept of Oncountry Learning has certainly caught on and raised the bar at the University of Melbourne. Other disciplines, including health, education, law, engineering, architecture, building and planning and cultural studies, have been inspired by the program. For five years I coordinated and taught an Oncountry Learning course for students in the Medical School. Local partnerships for this course were forged with community-based organisations, including Rumbalara Aboriginal Co-operative, Rumbalara Football Netball Club in Shepparton, Njernda Aboriginal Corporation in Echuca, and the Viney Morgan Aboriginal Medical Service at Cummeragunja. Again, the Oncountry Learning process produced positive outcomes for all parties involved.

There is still much work needed to provide pathways for Indigenous students in higher education. More Indigenous voices to teach Indigenous studies within the academy are required. The vision of those Indigenous education programs I studied in North America in the early 1980s is still relevant. We have made progress over the years, but there is still much groundwork to be done to put Indigenous education front and centre of education programs and curriculums in Australia.

In 2017, I was awarded the TG Tucker Medal for excellence in scholarship and teaching at the University of Melbourne at the conferring-of-degrees ceremony in the Royal Exhibition Building. I gave an address[2] to the audience of over 1000 people, and it was with immense pride that I drew attention to the educational methods and inspiration of Granpa James and the other Yorta Yorta leaders he worked with. They have influenced my lifelong journey of learning.

Teaching the Yorta Yorta struggle for land justice and taking students on Country is an overwhelming and empowering process for me and my people. As our activist elders taught us, we have reached many people through the power of the voice and the spear of the pen and collective organisation. Receiving the award for teaching excellence is a highlight of my career, but it is also an honour for all who have contributed to the Oncountry Learning program.

20

Andrew Bolt's Myths for Money

On 5 May 2011 I was teaching my large first-year course 'Indigenous People and the State' when one of my students asked, 'Wayne, have you read the *Herald-Sun* this morning?'

I replied, 'Thanks, Amy, but no, I try my hardest not to read it at all. Why? What was in it?'

She said, 'Andrew Bolt has had a go at you and your brother Graham about your Aboriginality. He says in the paper that you're not real Aborigines, or something to that effect.'

'Oh, we're not the real thing, hey? Okay, I'll check it out after the lecture.'

As I was heading home, my daughter Gabrielle rang with the same question: 'Hey Dad, have you seen today's paper? Andrew Bolt reckons you and Uncle Graham are not real Aboriginals.' I won't disclose what else my dear Gabby said, but she was offended and annoyed about the article and was sticking up for her dad and uncle.

The title of Bolt's article was 'Yorta Yorta Money for Myths'. Graham and I were two of eleven Aboriginal people named in what turned out to be a series of articles and blogs in which Bolt questioned our motives for 'choosing' to be Aboriginal, as he put it. He attacked the basis for us identifying with our tribal group and as Aboriginal people. He had other headlines in the paper too, such as 'It's So Hip to Be Black' and 'White Fellas in the Black'.

Bolt implied that we chose to identify as Aboriginal for financial and other benefits reserved for 'genuine' Aboriginal people, who are darker skinned rather than fairer. He then vilified a larger group of articulate Aboriginal people, including activist Pat Eatock, barrister Mick Dodson, Professor Larissa Behrendt and other well-known figures. Bolt had first targeted me and Graham with these offensive views back in 2005, and I used his articles to discuss the concept of race in my lectures. For whatever reason, he had quickly risen to the status of a serial offender on Indigenous issues.

It came to the point where Graham and I said enough was enough. We weren't going to let him get away with this—the consequences were too serious. Young Aboriginal people were being intimidated and confused about their identity. Bolt was causing distress and racial division and was getting paid for it.

Nine of us decided to lodge a group case on behalf of all people recognised under the law as Aboriginal and likely to be offended, insulted, humiliated or intimidated by the publication of the articles. One of my students who was studying law was quick to provide support. She contacted lawyers who might take on the case pro bono. Ron Merkel came on board and represented us. We were grateful that such an eminent former justice of the Federal Court agreed to be our legal counsel.

The case was called *Eatock v Bolt* and was heard in the Federal Court, Melbourne from March to April 2011—the same place we had sat through months of legal argument over native title. On the opening day of the case, all nine of us gathered from different parts of Australia to be present. We fronted the media outside the court holding a huge Aboriginal flag with an air of defiance. Bolt was powerful, with the backing of the *Herald-Sun*, but our very identity was on trial. Ironically, this time it seemed we were not being put down for being blackfellas but were accused of being too hip to be black!

As with the native title claim, most of our lawyers were Jewish. Uncle William Cooper had forged a historic link between First Nations and Jewish people on 6 December 1938 when he led a march from Footscray to the German Consulate in Melbourne to protest the violent and racist actions of Nazi Germany. Uncle William's letter of protest read:

> On behalf of the Aboriginal inhabitants of Australia, we wish to have it registered and on record that we protest wholeheartedly at the cruel persecution of the Jewish people by the Nazi government in Germany.

> We plead that you would make it known to your government and its military leaders that this cruel persecution of their fellow citizens must be brought to an end.[1]

The lawyers agreed to work pro bono, believing that our case served the public good. The team was led by Merkel and the cross-examination was carried out by Herman Borenstein SC. The law they used in the case was the *Racial Discrimination Act 1975*. It was powerful to listen to Borenstein as he forensically cross-examined Bolt, but it took my total concentration to follow his line of argument through, so complex was the web he wove. It was a web that captured Bolt, who appeared *golyinan* (agitated) in the witness box. Many times, he had to admit that he had made false claims about people's ancestry and had distorted the reality that they had grown up Aboriginal and suffered the consequences.

Justice Mordy Bromberg handed down the verdict in September 2011. He found that Bolt was guilty of breaching section 18C of the Act and that it was likely that a fair-skinned Aboriginal person would have been offended and insulted by the newspaper articles. In the case of Graham and me, Bromberg said,

> The facts given by Mr Bolt and the comment made upon them are grossly incorrect. The Atkinsons' parents are both Aboriginal as are all four of their grandparents and all their great grandparents other than one who is the Indian great grandfather that Mr Bolt referred to in the article.[2]

He said that Bolt had distorted the truth about matters of public importance and found that Bolt had written the articles 'because of the race, ethnic origin or colour of the Aboriginal persons there described'.[3] The *Herald-Sun* was ordered to publish a correction beside Bolt's column and had to pay our costs. It was with great rejoicing that we left the court that day to front the media.

~

After the Bolt case some extremist groups and the government tried to change section 18C of the Act to give it less power, and 18C became a catch-cry in the community. Thankfully they didn't succeed, and the Act prevailed. As an act of conciliation, I invited Andrew Bolt to come on Country to meet our people and share our culture and history. We never got the response of an apology from him for the hurt that he caused.

Thank goodness for the law coming down in our favour. Back in 1975 the Whitlam government had enshrined in legislation a human rights law that opposed all forms of racial discrimination in Australia, and it helped us now. Having the Act on our side was a humbling experience. The same protection hadn't been available in our parents' and grandparents' time. Our case showed everyone that there are limits to free speech and that racism and vilification don't have to be tolerated.

The Bolt case became a case study for students to examine, which they did with rigour and critical analysis. They wrote some excellent essays, a few of which are published on my website. Jerome Holleman's paper is an exemplary contribution. He argues that Bolt:

> would like what he calls 'political Aborigines' to be discredited, undermined and to eventually disappear. Preferring instead to forget that Aboriginal people have been defined by race, made inferior by race, segregated, and controlled because of race and assimilated in attempts to breed out race.[4]

Graham and I wrote a letter of explanation to the *Riverine Herald* (Echuca) that was published on 29 September 2011:

> We're very pleased with the outcome and the findings of the Federal Court in the Bolt Case. Free speech has nothing to fear from this Judgement. Justice Bromberg however found that there is a right and a wrong way to go about exercising the value of free speech. That is, it can't be done by getting it wrong when it comes to the use of factual information. It can't be done by 'distorting the truth' about matters of public importance and it definitely can't be done by using 'inflammatory and provocative language' to make personal attacks on individuals. Using value judgments to make false claims about people's identity and cultural background is another negative for free speech.
>
> That is the essence of the key findings and in the case of my brother Graham and I, we are both pleased with the outcome. We're pleased not just for us but for our family and the next generation

coming through who have been reared in an environment in which they have been taught to be proud of their Aboriginality and to walk tall wherever they may choose to go in life. We are indeed a proud people who are more than willing to share our unique identity, cultural heritage, and our family history with people from all walks of life.

21

Adventures Abroad: Travelling with Wayne

by Catherine Guinness

An account of our life together would be incomplete without tales of our adventures across the seas. We've travelled from Australia to the Pacific Islands and Asia, across the Indian Ocean to Mauritius and India, from England across the Channel to Ireland and Europe, and across the Atlantic to North and South America. Our planet is an amazing place peopled with welcoming and interesting people. We have been blessed to enjoy these travels and adventures across the globe. We have expanded our minds exponentially and are not finished yet.

But why have we done all this journeying?

It all started with Wayne's cultural exchange to Māori New Zealand in 1980 and his overseas study in North America in 1982. Wayne has focused on finding out about other Indigenous peoples and their history and pursuing his interest in archaeology. He has increased his knowledge about human rights and the impact of colonisation, particularly British colonisation, and has applied much of this in his teaching of Indigenous Studies.

Wayne's travels have built bridges with Indigenous communities and academic institutions. He has done research, given public talks, and collected genealogical data. He has presented papers at Cambridge and Leicester universities in the United Kingdom, the National University of Ireland in Galway and Trinity College in Dublin, Hokkaido University in Japan, the Monash University Prato Centre in Italy, and Jagiellonian University in Poland.

I will concentrate on three major journeys. The first was to Ireland, where the focus was on patterns of British colonisation. Second was to Mauritius and India to investigate a rich piece of family history about Wayne's great-grandfather. Third was a marvellous opportunity for networking at the Indigenous Peoples Summit in Japan. I will finish with brief comments on some other relevant trips.

~

In 2006 Wayne was invited to give a paper at the following year's Galway Conference on Colonialism, whose theme was settler colonialism. This led to a love affair with Ireland and a rich understanding of British colonialism there; it also led me to write a book about my Guinness ancestors. Wayne ended up becoming a visiting fellow at the University of Galway for eleven years, where he participated in the summer school program of Irish Studies and took the opportunity to complete an intensive course in human rights and advocacy. From these experiences, he produced a range of written work.

The history of British interaction with Ireland gave a startling insight into the long history of the reserve system. The *Act for the Settlement of Ireland 1652* gave powers to the British to forcibly remove Irish Catholic Traditional Owners to the west of the Shannon River. They were expected to survive in Connaught, the most isolated and poorest of the Irish provinces. If you did not move to Connaught, you were put to the sword under the violent 'to Hell or to Connaught' scheme.

Oliver Cromwell was the leader of this plan to force people to move. He undermined Irish sovereignty and imposed British law. The Cromwellian invasion replaced native Irish Catholic landowning classes with British colonists. Cromwell is notorious in Irish history for his legacy of terror, bloodshed and violence. Over 600,000 men, women and children died during his invasion. Learning about this gave Wayne evidence to argue that the formula of segregation and control was well oiled before it reached Australia—the British had practised this strategy in Ireland, North America and other colonies.[1]

With the shameful history of British colonisation, Wayne would rather me be Irish than English—and of course my surname is famously

Irish: Guinness! We had such an enjoyable and meaningful trip in 2007 that we returned to Ireland over their summer months for the next ten years. I became quite immersed in my Irish history and was delighted to celebrate my Irish roots. Wayne jokes about my Guinness heritage: he says he had no idea that our relationship would take him to the place that produces over 10 million pints of the dark stuff every day. His Itchica friends Simon O'Toole and Paddy Malone had told him that the only way to enjoy Guinness at its best was to drink it in Ireland. Indeed, Wayne proved them to be exactly right.

We had free entry to the brewery in Dublin courtesy of my great-great-great-grandfather Arthur, the founder of the Guinness business, and our Montmorency home in Melbourne started to fill up with those famous posters advertising Guinness, like 'My Goodness, My Guinness'. We also collected posters about the Irish struggle and Irish culture and to this day have a poster of the 1916 Irish Proclamation on our wall. This is an inspirational document for Indigenous sovereign rights in Australia. Wayne's interest in the Anglo-Irish Treaty of 1921 took up much of his time reading and doing research into the Irish struggle for sovereignty and Home Rule. We visited many of the places and sites connected to the civil war that followed the signing of the treaty. Michael Collins became a powerful figure in the Irish story and our journey of learning in Ireland culminated in a visit to his homeplace in Clonakilty, County Cork.

I can claim to be Irish when it suits—after all, no one can tell from my looks. For Wayne, however, ethnicity is not a choice when we are in Australia because being Aboriginal is such a big deal that his background soon comes up in conversation. But in Ireland and anywhere else overseas, he can be anonymous—being Aboriginal is not a barrier.

Ireland became a refuge for Wayne, the place where he felt most at home apart from the times with his own community and at Dungula. Here was a rich musical heritage to be shared, and a tradition of storytelling and the sense of humour that both Kooris and Irish use to deal with adversity. But it was much more than this for him. The paper he gave to the conference in Galway was about the connection between Irish and Aboriginal history, about how they share a common heritage of aggressive British colonial oppression. It was a way of giving a global context to the appalling reserve policy under which his parents and grandparents suffered.

Many Irish people are aware of this comparative history and often talk about Aboriginal history and British colonisation. Some openly admit that Irish settlers in Australia could have done better in recognising Indigenous people's rights to the soil. We are reminded of John O'Shanassy, who leased the Moira pastoral station in Yorta Yorta Country.

Our Irish connection took another turn when Wayne met historian Angus Mitchell in Galway. Angus was keen to meet me to discuss my grandfather Dr Harry Guinness's involvement with Roger Casement, whose life he was writing about. Casement was British consul in East Africa and the Congo Free State from 1895 to 1904 and gained international fame for revealing atrocious cruelty in the exploitation of native people by white traders in Congo and Peru. One of his reports led to major changes in how Belgium ruled in Congo. Casement inspired Edmund D Morel and Grandfather Harry to form the Congo Reform Association in Britain. Angus later wrote the book *Roger Casement: 16 Lives*, an epic account of Casement's support for the Irish rights struggle.[2] Casement was executed for treason and became one of the principal Irish martyrs in the revolt against British rule. His role in the fight for Ireland became a major interest for us.

Angus encouraged me to write about my grandfather and his missionaries' involvement in the Congo Reform Association, and his academic interest in my family story made me realise that this history may be of broader interest. I discovered that my grandfather gave years of his life to the Congo Reform campaign. The endpoint was my own book, *Rubber Justice*, which is about the Congo when Belgium invaded under King Leopold.[3] His brutal exploitation of Congolese people to harvest rubber, or 'black gold', led to the death of 10 million Congolese. Here was another example of European colonial practice.

Another intriguing link to Irish history takes us back to my great-great-grandfather Captain John Grattan Guinness, youngest son of Arthur Guinness of the Guinness Brewery. I would not be here were it not for a duel between The Liberator, Daniel O'Connell, and

John D'Esterre in Dublin in 1815, in which O'Connell mortally injured D'Esterre and left his wife, Jane Lucretia D'Esterre, a widow. Jane later became John Guinness's wife and, with the birth of Henry Grattan Guinness, my great-great-grandmother.

~

Wayne always knew that Granpa James had come to Australia from Mauritius, but there were many mysteries to his story. One of these was the oral account that his family name had been Peersahib but that he changed it to James when he arrived in Australia. From 2012 to 2016, Wayne did a family history project to trace the origins of his great-grandfather that took us to Mauritius, Chennai (formerly Madras) in India, and Sri Lanka.

Past connections can be invaluable. We had welcomed a Mauritian student, Tali, into our home some years before. She had stayed with us for three years while undertaking computing studies at La Trobe. Now she invited us to stay with her and her husband and two boys in Mauritius, where they were going for a holiday. What a wonderful idea. We loved Tali. The thought of spending this holiday with her was enticing, and we would be able to do all our research while there for a month.

We rented a house with Tali in Flic-en-Flac, a seaside village with a white sandy beach and palm trees that is very popular with tourists. When not being tourists ourselves, we became serious researchers, travelling to archive offices, the Mahatma Gandhi Institute (MGI) and the registry of births, deaths and marriages. We were hunting for any information about Granpa James's father, with a family name of Peersahib or Pursaib. We drew a blank at the Indian Immigration Archives at MGI, which was puzzling, because we knew he was a Tamil Indian who had come to Mauritius before Granpa James was born in 1859. We also knew he had been an interpreter.

One day we were in the National Archives office methodically going through the huge annual Blue Books, which recorded the names of the British colonial government officers, when it happened. 'Eureka!' I whispered excitedly.

> Peersahib, James
> Interpreter, Stipendiary Magistrate, Plaines Wilhems
> Date of appointment: 1/2/1859. Annual salary: £72
> Place of birth: India

This was the first definite sighting of him. From there, we traced his career as interpreter in the Stipendiary Magistrates' Courts to interpreter in the District Courts, where the skills demanded were higher and the annual salary was 1500 rupees. His eventual retirement at age sixty-seven was 'due to old age'. We were able to imagine his contribution to justice for Indian labourers in the sugar plantations, using his linguistic skills in Tamil and English to ensure their story was heard accurately. Indentured labourer Pursaib 132719 had, like them, been enticed to leave India, as we discovered to our amazement at MGI, which listed him as James Pursahib.[4]

We can only guess that his employment and connections helped him to educate Granpa James in good schools. Granpa had been a well-educated man when he arrived on Australian shores aged about seventeen and took up teaching and medical studies. He went on to become part of the Yorta Yorta community as a teacher at the Maloga Mission. In 1885 he married Wayne's great-grandmother Ada Cooper, daughter of Granny Kitty.

On our way home from Mauritius in 2012 we spent a month as tourists in India. I was turning seventy that September and had set my heart on seeing the Himalayas. We got up to the hill station of Mussoorie in the foothills of the great mountain range, 300 kilometres north of New Delhi. We then joined an Intrepid tour to Rajasthan, which was wonderful, but a sideline to Wayne's family history. So after that we flew to Chennai to see what we could find out about James Peersahib the indentured labourer. We had hoped to get a better understanding of his Muslim identity but only knew he spoke Tamil and was born in about 1832. Despite our visit to the records office, we were unable to learn any more about his background.

It is challenging to think that my own great-great-grandfather Captain John Grattan Guinness spent time in Chennai as a British soldier. He was there from 1800 to 1824 and was involved in defeating the rule of the maharajas. There you have the irony of our family histories: our great-great-grandfathers were in Chennai within eight years of each other but one was enforcing British rule and the other was a victim of that rule.

In 1877 Queen Victoria was proclaimed Empress of India just as Granpa was setting out for Australia. There was no escaping the British Empire—he arrived in another British colony on the other side of the world. He then spent his life with the Yorta Yorta people, quietly using education to subvert the power of the Aborigines Protection Board.

~

Our visit to Japan in 2008 is an example of the important friendships Wayne has forged. He had mentored some Japanese students at University of Melbourne, one of whom, Tako, was a teacher who asked to sit in on his lectures and camped with us in the Barmah Forest. Another, Yugo, was doing a comparison between the Cummera community and his own burakumin identity. Through these contacts, Wayne was invited to participate in the Indigenous Peoples Summit on Ainu Country in the northern island of Hokkaido. He presented a paper at an ecotourism workshop at Hokkaido University, and later in Osaka.

The summit took us to a new level of understanding of the international Indigenous rights movement. Twenty Indigenous people attended from eleven countries. It was held at the Nibutani Culture Museum in the heart of Ainu Country. We participated as honoured guests at a ceremony to launch the summit and welcome Indigenous visitors. The ceremony was in a thatched hut with a sacred fire in the middle. We all sat around the walls and the Ainu leaders sat around the fire conducting the traditional calling on the ancestors. The unexpected happened when one of the visitors from New Mexico, a Pueblo elder, came forward to contribute a Native American blessing to the ceremony, bringing with him an eagle feather and praying in his language.

The summit developed the Nibutani Declaration on Indigenous Peoples Rights to present to the G8 Summit, which was to take place in Hokkaido the following weekend. It was terrific to hear from Indigenous people from Hawaii, Aotearoa, North America, South America, Finland and Bangladesh. The most exciting time of the summit was the final concert. It is impossible to convey the intense joy in the air when the whole hall, full of hundreds of people, danced together in Ainu fashion right around the space.

Wayne not only supported the Ainu people's struggle and the Nibutani Declaration but also gained their support for the Yorta Yorta struggle. He was successful in getting relevant clauses added to the declaration and later used the declaration in press releases to hail its support of the Yorta Yorta as a major victory.

We were changed by the experience. We met Japanese people and discovered their graciousness and generosity. We met the Ainu and shared their love of their land and forests and their resilience in the face of Japanese colonial domination. We met the burakumin people, the 'untouchables' of Japan, and gained inspiration from their community. And we tasted exquisite Japanese food. Such were the reciprocal gifts from Wayne's teaching.

My confidence as an Anglo-Celtic supporter also developed further. I was accepted as a working member of the summit. That inclusiveness was very special for me as I felt I had a legitimate place in the Indigenous rights movement.

~

Our travels have largely focused on learning about European colonisation of Indigenous peoples and the impact of genocides, as well as human rights and cultural heritage. However, we have also expanded our worldly knowledge with visits to China, Vietnam, Cambodia, Laos, Thailand, Cuba, Ecuador, Peru, Italy, Spain, Portugal, Croatia, Bosnia and Herzegovina, Poland, the Baltic States, Russia and France.

Our Asian journeys opened our eyes to our neighbours in the north. Later, in South America, we were curious to see how Spanish colonisation had panned out for the Indigenous people there. Much of the information gained from these visits has an archaeological focus, and Wayne has used it in his teaching. For example, he compared cave paintings in Spain and France with the antiquity of Aboriginal rock art in Australia. The Murujuga rock art in the Burrup Peninsula, Western Australia is considered to be the world's largest and oldest, dated at 50,000 BP.[5]

In Spain we followed in the footsteps of Christopher Columbus and Wayne studied the legal aspects of Indigenous rights at the time of Columbus's voyages to the Americas (1492–1502). Outrageously, the 1494 Treaty of Tordesillas divided the 'New World' into two: the land, resources and people were divided between Spain and Portugal. Portugal wasn't happy with the deal and eventually had Brazil included in its empire, which is why Portuguese is the official language of Brazil.

Our respect for Islam was heightened by our visit to Andalucía in Spain. This led me to investigate the contributions of Islamic civilisation to science and medicine, mathematics, architecture and law, providing a respectful basis for my work with Muslim communities in Australia. In Poland, the Baltic States and Russia we learned about the legacy of Nazism and Communism as well as some features of contemporary nationalism. I was pleased to go back to Poland after more than fifty years, having first visited as a student seeking understanding of Communism.

In Poland, Wayne organised a meeting at the famous 14th-century Jagiellonian University in Krakow, where Professor Pawel Nowak was keen to show us something of relevance to Indigenous Australia. He produced an object wrapped in protective cloth and asked Wayne to examine it. The professor told us how they had found this fragment of mammoth tusk shaped like a boomerang and showing signs of having been manually shaped and polished. After demonstrating how it may have been thrown, Wayne surmised that it looked like a hunting boomerang. A Polish archaeologist showed us pictures of the cave where the mammoth tusk had been excavated, and Professor Nowak explained that the material from the cave had been dated to about 23,000 BP.[6] There had also been skeletal materials and decorative objects surrounding the boomerang. Was it a burial? There were still many questions about the nature and context of the boomerang and whether the cultural practice of boomerang making continued or ended during the Stone Age. These are questions that remain part of a work in progress as more evidence is found.

Wayne then gave a lecture on Aboriginal archaeology at the University. There was a lot of interest in the diversity of languages and territorial groups in Australia, and their timeline. In his discussion of the boomerang, Wayne took the opportunity to connect the story with the work of Uncle Bill Onus, the famous boomerang maker, and included the tale of how Uncle Bill threw a boomerang at the Tivoli Theatre in Melbourne (see Chapter 7), which went down very well.

In all our travels, Wayne's strong incentive was closing the gap in his knowledge of the origins of the reserve system. The story of reserve life is much more than a story of survival and resistance, and his search for the bigger picture launched him on a journey of discovery of global proportions. The search for the roots of the notorious policies of segregation and control took us first to North America, then to England, and eventually to the Celtic regions of Ireland and Scotland. Understanding British colonial policy in its global reach connects Wayne to other Indigenous peoples who were treated similarly. It authenticates the Aboriginal experience and puts together a clear picture of the way the British acted as imperial colonisers.

PART VI
Unfinished Business

22

Truth, Justice and Self-Determination

In the long and continuing struggle for First Nations peoples' fundamental rights, it is true to say that there is still much unfinished business to be dealt with in Australia. The call for a treaty as a means by which greater justice and equality can be achieved came to the fore in 1988 in the Northern Territory at the Barunga Festival.

The Barunga Statement was presented to Prime Minister Bob Hawke as a collective statement that called for a treaty with the Commonwealth of Australia. It was focused on the rights of mob and called for land, social and economic rights, self-determination and compensation, among other things. In response to the statement, Hawke claimed he would have a treaty created between Aboriginal people and the Australian Government by 1990—this promise has still not been fulfilled.

This call, another betrayal of our hopes that failed to deliver, was followed by the Uluru Statement from the Heart in 2017. With renewed hope, the Uluru Statement reiterated First Nations' aspirations for a treaty as one of its three core elements: Voice, Treaty and Truth.[1]

Victoria's First Peoples' call for a treaty arose out of a community forum hosted by the Office of Aboriginal Affairs (OAAV) in Melbourne in 2016. At this meeting, some 500 Aboriginal and Torres Strait Islander people unanimously voted against constitutional recognition, arguing instead for a treaty and self-determination. Subsequently, the Victorian Aboriginal Affairs minister and the Victorian Government committed themselves to develop a statewide treaty process. Consultations saw

Victoria become the first state to pass legislation on a proposed treaty, the *Advancing the Treaty Process with Aboriginal Victorians Act 2018*.

In 2019 a statewide election set up the First Peoples' Assembly (FPA) of thirty-two members to be the voice of First Peoples in the Victorian treaty process. Membership was increased to thirty-three in 2024 when the FPA voted to create a new reserved seat for representatives of the Wamba Wamba peoples.[2] In a significant first, the FPA and the Victorian Government agreed to set up a truth-telling process as a basis to inform the treaty negotiation process. In May 2021, towards the end of my teaching career at the University of Melbourne, the Andrews Labor government announced a truth justice royal commission. The Yoorrook Justice Commission, to run from 2021 to 2025, was to be the instrument of truth-telling, mandated with the powers of a royal commission.[3] The assembly chose the name 'Yoorrook', which means 'truth' in Wamba Wamba language.

Being the first of its kind in the Australian context, the commission attracted much attention. The terms of reference[4] outlined how it would conduct its business and authorised what it was empowered to do. Under these terms of reference, it is empowered to inquire into and report on the historic injustices perpetrated by state and non-state entities against First Peoples of Victoria since the start of colonisation. At the end of the truth-telling process, the commission's main function is to produce recommendations that will feed into treaty negotiations with the state. Its final report is due in mid-2025.

This historic truth justice process and its overarching royal commission powers grabbed my interest. I thought it was necessary, and something to which I believed I could make a contribution as a senior Yorta Yorta elder with many decades of study, teaching, writing, international experience, human rights advocacy and analysis of the subject matter.[5] It raised my hopes, and I'm sure the hopes of many other community members, that the process would expose the systemic injustices perpetrated on First Peoples since the start of colonisation. Its mandate was broad and inclusive of historic and ongoing injustices; some of these are the continuing high numbers of our people in jails, the deplorable number of deaths in custody, and the low age of criminal responsibility leading to Aboriginal children being held in jails.

My immediate attention was grabbed by the promise that the process would lead to a treaty outcome and the full realisation of self-determination, as enshrined in UNDRIP's articles 3 and 4. It had the potential to produce strong recommendations for action against systemic racism, structural barriers and institutional racism entrenched in the government system. The acknowledgement in the commission's letters patent of First Peoples not ceding their sovereignty[6] raised the truth justice bar to its highest point, at least in my lifetime. Unceded sovereignty to me was sufficient truth in itself, without fear or favour.

With knowledge of and commitment to these important issues, I applied for a position and was appointed as a commissioner to the Yoorrook Justice Commission, which was formally launched in Melbourne in May 2021. My expectations, as set out in the terms of reference, were that its powers would allow us to:

- provide substance about the legal enforcement of unceded sovereignty and what should be included in a treaty or treaties being negotiated
- gain reparative justice for the harm done to First Peoples through past and ongoing colonisation and the attempts to eradicate language, culture and identity
- deliver real self-determination and the transfer of power and resources to First Peoples under community control measures
- identify, document and challenge the ongoing and detrimental effects of racism, with strong recommendations for action
- inquire into and make recommendations on the gross over-representation of First Nations Peoples in the criminal and juvenile justice systems
- inquire into the theft, misappropriation and destruction of cultural property and the dispossession of First Peoples of their ancestral land, water and resources.

I sought to include another important point of community reference: investigate matters relating to the systemic injustice of fraudulent claims of Aboriginality being engendered by people seeking to advance their interests through career opportunities in First Nations Peoples affairs without meeting proper bloodline selection criteria. This inclusion in the mandate was not supported.

The letters patent of the governor in consultation with the premier authorised the appointment of the Yoorrook Justice Commission and acknowledged that the sovereignty of the Traditional Owners of Victoria was never ceded.[7] This fundamental declaration of truth is in the pudding, as the saying goes. It gave me hope that Yoorrook would lead to a treaty that recognises Victoria's First Peoples as the sovereign owners of their land, water and resources. That would be the basis for the FPA to negotiate the treaty's full legal meaning in terms of what it delivers to First Peoples of Victoria under tradition-based lore.

The acknowledgement of unceded sovereignty goes beyond the letters patent to the truth of the matter as it exists in the here and now. It invokes a factual truth sanctioned by at least 60,000 years of occupation and use of the ancestral land and waters. Nothing can change what always was and always will be ours by right of sovereign occupation.

The Uluru Statement from the Heart endorses this fundamental truth. It came from over 250 Aboriginal and Torres Strait Islander delegates and Traditional Owners from all points of the southern sky who gathered at Uluru and put their signatures to the historic statement in 2017. The Uluru Statement verifies the ownership and sovereignty of Indigenous Australia from creation to the present. It is validated by scientific timelines, Indigenous worldviews and tradition-based lore and customs. It confirms the origins and continuity of occupation as the basis of sovereign ownership of the soil when it says that sovereignty 'has never been ceded or extinguished, and co-exists with the sovereignty of the Crown'.[8]

How could it be otherwise, the Uluru Statement rightly asks? It challenges the way the colonial mindset denied the fact of possession and the sacred link that continues. It proposes a remedy for the Australian people to come together through a truth justice process. A representative voice in parliament, constitutional change and structural reform are the requirements put forth. This would allow the 'ancient sovereignty' to 'shine through as a fuller expression of Australia's nationhood'.[9]

Powerful words like these coming from Indigenous voices from all points of the country should not be ignored or diminished. Furthermore, they add substantive weight to the treaty and truth-telling process in Victoria. Having the letters patent declare that we have never ceded sovereignty was a strong start for Yoorrook. It lifted my faith in the process and in what could be delivered at the end of the truth justice journey.

~

Our survival and resilience against the impact of colonisation, dispossession and forced removal are remarkable achievements. A key role of Yoorrook is to examine the impacts of colonisation caused by policies and actions like massacres, genocide and frontier violence. As I have touched on in earlier chapters, a lot of research and reports give detailed information about Stolen Generations, frontier violence and massacres.[10] Yoorrook researchers will also be familiar with the violent history of colonisation in Tasmania, which continued on the mainland as people like Edward Curr Junior moved to Victoria and to Yorta Yorta Country, where the Moira Swamp massacre took place in 1843 (see Chapter 2).

The impact of colonisation in Australia is a harrowing story of violence and terror. I have studied in detail the multitude of laws that gave powers to the reserve system and the policy of segregation and control.[11] They were carbon copies of the laws used by the British to invade and plunder other First Nations Peoples' territorial sovereignty in North America and Ireland. I have also studied the powers of the Aborigines Protection Board administration in Victoria from 1869 to 1957. From these studies it was clear to me that the Protection Board was nothing less than a front organisation for the colonial project aimed at eradicating our culture and identity as First Nations Peoples. The government of the day made the laws and the Protection Board enforced them through the managers of the reserves. The impact of colonisation over a century of life under the control of the Protection Board is the underlying history being uncovered and put on the table. This is the subject matter that confronts the truth justice inquiry.

Cummeragunja, Coranderrk, Framlingham, Lake Condah, Ebenezer and Lake Tyers are prime examples of where Protection Board human rights violations took place. They all have their own stories to tell about the policies of segregation and reserve life. Protection Board management is clearly one of the systemic injustices perpetrated by state and non-state entities referred to in Yoorrook's terms of reference, which state that the commission is to inquire into and report on 'protectionist and assimilationist policies, including forced removal of children and attempts to eradicate language, culture or identity'.[12]

My Chapter 4 on Cummeragunja history explains how the constant battles with Protection Board policies culminated in the walk-off in 1939. It also examines the way Aborigines Protection Acts were designed to forcibly move First Peoples onto reserves and take their children, and to classify residents on the basis of their skin colour. The 1886 Absorption Act was used to divide and assimilate lighter-skinned residents into the general community.

Ironically, the role that reserves played in the oppression and denial of our rights remains culturally and strategically important. Reserve lands confirm our connections with the ancestral lands and with the apical ancestors who were on Country before the British imposed their sovereignty over tradition-based law. While the British Crown tried to claim land and remove Traditional Owners to reserves, the traditional connection with Country was maintained. Cummeragunja is an example of how reserve culture enabled the Traditional Owners to keep their cultural connections with the ancestral lands.

British laws were used to justify the pretext of terra nullius and the land theft that followed. This provided the basis to implement the policy of racial segregation. This policy was enshrined in generic laws that spread across Australia like an uncontrolled bushfire from Tasmania and Victoria into the mid-twentieth century and beyond. Racist policies of segregation were repeated in South Africa in 1948. In 1996, Nelson Mandela authorised the South African Truth and Reconciliation Commission to examine that nation's violent history of apartheid.[13] European colonisation has left a track record for truth-telling on a global scale.

The extent of violence and the impact of colonisation on Yorta Yorta people and First Peoples of Victoria has been horrendous and well documented. Our people have survived and thrived, but this is despite the brutality of colonisation and ongoing injustice and inequality. I hope the truth justice process can find ways to redress the magnitude of the impact of colonisation. The 2021 article 'From dispossession to massacres, the Yoo-rrook Justice Commission sets a new standard for truth telling' by five Yoorrook commissioners, including myself, provides the context for examining and making strong recommendations on the impact of colonisation.[14]

From 1837 to the present there have been hundreds of different inquiries, strategies, reports, reviews and laws passed about First Peoples of Victoria. Historically, we are the most legislated, examined, managed and regulated people in the country. No other cultural or ethnic group has been subjected to the degree of paternalistic domination and control that Victoria's First Peoples have. The ongoing structural barriers that perpetuate inequality and disadvantage will be named and addressed by Yoorrook. I have already laid out the past and ongoing structural barriers in my own people's struggle for justice. It's a long road that many have already travelled and one that confronts us in the work ahead in the truth justice patch.

Yoorrook has the opportunity to make recommendations about a whole range of reparations to include in the treaty process. Reparative justice focuses on repairing past harms, stopping present harm, and preventing its reproduction in the future. But real outcomes from commissions are not guaranteed. The recommendation from Yoorook to raise the age of criminal responsibility from ten to fourteen years comes to mind.[15] The Victorian premier has already walked back the government's commitment to do so, settling instead for keeping it at ten.[16] This clearly illustrates the limited influence of royal commission findings on which Yoorrook has been given its mandate. The hope is that a treaty will be more effective in holding the government to its commitments.

~

The impact of colonisation and its effects on culture and language was discussed in 2021 by two leading Victorian authorities on language rights: Wurundjeri Mandy Nicholson of the Woiwurrung language group and Dr Vicki Couzens, Gunditjmara language custodian and co-chair of the Victorian Aboriginal Corporation for Languages. In *The Age* article by Jack Latimore, Mandy talked about the impact of colonisation and the forced removal policies that attempted to break the link between language and cultural identity. She argued that both impacts happened at the same time, and explained that the key to breaking a person's cultural identity is to 'get rid of the way they communicate with each other. The thing that makes Aborginal people who they are is language.'[17] Vicki used the word 'linguicide' to describe the decimation of Indigenous languages by colonial agencies and argued that this 'continues through inertia, low-level prioritisation of language, lack of policy implementation and paucity of resource allocation'.[18] She further noted the lack of resources for language work:

> There's no adequate resourcing for any of that. The state doesn't have an identified bucket of money for Aboriginal languages. Language that is supported by government funding is usually part of another priority strategy, for example, language in schools. While these programs have value as part of a strategic language revitalisation approach, the work required to support these programs is not funded.[19]

Latimore's article is relevant for the Yoorrook Justice Commission's mandate on cultural matters. It points to the work of language revitalisation, especially in the south-eastern region of Australia, and highlights the comprehensive spectrum of work to be undertaken. This includes research and sourcing language held in community and historical archives; community protocols around language development, uses and sharing; recording and documentation; development of orthographies; learning and teaching; and so on.

Other issues raised by Traditional Owners in the Yoorrook consultation process are relevant to this discussion. The relationship between language and wellbeing was discussed by a Traditional Owner of the Latji Latji western central Murray language group who spoke passionately about his experience of language deprivation and the social and emotional wellbeing aspect of language loss. This was noted by the commission as an issue of relevance to the truth justice inquiry.[20]

Many communities have done extensive research into language revitalisation, publishing booklets and vocabulary dictionaries. These are being used to reconstruct and articulate language through different media, including in children's books, Welcome to Country ceremonies, place names, sporting events and daily conversations. Australia stands to be enriched by the diversity of First Peoples language programs and the reintroduction of language to education. Much research has also focused on retrieving language from early missionary and colonial records, adding to the language retrieved from community sources. Many talented Aboriginal artists, musicians and writers are seeking inspiration from the power and meaning of traditional language.

The revival and restoration of language is vitally important for many reasons. It helps to keep people connected to culture and to ground our identity in who we are as a community. Keeping cultural connections strong through language is also important for education and cultural awareness programs. Importantly, it is now being used inclusively in treaty and truth-telling education and cultural awareness. The Yoorrook Justice Commission uses some language in its truth-telling work. The foreword to the June 2021 *Tyerri Yoorrook 'Seed of Truth'* report by FPA includes a message on the importance of language:

> Using Aboriginal language in Victoria shows the value and contribution of our living culture and is a reminder that Community must be front and centre of this process. Combining these words along with English symbolises the coming together of First Peoples and non-Aboriginal Victorians throughout this process.[21]

The Yoorrook terms of reference specify the need for reparative justice in relation to attempts to eradicate language. Vicki Couzens offers a way forward through the adequate resourcing of language programs and educational material. She also highlights the low level of priority that language work receives and the lack of policy implementation. These are practical ways to provide some reparation for language loss. Other mechanisms that can be drawn on for the process of language rights ownership, protection and restoration are from the relevant human rights instruments. These include Article 13 of UNDRIP:

> Indigenous peoples have the right to revitalize, use, develop and transmit to future generations their histories, languages, oral traditions, philosophies, writing systems and literatures, and to designate and retain their own names for communities, places and persons.[22]

The Global Action Plan of the International Decade of Indigenous Languages (2022–32) fits within the mandate of the Yoorrook Justice Commission's letters patent and human rights instruments.

~

In the reforms that the Koori Heritage Working Group achieved in the early 1980s, we used the United Nations' social, cultural and political declarations as a framework for asserting our right to self-determination. This is a vital part of the truth justice process. Control of our own affairs rather than by government and state entities is what the right of real self-determination is about. The grassroots version of the same principle is community control, which has been a core policy goal in our ongoing struggle for equality and autonomy.

Self-determination is not something we have to wait for government to deliver: it is a natural entitlement that we should be able to bring to the table as equals. To achieve an agreeable treaty outcome, we need governments to use the language of real self-determination. The Victorian Government's Aboriginal Affairs Framework 2018–2023 (which has been extended to 2025) includes self-determination reform measures.[23]

The objectives as stated in the letters patent provide a mandate for Yoorrook to 'identify Systemic Injustice which currently impedes First Peoples achieving self-determination and equality'.[24] As a long-time campaigner for self-determination, I see this as a clear instruction for the powers of a royal commission. Naming the impediments will be the easiest part of the process. In simple terms, it requires removing the blockages and handing the reins to First Peoples. I think Commissioner Lovett's examination of government policy in the Yoorrook hearings, nails the transition of the power relationship needed. I will return to this shortly.

In her evidence to the Yoorrook hearings at Charcoal Lane in Fitzroy in 2022, Minister for Aboriginal Affairs Gabrielle Williams strongly endorsed First Peoples' right to self-determination. To make this happen, she stated that the government acknowledged that 'to achieve true self-determination and justice, reform and structural change is needed' and that 'the government is committed to action'.[25] Backing the minister's support for real self-determination is the government's *Wirkara Kulpa: Aboriginal Youth Justice Strategy 2022–2032*. Self-determination is a cornerstone of its 'journey towards a justice system that values and promotes Aboriginal children and young people'.[26]

A whole-of-government commitment to self-determination sounds fine on paper, but, given the overdue status of required reforms and commitments, the question of where accountability lies for its implementation is unclear. The Yoorrook hearings with government and departmental heads on 15 April 2023 threw more light on the delivery of the commitments made. Minister for Corrections Enver Erdogan was asked for his definition of self-determination for First Peoples of Victoria. He said it meant Aboriginal people making decisions about themselves and matters that affect them. He qualified this by adding that it was not just about consultation. When further questioned on what actions have been taken to put into effect that aspiration by transferring power and resources to Aboriginal people, the minister replied that he hadn't seen a transfer of power and resources. He suggested that the transfer would occur through the treaty process. Commissioner Lovett's statement that 'a vision without a plan or strategy in how to get there is just an illusion' is well put.[27] Indeed, it sums up the gap between the rhetoric of real self-determination and its implementation as a policy commitment.

The minister's seemingly vague understanding of self-determination was clarified somewhat by Minister for Treaty and First Peoples Natalie Hutchins in her evidence to the commission in April 2024. She said she was committed to 'working towards a future, through Treaty, where self-determination is not an aspiration, but a reality for First Peoples'.[28] She also said that with the 'genuine self-determination commitments that the Government has made, it's not just around consulting First Peoples; it's about embedding change and handing over power and handing over resources'.[29]

The question of whether there are adequate checks and balances and duty-of-care mechanisms for the delivery of real self-determination within the Victorian Aboriginal Affairs Framework is problematic. A whole-of-government approach surely means having senior ministers and the cabinet on the same page.[30] Discrepancies in policy commitments have to be readily identified and remedied. Hutchins' predecessor as minister, Gabrielle Williams, did tell a Yoorrook hearing that structural change is 'indeed overdue'.[31]

The government says it is committed to uncovering truth, providing justice and reparation, and preventing further harm to First Peoples.

The Yoorrook process could help Victoria reach an agreeable treaty that includes self-determination, sovereignty and recompense for dispossession. But an unequivocal commitment to the right of real self-determination does not happen through the treaty process when it is a preconditional stepping stone to the treaty. It really should be in place now. Given that much is hinging on the treaty and reparative justice, Victoria is poised to be the state in a position to set a precedent for other jurisdictions.

In 2020 the Australian Government co-signed the National Agreement on Closing the Gap—a historic agreement with the Coalition of Peaks, a representative body of more than eighty Aboriginal and Torres Strait Islander community-controlled organisations. Closing the Gap is a federal and state government strategy that aims to reduce the differences between Indigenous and non-Indigenous Australians on key health, education and economic targets.

But a 2024 progress report on the last three years presents a damning review of government efforts to close the gap.[32] The report argues that the gap is a direct result of the ways in which governments have used their power over many decades. In particular, it stems from a disregard for Aboriginal and Torres Strait Islander peoples' knowledges and solutions. Most critically, it argues that the Agreement requires government decision-makers to accept that they do not know what is best for Aboriginal and Torres Strait Islander people.[33]

The crux of the issue is that governments have failed to hand over decision-making powers to Aboriginal communities. Government decision-makers need to accept that they do not know what is best for Aboriginal and Torres Strait Islander people. Community control is an act of self-determination, and community-controlled organisations need to be further strengthened and adequately resourced. In achieving the ultimate goal of self-determination as agreed to in UNDRIP, the report argues that the power imbalance must change. This supports Commissioner Lovett's view that the 'illusion' between the transfer of power and resources from government to the community is still a barrier to the right and practice of self-determination.

~

In its terms of reference, the commission has a mandate to extend its inquiry into other matters considered appropriate.[34] Community consultations and some submissions have raised the matter of the alarming increase in fraudulent claims of Aboriginality being made. As a commissioner I raised the divisive way many people are falsely claiming Aboriginality to gain jobs in Aboriginal affairs and Indigenous education. It was further noted in the *Australian* newspaper 'that the sheer number of people now laying claim to an Indigenous identity has begun to distort national statistics'.[35]

The systemic and divisive nature of identity politics calls for the inquiry to be appropriately applied to the matter of false claims of Aboriginality. Yoorrook needs to be a role model in recommending proper measures to deal with this ongoing problem. Community leaders are concerned that people who have no depth of experience living as Aboriginal people are claiming status and jobs that require genuine experience. In her witness statement to the Yoorrook public hearing on 29 April 2024, my sister Fay Carter gave evidence on the way Aboriginal people are affected by those who claim to be Aboriginal to get a good job.[36] Citing a particular incident, she talked about the divisive and fraudulent claims being made and said she had real concerns about non-Aboriginal people claiming Aboriginal identity just to make money. It was a key issue she had discussed with me and other family and community members, letting us know that she was going to raise it as a major issue in the hearing process. Although this matter was included in her written statement, it was not raised or examined in the hearing.

There must be clear accountability to the community for people claiming Aboriginality. There need to be clearer guidelines and criteria for Aboriginality in the employment and appointment of staff, but there is currently no formal structure or accountability for dealing with this important matter. There are no formal procedures to check whether people who claim Aboriginality actually fulfil the three-point definition. The federal government definition of Aboriginality is based on three criteria: descent, self-identification and community acceptance.[37] In Chapter 1, I aimed to provide clarity on the way Aboriginality is defined from a Koori community perspective: validation of identity comes from bloodline connections with the apical ancestors of the

Traditional Owners of the Country from which Aboriginality is being claimed. If you can't provide evidence for your bloodline connection, you don't meet the full requirements.

~

The statement 'without Truth, there can't be Treaty' came from the First Peoples' Assembly.[38] Honourable words as they are, the underlying assumptions in the statement leave questions unanswered, like:

- Who wrote the letters patent and the terms of reference for Yoorrook?
- Where did approval come from to include the 'immunity clause' section 4, Conduct of the Inquiry: to 'not inquire into, or report on, any executive decisions or specific outcomes which have been settled or determined' in relation to land and cultural heritage laws?[39]
- Was approval given by the FPA and Traditional Owners for the inclusion of the immunity clause?

In *Arena* magazine in September 2021, Bhiamie Williamson, researcher at the Centre for Aboriginal Economic Policy Research at the Australian National University, pointed the spear of the pen at Yoorrook's letters patent for granting immunity to past governments from legal proceedings. He argues that the immunity clause 'jumps out, like a lemon growing on a peach tree'.[40] Section 4(m) of the letters patent refers to historical decisions in relation to the recognition of Traditional Owners in land and cultural matters. These include, but are not limited to, government decisions made in relation to the *Native Title Act 1993*, the *Traditional Owner Settlement Act 2010* (TOSA) and the *Aboriginal Heritage Act 2006*.

As a commissioner, I rejected the way this immunity clause was included. In a truth justice context, I strongly believe that all legislative processes aimed at Victorian First Peoples' land and cultural matters should be transparent and not exempt from scrutiny and accountability. After all, isn't that what we fought for in the long and continuing struggle for land rights and the return of cultural heritage ownership to Traditional Owners?

While these matters seem to be a no-go zone for the inquiry process, Yoorrook has heard evidence of community concerns about cultural heritage and land justice matters. Like the Treaty Assembly, Aboriginal Heritage Council members are not democratically elected but selectively chosen by the minister. They get to make decisions on heritage matters, heritage boundaries, and Registered Aboriginal Parties under the Heritage Act. These are cultural and jurisdictional matters that require proper democratic processes of representation.

Conflicts of interest have arisen. For example, there is no clear demarcation between Aboriginal Heritage Council matters and land justice matters, which allows for undue influence by Aboriginal Heritage Council members in land justice processes. This can have the effect of undermining Traditional Owners' rights to represent themselves in land jurisdiction matters. While there is an inseparable relationship between land and heritage rights under tradition-based lore and custom, in practice they are divided between two different imposed jurisdictions.

Another example of conflict of interest in land matters arises from TOSA. Under that Act, the government can make out-of-court settlements with Traditional Owners, who are then required to withdraw any native title claims and not to lodge any future claims. This law does not respect our fight for land rights in the 1970s and 1980s. It's a long way short of rectifying our unceded sovereign rights to our traditional land. It means that despite proving bloodline connections with the apical ancestors, tradition-based rights can be negotiated away with the stroke of a pen. Settlements can be made, with the subtext that if you don't sign away your rights you get nothing. Under this regime, Traditional Ownership is reduced to the status of conditional-use rights controlled by the government.

This issue was brought home in the Yoorrook public hearing of 18 April 2024 with Minister for Treaty and First Nations Natalie Hutchins. It was pointed out to her that the government's ability to deliver land to First Peoples that they can own and on which they can live and practise culture is hard to imagine when less than 1 per cent of their former lands have been returned. The minister accepted this proposition and, in her response, defaulted to the treaty process as a remedy for outstanding land-justice and other relevant First Peoples matters. Defaulting to the treaty process as a remedy for outstanding justice matters has been a regular avoidance strategy by ministers in the hearing process.

The minister then committed herself to making some amends for the dismal state of freehold land returned in Victoria, saying her ministerial aims are to ensure all Traditional Owner groups have access to Country that fulfils their right to culture and social and economic aspirations. This includes rights to land for ceremony and culture, to build housing, and to generate collective wealth that sustains the communities and contributes to regional economies and a better future.[41]

The community is also concerned about the whittling-away of rights to water and resources under TOSA. The inseparable nature of land, water and resource rights under tradition-based lore has not been extinguished.

From my experience, there is simmering dissension and division within the community between those who have achieved some remedial land justice and those who have not. That is, people are not enjoying equally the benefits of those government structures designed to give some form of reparative justice and land to First Peoples so they can own and live on that land as inherent rights. The government as representative of the Crown already owes a huge debt for stolen Indigenous lands in Victoria. The fact that it granted most of the land owned by Traditional Owners to settlers without consent or compensation is an important matter on the table for truth justice deliberation. Yoorrook faces choices in examining First Peoples' experiences of these processes. Returning the remaining Crown lands, water and other resources and providing compensation for land stolen from Traditional Owners would be an act of reparative justice.

~

Addressing racism is an important part of the truth justice process. There is a large body of evidence showing that the racial ideology of colonisation continues to have a wide range of detrimental outcomes for individuals, communities and societies. Moreover, racism has a significant negative impact on self-esteem and life satisfaction, and can lead to depression, anxiety and psychological distress. Unfair policies and practices have caused exclusion of First Peoples from economic, social and political life.[42]

The recent book *Dhoombak Goobgoowana* takes up the challenge of truth-telling about the history of the University of Melbourne in its engagement with Indigenous people. One of the issues it examines is scientific racism, or eugenics. The editors, Ross L Jones, James Waghorne and Marcia Langton, show that 'teaching and promoting discredited eugenic theories to generations of impressionable students and publics' led to racist public policies.[43] For example, Professor Richard Berry in the medical school (1906–29) claimed that most criminals, slum dwellers and 'pure-bred' Aboriginal people were mentally and racially deficient.[44] These views were based on the 'science' of eugenics and received almost total consensus in the newspapers of the day. In alliance with Berry was Frank Tate, whose position as director of education in Victoria from 1902 to 1928 shaped policies. Tate believed that the education of the poorer classes should be vocational, because they could not profit from an academic curriculum. He had no belief that Indigenous Australians should attend university.[45]

It wasn't until after the full horror of the application of these ideas, when the Nazis used eugenics in the mid-twentieth century to support the elimination of whole races, that eugenics was thoroughly discredited. In the meantime, this thinking had been incorporated into government policies, including those of state departments of education. For example, we have seen how Aboriginal reserve schools only taught the students to Grade 3 standard, assuming they were less intelligent than other children. Another major impact of these beliefs was the separation of Aboriginal children with mixed parentage from their communities and their adoption by white families, with the expectation that the 'inferior' Aboriginal race would be bred out—another form of genocide.

Dhoombak Goobgoowana provides an example of the work ahead for institutions more broadly, not just government institutions. It concludes:

> We must not stop at acknowledging failures and triumphs but address injustices and violations with corrective actions that engage our community. Not only must we talk, but we must also help to overcome the often-traumatic historical legacies and contribute to initiatives that redress the wrongs with respect and with regard to the rights of Indigenous peoples, as they are now elaborated in the *United Nations Declaration on the Rights of Indigenous Peoples*.[46]

On the question of racism, Yoorrook invited eminent epidemiologist Sir Michael Marmot, a world authority in the specialist field of health inequalities and world health, to an online briefing session on 28 September 2021. His answer to the question of whether there is a correlation between racism and ill health was rather daunting: he replied categorically yes, and added that racism can badly damage your health.[47]

From a Traditional Owner worldview, there is much to reflect on with the truth justice process. The racism that drove the policies and practices of colonisation is also the cause of ongoing harm. It needs to be understood from the experience of those on the receiving end, whose lives and wellbeing continue to be affected. We know that the most effective way to challenge racism is through education and cultural awareness. Knowledge gathered through Yoorrook could be used to develop learning programs in primary, secondary and tertiary education, in addition to generally raising the level of public knowledge. This could help to reduce government spending on social programs, corrections and health.

Many First Peoples have experienced racism or other trauma through the justice system, so we would also need reassurance that things will be different there. Aboriginal and Torres Strait Islander people are fourteen times more likely to be imprisoned than the general population.[48] For Indigenous young people, the detention rate is twenty-nine times higher than non-Indigenous people.[49] This contributes to social disadvantage, family dislocation, intergenerational trauma and cultural deprivation. We need systemic change to address the barriers causing Indigenous people to have a historical distrust of the system. Racism is implicit in the rising over-representation of Indigenous peoples in custody today, as shown in the report of the Royal Commission into Aboriginal Deaths in Custody[50] and the Stolen Generations report.[51] These are legacies of human rights violations that continue to be reflected in current reports and statistics on juvenile justice and Closing the Gap indicators.

Harmful media conceptions of First Peoples add to the burden of racism. In 2024 we saw a very negative campaign against the Voice. A counter media campaign to balance the over-representation of misinformation and fear-driven messages was missing. This book has discussed similar harmful misinformation campaigns that were waged against the Yorta Yorta in their struggle for land rights and in the native title claim. Yoorrook is empowered with the relevant human rights tools to examine the causes and effects of racism. Community consultations are revealing the many ways First Nations people experience racist attitudes and practices in their daily lives. Racism is reflected in the historical and ongoing systemic injustices that Yoorrook will be required to make recommendations about. It is an opportune time to put racism up-front as a priority. By taking a strong and informed stand against it, we can build a better society for the future.

This is an opportunity for justice to be delivered rather than paying lip service to the nice words in the letters patent. For many decades, the Aboriginal and Torres Strait Islander community has had to deal with many past and ongoing issues that are now before the Yoorrook Justice Commission.

The defeat of the Voice referendum in October 2023 was another disappointing blow to First Nations Peoples of Australia. The lack of understanding by the public about the structure and powers of the Voice created a political quagmire, and finding a pathway through the fear campaign and politicisation of the referendum proved to be impossible. Having discussed racism as an ongoing systemic barrier to First Peoples' human rights, to see it raise its ugly head again in the referendum process was staggering. It is still a structural barrier to an Indigenous voice as it was nearly a century ago when Uncle William presented his petition for a voice in parliament in 1938.[52] The matter was brought home by Race Discrimination Commissioner Chin Tan, who expressed his disappointment at the way the race card was played in the referendum media coverage, calling it a 'tentacled monster' that was used to create division and discord in the community. He reminded us that tackling racism needs a national anti-racism framework and a bipartisan response.[53]

The outcome of the Voice referendum highlights why racism must be a major focus for Yoorrook. It will take time to heal and to move forward. In Victoria we can continue to focus on treaty, self-determination and sovereignty issues at the local level. Retreating to local issues is a fight-back position that will allow more energy to be concentrated on treaty matters and the truth justice process.

~

While the outcome of the Voice referendum was disappointing, there is an alternative pathway. As I write, much attention is being focused on UNDRIP, which was adopted by the UN General Assembly in 2007 after twenty years of negotiation by Indigenous peoples and governments around the world. It is essentially a list of human rights Indigenous peoples have under international law. UNDRIP has garnered strong support among Indigenous communities in Australia and is uppermost in the human rights instruments in the Yoorrook Truth Justice Commission letters patent.

In 2023 the Joint Standing Committee on Aboriginal and Torres Strait Islander Affairs presented a report to federal parliament calling for implementation of UNDRIP in Australia.[54] A strong majority of the standing committee, including the Greens members, supported the implementation of the declaration, while the Liberal-National coalition members dissented on the key recommendations. Djab Wurrung Gunnai Gunditjmara senator Lidia Thorpe supported the recommendations and went further to propose that UNDRIP be enshrined in federal legislation as an absolute minimum.[55] While her proposal was rejected by parliament, it is still active in the community.

In this book I have given many examples of Indigenous peoples' human rights being violated by colonisation, which resulted in past and ongoing injustices. UNDRIP recognises and lists those rights with the purpose of addressing those injustices. A key right is self-determination, as affirmed by the UN General Assembly, which says that by virtue of that right, Indigenous peoples should be able to 'freely determine their political status and freely pursue their economic, social, and cultural development'.[56]

In exercising our right to self-determination, First Nations Peoples have the right to autonomy or self-government in matters relating to our internal and local affairs, as well as ways and means for financing our autonomous functions. The Joint Standing Committee report noted the advantages that could be gained from states applying UNDRIP. These include improved access to land rights, help in combating racial discrimination, and support for Indigenous businesses, social services and cultural organisations. Applying UNDRIP would also add momentum to historic processes already underway, such as the truth-telling and treaty-making processes in Victoria. The main purpose of treaty-making is to give effect to Indigenous peoples' self-determination. Implementing UNDRIP would support treaty-making because it would involve recognising self-determination as a fundamental right.

The Joint Standing Committee report examined how UNDRIP could be implemented in Australia and whether it should be through legislation, under policy, or both. The majority of the committee decided against supporting Thorpe's legislation approach. They examined Canada's and New Zealand's legal and policy-based approaches for implementing the declaration, which appear to have been effective, but recommended instead that Indigenous peoples have a choice of approach, through negotiations with governments and others, based on their right to self-determination.[57] Whether this would need at least the minimum standards and essential framework to be set down in legislation is an open question.

On reflection, the Voice offered a bold vision of a constitutionally protected say for Indigenous peoples in federal law-making and administration. This would have been consistent with the right to self-determination and to participation in decision-making specified in UNDRIP. The standing committee's report, however, asserts that the declaration offers a bigger vision than the Voice: it recognises not only the importance of First Nations Peoples' self-determination and participation in decision-making, but also rights to housing, health, work and freedom from discrimination and other human rights contraventions. While the Voice would have given Indigenous people a say in those areas, implementing UNDRIP could elevate that say and those areas to the level of human rights. This is greatly needed in the aftermath of the disappointing and painful referendum result.

There are no constitutional impediments to implementing this wider vision of UNDRIP as proposed by the standing committee. Federal, state and local governments have ample power to bring it about. In the after-shadow of the Voice referendum result, the standing committee's report makes a strong call for this to happen.[58] Through its passage into Australian law and public policy, UNDRIP would offer a workable alternative and a much bigger vision than the proposed Voice. We need the federal government to implement it into law, policy and practice as an alternative to the Voice.

The main issue plaguing the Yes campaign was the late withdrawal of Liberal Party support by Opposition Leader Peter Dutton. As Prime Minister Anthony Albanese acknowledged, 'The truth is that no referendum has succeeded without bipartisan support.'[59] It is alarming that a similar withdrawal of support has recently occurred in relation to the Victorian treaty process. The Liberal and National party room originally supported the advancement of the process, as set out in the *Treaty Authority and Other Treaty Elements Bill 2022*, but a news article of 21 January 2024 headed 'Opposition dumps vow to back First Nations treaty process'[60] indicated an act of betrayal of the clear goodwill that forged the bilateral relationship. The *Age* newspaper editorial the following day condemned this betrayal of the agreement as an act of 'political opportunism'. It said that the Opposition had clearly made a political calculation that 'the best move now is to crabwalk away from a treaty, using a series of flimsy and tortured justifications. In doing so, the Opposition has embraced political opportunism in a disgraceful breach of faith.'[61]

In the absence of further information on the matter, we will have to wait and see how politics are played out in Victoria in light of the damaging Voice saga. The underlying question is whether the long-held track record of the race card, which I have continually exposed in this book, is played out again in the treaty scenario. Like many other members of Victoria's First Peoples, my hopes have been raised with what has unfolded through the historic treaty and truth justice process. It has been a long time coming, and the flow of evidence has put much emphasis on what the truth justice process and treaty negotiations will deliver. On that note, it is very much a wait-and-see proposition that will require full community support for a positive outcome.

~

My role as a Yoorrook commissioner was a good opportunity to apply my knowledge and experience in statewide community consultations and the collection and storage of cultural knowledge. The Yoorrook inquiry includes the theoretical concept of data sovereignty, which is aimed at protecting Indigenous ownership of data, including oral knowledge. It has a mandate to inquire into the destruction of cultural knowledge and property, which includes written and oral knowledge.

Community consultations across Victoria have been carried out as a way of hearing stories and gathering information from First Peoples on our experience of past and ongoing injustices and how our cultures and knowledge have survived. In gathering stories, Yoorrook visited my birthplace, the Mooroopna Flat.[62] I shared many stories about life on the Flat and we talked about its relationship with Daish's Paddock, where people moved when the river flooded. I was also able to discuss the historic connections between the Flat and the Cummeragunja walk-off.

I hope the final recommendations provide ongoing solutions for cultural matters like oral history recording and management, and the continuity of existing oral history programs. To enhance the cultural program, the treaty process proposes the concept of a cultural institute, which was part of the Koori Heritage Working Group's agenda back in the 1980s. This would bring cultural programs into the modern era of digital technology and cultural resource management. The vision is commendable and worthy of support from the commission under its mandate for the restoration of cultural materials and property, including archival materials.

After serving for twelve months on the Yoorrook Justice Commission, I chose to step down. It wasn't an easy decision to make, and I have alluded in these pages to many of the things that contributed to my decision. I hope the contribution I made and the submissions I presented to the inquiry were worthwhile.

23
Reflections

There is a clear pattern to the history of our Yorta Yorta people. As I reflect on the course of my life and the lessons I have learned about history, politics, truth justice, I am reminded of the story of the ten-year-old boy who replied to the question I asked about native title—he said it is 'something that the Aborigines want but the government won't give it to 'em'.

I've talked of change being two steps forward and one step back. I've described our battles to dismantle the barriers put up in front of us. I've looked at successful campaigns and some big chips being knocked off in the chipping-away process. Looking back, a much bigger pattern emerges.

I think of our early petition for land in 1881. It started with frustration, a vision of a better life if only we could be granted land to become independent farmers. We organised ourselves and translated our vision into language that would persuade the government to give us land. We presented a petition to the top power of the state, the NSW governor. We hoped. We waited. Years later a partial answer came in the form of farm blocks at Cummera: not a recognition of our right to land, not ownership of land, not enough land to make a go of it, but a small parcel to test whether we could adapt to farming. Then it was taken away. The struggle for land justice was not abandoned; it continued and will continue beyond my lifetime.

I think of twenty years living in shacks on the riverbank Flat. In 1956 we presented the McLean Inquiry with our acute need to be allocated proper housing. What did the community get? We got Rumbalara housing on the edge of Mooroopna. The government response was a betrayal. They built small huts without bathrooms and reinstated welfare inspections to watch over and intimidate us.

What was the meaning of the discriminatory treatment imposed on us by governments for all these years? Through travel and study, I came to understand the bigger picture of Indigenous-rights-based struggle and colonisation. Law professor Irene Watson wrote: 'The colonial project has embodied a centuries-long, ongoing campaign to annihilate, define, subordinate and exclude the "native", and an arsenal of tools has been applied to these ends.'[1]

It has been the community's task to evaluate and dismantle these destructive tools of control and oppression. In the long run we dodged the genocidal assimilation that governments had in mind. Our protests, our aspirations, finally found common ground with the vision of the late, great prime minister Gough Whitlam. Thanks to the deep reforms of the Whitlam government in the 1970s, we experienced a great leap forward. With the policy of self-determination (or at least the government's version of it) and funding for community organisations, we saw gains being made. We took full advantage, setting up numerous Aboriginal organisations. Our elders who led the walk-off continued to fight for the rights of our community and led the way to the creation of organisations to meet our needs in the areas of legal assistance, health, housing, land management, sport, education, culture and elder care.

These organisations were driven by a commitment to run our own affairs where governments have dismally failed. Community control became the goal of Koori politics in Victoria. In the journey of education, those of my generation benefited from Whitlam abolishing tertiary tuition fees and Premier Don Dunstan's support for the Aboriginal Task Force in Adelaide. The era of tertiary education for Aboriginal people began in earnest.

Reflecting on my personal experience of working for change, it too started with a vision. The seeds were planted by elders such as Uncle Bill Onus, Uncle William Cooper, Uncle Shadrach James, Aunty Marge Tucker and Aunty Geraldine Briggs. That vision grew within me at the Task Force, where I was united with Aboriginal people from around

Australia. We were like brothers and sisters coming together. It was strengthened when I visited First Nation communities around the world and saw their treaty lands, their strong cultural heritage, their oral history programs, their Indigenous Studies programs in universities, and their positions as lecturers, professors and heads of education programs.

Ongoing higher education gave me the tools to contribute to the struggle. I returned again and again to the teaching of Uncle William: 'the power of the voice, the spear of the pen and collective organisation'. Achieving a PhD empowered me to stand as an equal in academic and government circles of power and to assert authority to tell our story our way. This wasn't a handout, but a goal that required rigorous study, hard work and perseverance.

I have been able to use my education in several Koori campaigns, developing the political vision and strategies to take us forward. We formed organisations like the Koori Heritage Working Group and we ran community meetings to consult across Victoria. We worked with sympathetic state Labor governments to change the Heritage Law to include ownership and control of our heritage. We achieved real change with the formal recognition of traditional cultural organisations such as the Yorta Yorta Tribal Council, which grew into the Yorta Yorta Nation Aboriginal Corporation.

Yorta Yorta work on land rights has been a long, gruelling journey. Much of this book is dedicated to the Yorta Yorta struggle for land justice that culminated in our native title claim. My role as a member of the Nations and a principal claimant allowed me to reflect on the claim. I challenged the notion of the 'tide of history' as gammin words used to try and erase our proud ancestral connections and to deny us land justice. At the end of the journey, what we achieved from the ten-year campaign for the Barmah–Millewa National Park was rewarding. Through solidarity with like-minded activists, the Yorta Yorta achieved traditional-owner joint management of the national park. Our vision was very much greater than this—we wanted our Yorta Yorta lands restored to our ownership. This was not achieved, but at least we won the fight for a say in the protection of our heartland, the Barmah–Millewa Forest. A big chip. The return of the land under a leaseback arrangement is still on the agenda.

The fragile nature of these changes throws up the need for a more robust framework to ensure continuity of purpose and a guarantee that what has been achieved will not be whisked away by the next government in power. Our generation has benefited from the United Nations Declaration on the Rights of Indigenous Peoples. When we are accused of wanting too much, we turn to it to support our claims. We stand on our belief in justice, as did our elders, but with a stronger foundation. In the absence of success with the Voice, we bounced back and presented the alternative of UNDRIP, which does not require amending the Constitution.

The Rumbalara Football Netball Club is showing the way to a different future, led by the visionary Paul Briggs and his team. In 2023 the Munarra Centre for Regional Excellence was launched in Shepparton. The first sod was turned using four traditional digging sticks, and I shared the story of the Scholars' Hut and the role our elders played in inspiring us. The project is a partnership between Rumbalara Football Netball Club, Kaiela Institute, the University of Melbourne and Greater Shepparton City Council, and it is supported by the Victorian Government. It offers opportunities to enhance Aboriginal cultural identity, expression and celebration; to grow in our leadership; improve our health; build our education aspirations; advance our employment options; and move towards equitable social inclusion and reconciliation. The project will work towards the region's prosperity and its capacity to close the gap. By combining education, culture, the arts and sport, it aims to create healthy people, healthy communities and the leaders of tomorrow.

Thanks to our extraordinary expressions of pride in our Aboriginal identity, our unique contribution to Australia has taken centre stage. Our sportspeople have led the charge against racism. Our songwriters, our playwrights, our filmmakers, our visual artists, our dancers, our languages—it is no longer possible to deny our history and culture. Assimilation failed to extinguish our unique Aboriginal identities. There is much optimism that the benchmark of hope has been raised higher than the raft of broken promises of the past.

Looking to the future, it is inspiring to see the talented and capable generation of young leaders coming through, taking the spear of the pen and using their voices to articulate the struggle within the treaty, truth-telling and justice process. It is a reassuring message for those of my generation to see that the flag of justice will continue to fly up front.

Appendix: Aboriginal Protection Laws and Government Policy, Victoria and New South Wales, 1869–2021

The legislation and policies included here were used, in some cases until the 1980s, as a means of implementing policies of protection, separation, absorption and assimilation of Indigenous populations depending on the prevailing ideology and political views of governments at the time. Those in the Aboriginal welfare system were generally excluded from the provisions of the mainstream Australian welfare system by their separate legal status.[1]

NOTE: The racist terminology used in some of the legislation and in classifications of Aboriginality are abhorrent to First Peoples of Australia.

Victoria

In the early years of the colony, interaction between settlers and Indigenous people was officially discouraged and a policy of segregation was adopted. This involved establishing reserves and encouraging Indigenous people to settle down to a life of farming. The reserves were mostly run by missionaries, who also established schools designed to pull Indigenous children away from tribal influences.

1860: The Central Board Appointed to Watch over the Interests of Aborigines was established. It is responsible for managing the reserves, including two larger ones at Framlingham and Coranderrk. During this time, the removal of Indigenous children is informal. The manager of Coranderrk Reserve would travel around Indigenous communities removing 'neglected' children without any legal authority.[2]

1869: *Aborigines Protection Act 1869*. The Act to Provide for the Protection and Management of the Aboriginal Natives of Victoria (No. CCCXLIX (349)) becomes effective from 11 July 1870. It establishes the Aborigines Protection Board and gives powers to state entities for the purpose of 'prescribing the place where any aboriginal or any tribe of aborigines shall reside' and 'for the care custody and education of the children of aborigines'.[3]

1882: Inquiry by the Protection Board into the condition and management of Coranderrk Aboriginal station. My grandmother Caroline Morgan gave evidence to this inquiry. She spoke about the conditions at Coranderrk and having to nearly beg for blankets to keep children and herself warm.[4]

1886: *Aborigines Protection Act 1886*. Otherwise known as the 'Half-Caste Act' or 'Absorption Act', it makes a distinction between colour and race by changing the definition of Aboriginal to exclude 'half-castes'. It gave the Aborigines Protection Board extensive new powers over the lives of Aboriginal people, including regulation of residence, employment and marriage. In particular, under the Act Aboriginal people of mixed descent, known as 'half-castes', begin to be removed from Aboriginal stations or reserves to force them to assimilate into European society. These expulsions separate families and communities, causing distress and leading to protests. Nevertheless, the Board refuses to assist the expelled people. It is assumed that the expulsions will lead to a decline in the population of the reserves and their eventual closure.[5]

1910–15: *Aborigines Act 1910–1915*. This Act abandons the distinction in law between 'full blood' and 'half-caste' in terms of defining Aboriginality. The Aborigines Protection Board continues to make regulations that extend its powers of removal. If families refuse to consent to the removal of their children, they are threatened with being forced to leave the station or being denied rations.[6] The Board has the power to take any Aboriginal child from their family at any time for any reason. Similar policies are brought in by Australia's other states and territories.

1955–57: Board of Inquiry Upon the Operation of the Aborigines Protection Act 1928, otherwise known as the McLean Inquiry. In 1955, the premier appoints Charles McLean to review and recommend changes to the state's Aboriginal affairs policy. Soon after his appointment, McLean reports back on the dire conditions in which many Indigenous people lived: 'On these two areas [at Mooroopna] live about 59 adults and 107 children, in most squalid conditions. Their "humpies" are mostly constructed of old timber, flattened kerosene tins, and hessian … They are not weatherproof, have earthern floors, very primitive cooking arrangements, and no laundry or bathing facilities except the river.'[7] The Aborigines Advancement League expresses its concerns to McLean about the physical and cultural future of Indigenous people. It also advocates self-government for the communities. McLean rejects these claims and calls for a policy of assimilation.[8]

1957: *Aborigines Act 1957*. This Act abolishes the Protection Board originally formed in Victoria in 1860. The new Aborigines Welfare Board has the function 'to promote the moral, intellectual and physical welfare of aborigines [full blood and half-caste] … with a view to their assimilation in the general community'.[9] It retains many of the far-reaching powers exercised by the previous Protection Board. One significant change is that the Welfare Board does not have specific powers in relation to children. From 1957, any removal of Aboriginal children from their family and community by government agents takes place under the provisions of the *Children's Welfare Act 1958*.[10]

1972: *Archaeological and Aboriginal Relics Preservation Act 1972*. Establishment of the Archaeological Relics Advisory Committee with ten members, one to be Aboriginal. The director of the Museum of Victoria is appointed Protector of Relics.

1980: *Archaeological and Aboriginal Relics Preservation Act 1980*. Aboriginal membership on the twelve-member advisory committee is increased to three.

1987: *Australian Government Aboriginal and Torres Strait Islander Heritage Protection Amendment Act 1987*: Part 11A: Victorian Aboriginal Cultural Heritage. This amends the *Aboriginal and Torres Strait Islander Heritage Protection Act 1984* to make provision for the preservation of the Aboriginal cultural heritage in Victoria and for related purposes.

The Act strengthens the protection of Aboriginal cultural heritage and gives Victoria's First Peoples a greater role in the management and protection of their heritage.

1987: *Victorian Aboriginal Cultural Heritage Act 1987*. Decolonises the Anglocentric Aboriginal relics laws of the 1970s and empowers First Peoples of Victoria to have ownership and control over their heritage—a watershed achievement in Indigenous heritage reforms in Australia.

2006: *Aboriginal Heritage Act 2006*. In response to the reforms embedded in the 1987 legislation that gave greater power to Indigenous voices, the 2006 Act establishes the Victorian Aboriginal Heritage Council, a body of Victorian First Peoples not democratically elected by Traditional Owners but appointed by the Minister for Aboriginal Affairs. The Act is later given immunity from the Yoorook Justice Commission inquiry into heritage matters under the 2021 letters patent.[11]

2010: *Victorian Traditional Owner Settlement Act 2010* (TOSA). Provides for out-of-court settlements of native title. It allows the Victorian Government to recognise Traditional Owners and certain rights in Crown land. In return for entering into a settlement, Traditional Owners must agree to withdraw any native title claim pursuant to the *Native Title Act 1993 (Cth)* and not to make any future native title claims. TOSA is also later given immunity from the Yoorrook Justice Commission inquiry into heritage matters under the 2021 letters patent.[12]

2018: *Advancing the Treaty Process with Aboriginal Victorians Act 2018*. The purpose of this Act is to advance the process of treaty-making between Traditional Owners and Aboriginal Victorians, and the state.

2021: Yoorrook Justice Commission is established—Australia's first formal truth-telling process established by a state government. It aims to fully examine the historic and systemic injustices experienced by Victoria's First Peoples since colonisation.[13]

New South Wales

1883–1940: The NSW Board for the Protection of Aborigines is established in 1883 and reconstituted under the *Aborigines Protection Act 1909*. Initially, its activity is limited to those areas identified by the premier, such as issuing rations (though the amounts issued are less than those issued to white people), clothing and blankets, and the creation of reserves for Indigenous people.

1909: *Aborigines Protection Act 1909.* This Act has wide powers over the lives of Aboriginal people, including the power to remove children from families because their parents are Aboriginal, and to dictate where Aboriginal people live to ensure protection from violent colonialists and provide education in the face of European opposition.

1911: Amendment to the *Aborigines Protection Act.* Establishes Kinchela Boys Home and Cootamundra Domestic Training Home for Aboriginal Girls. Aboriginal children are removed from their homes for various welfare reasons and transported to Kinchela and Cootamundra, where they are often abused and neglected while being taught farm labouring and domestic work. Many end up as servants in the homes of wealthy Sydney residents.

1915: *Aborigines Protection Amending Act 1915.* Gives the Board authority to remove Aboriginal children without having to establish in court that they are being neglected.

1938: Inquiry by Legislative Assembly Select Committee on the Administration of the Aborigines Protection Board. This is relevant to Cummeragunja, which is located on the NSW side of Murray River. The walk-off in 1938 in protest against Protection Board administration brings pressure for policy change following the inquiry.[14] Many people move from Cummera and set up camp on the riverbank of the Goulburn River in Victoria, named the Flat.

1940: *Aborigines Protection (Amendment) Act 1940.* The Protection Board is renamed the Aborigines Welfare Board, which stipulates that Aboriginal people should be assimilated into mainstream white society. It intends that Aboriginal culture will evaporate and Aboriginal people will eventually become indistinguishable from Europeans. Another amendment in 1943 stipulated that the Board should have eleven members, including two Aboriginal people—one being 'a full-blooded aborigine, and the other being either a full-blooded aborigine or a person apparently having an admixture of aboriginal blood'.[15]

1969–83: *Aborigines Act 1969.* A landmark Act that abolishes the Aborigines Welfare Board and moves all Aboriginal children into the same welfare system as non-Aboriginal children. It makes Aboriginal children who have been under the care of the Welfare Board wards of the state. The Aborigines Welfare Directorate replaces the Board. Responsibility for Aboriginal children is then transferred to the Department of Youth and Community Services.

1983: *Aboriginal Land Rights Act 1983.* Returns land to Aboriginal peoples through a process of lodging claims for certain Crown lands and former reserves like Cummeragunja. Aboriginal land councils run by Traditional Owners are established.

National policies, conferences and inquiries

1937: Commonwealth Government Conference on Aboriginal Affairs. This first conference of federal and state government authorities agrees that 'the objective should be the absorption at least of "the natives of Aboriginal origin but not of the full blood"'.[16] The third Native Welfare Conference, held in 1951, agreed that 'assimilation was the aim of "native welfare measures"'[17] and the federal minister for territories, Paul Hasluck, said, 'Assimilation means, in practical terms, that, in the course of time, it is expected that all persons of aboriginal blood or mixed blood in Australia will live like other white Australians do.'[18]

1940s: Commonwealth welfare payments—child endowment, pension and benefit payments become payable to Aboriginal people who live away from reserves. Australian social security legislation has until then specifically disqualified them from eligibility.

1972: Whitlam government reforms. The Whitlam government adopts 'self-determination' as the central term for Aboriginal policy. The federal Department of Aboriginal Affairs is established, as is the National Aboriginal Consultative Committee (NACC). Aboriginal community-based organisations are encouraged to legally incorporate and receive funds.

1979: NACC replaced by the National Aboriginal Conference (NAC). Both the NACC and NAC are advisory bodies to the federal government on Aboriginal affairs.

1990: NAC replaced by the Aboriginal and Torres Strait Islander Commission (ATSIC). (ATSIC is abolished by the Howard government in 2005.)

1987–91: Royal Commission into Aboriginal Deaths in Custody. Appointed by the Australian Government in October 1987, chaired by Federal Court judge James Henry Muirhead QC, to study and report on the underlying social, cultural and legal issues behind the deaths in custody of Aboriginal and Torres Strait Islander people in light of the high level of such deaths in the 1980s. The final report makes 339 recommendations, mainly concerned with procedures for persons in custody, liaison with Aboriginal groups, police education and improved accessibility to information.[19]

1995–97: National Inquiry into the Separation of Aboriginal and Torres Strait Islander Children from Their Families. Established by the federal attorney-general in 1995 and conducted by the Human Rights and Equal Opportunity Commission (HREOC).

1997: Publication of *Bringing Them Home: Report of the National Inquiry into the Separation of Aboriginal and Torres Strait Islander Children from their Families* by HREOC. Fifty-four recommendations are made in the final report to redress the impact of removal and intergenerational trauma. The report identifies a strong need for reparations, and support services and processes to monitor the ongoing implementation of the recommendations. Some recommendations are supported, including funding link-up services across Australia to support reunification of family, and wellbeing programs. The recommendations about compensation and reparations are ignored, and the call for a national apology is actively resisted for a decade by the then conservative government.

Acknowledgements

This book has been inspired by the leaders of Yorta Yorta resistance over the generations. Thanks to Yorta Yorta Nations, family groups and ancestors past and present who have contributed to the spirit and vison of the story. They have been with us on the journey and their storylines will pass on to the next generation.

We have been very fortunate to be able to turn to our friend and fellow writer Val Noone, who gave us early feedback and followed the journey of this book with great interest. He and Catherine Noone helped us with the first draft.

We are also most appreciative of the staff at Melbourne University Press, who have been enthusiastic and encouraging throughout the editing and production process. Publisher Foong Ling Kong recognised the importance of this history and so gave us the confidence to trust the editorial process. Her suggestions were always helpful. Senior Editor Louise Stirling and her team were similarly encouraging and easy to work with.

The writing group in Eltham whom Cathy meets with have given ongoing support, believing that this was an achievable and worthwhile goal.

Special acknowledgement to Clive Atkinson, Wayne's elder brother, whose artwork covers the book in recognition of his admirable contribution to Indigenous art as a Yorta Yorta/Dja Dja Wurrung artist and graphic designer.

Further Reading

Atkinson, Roxanne (comp.), *Yorta Yorta Language Handbook*, included in *The Yorta Yorta Dictionary App* [online app], Wiradjuri Condobolin Corporation, 2022.

Atkinson, Wayne, 'Yorta Yorta occupation and "the search for common ground"', *Proceedings of the Royal Society of Victoria*, 117(1), 2005: 1–22.

——'Speaking strong for Country', in R Perkins and M Langton (eds), *First Australians: An Illustrated History*, Miegunyah Press, 2008: 295–337.

——'Victorian Government's treaty: Process & representation', research paper, School of Social and Political Sciences, University of Melbourne, OnCountry Learning website, 2019.

Bowe, H, L Peeler and S Atkinson, *Yorta Yorta Language Heritage*, Department of Linguistics, Monash University, 1997.

Clark, Mavis Thorpe, *The Boy from Cumeroogunga*, Hodder & Stoughton, 1979.

Forrest, James, Garth Lean and Kevin Dunn, 'Challenging racism through schools: Teacher attitudes to cultural diversity and multicultural education in Sydney, Australia', *Race Ethnicity and Education*, 19(3), 2016: 618–38.

Hagen, Rod, 'Ethnographic information and anthropological interpretations in a native title claim: The Yorta Yorta experience', *Aboriginal History*, 25, 2011: 216–27.

Perkins, Rachel and Marcia Langton (eds) with Wayne Atkinson et al., *First Australians: An Illustrated History*, Miegunyah Press, 2008.

Reynolds, Henry, *The Law of the Land*, Penguin, 1987.

Yoorrook Justice Commission, Public Hearings, 1–9 March 2023 (on the child protection and criminal justice systems), Yoorrook Justice Commission website.

——Public Hearings, 15–18 April 2024 (on injustices against First Peoples related to land, sky and waters), Yoorrook Justice Commission website.

——Public Hearings, 29 April – 3 May 2024 (evidence from Premier of Victoria and representatives from Uniting, Anglican and Catholic churches on injustices against First Peoples), Yoorrook Justice Commission website.

Legal cases

Onus v Alcoa of Australia Ltd (1981) HCA 50; 149 CLR 27

Mabo and Others v The State of Queensland [No. 2] (1992) HCA 23; 175 CLR 1

The Wik Peoples v State of Queensland & Ors; The Thayorre People v State of Queensland & Ors (1996) HCA 40; 187 CLR 1

Members of the Yorta Yorta Aboriginal Community v Victoria (1998) FCA 1606

Members of the Yorta Yorta Aboriginal Community v Victoria (2001) FCA 45

Members of the Yorta Yorta Aboriginal Community v Victoria (2002) HCA 58; 214 CLR 422

Eatock v Bolt (2011) FCA 1103

Notes

Introduction: Gulpa Gaka Yorta Yorta Woka

1 Personal communication, 2004.
2 Deborah Hoger, 'How incorporating Indigenous place names can strengthen community connections and promote reconciliation', *Amplify!* (blog), Community Early Learning Australia, 21 January 2022.
3 Wayne Atkinson, *A Picture from the Other Side: Cummeragunga and Its Historical Connections with Coranderrk from Written and Oral Sources*, 1981 (AIATSIS MS 1598).

Chapter 1 My Mob, Our Country

1 Wayne Atkinson, *A Picture from the Other Side*, 1981: 153.
2 *Genealogical Data: Yorta Yorta Native Title Claim, 1994–2002*, Document Library, Yorta Yorta Nation Aboriginal Corporation website; *Report of the Board Appointed to Enquire into, and Report upon, the Present Condition and Management of the Coranderrk Aboriginal Station*, Government Printer Melbourne, 1882: 20.
3 Early white settler Edward Curr called Barmah 'Pama' in his *Recollections of Squatting in Victoria*, Melbourne University Press, 1965 [1883]: 77.
4 G Singh and AP Kershaw, 'Quaternary vegetation and fire history in Australia', in AM Gill, RA Groves and IR Noble (eds), *Fire and the Australian Biota*, Australian Academy of Science, 1981: 45–6.
5 'Australia's earliest humans? The case for Moyjil', Royal Society of Victoria website, 4 March 2019.
6 WEH Stanner, 'The Dreaming', in WH Edwards (ed.), *Traditional Aboriginal Society*, Macmillan, 1987: 225; Josephine Flood, *Archaeology of the Dreamtime*, Collins, 1983: 239.
7 K Martin and B Mirraboopa, 'Ways of knowing, being and doing: A theoretical framework and methods for indigenous and indigenist re-search', *Journal of Australian Studies*, 27, 2003: 203–4.
8 B Gott, 'Koorie use and management of the plains', in R Jones (ed.), *The Great Plains Crash: Proceedings of Conference on the Grasslands and Grassy Woodlands of Victoria*, Indigenous Flora and Fauna Association & Victorian National Parks Association, 1992: 43–4.
9 Stanner: 225; Bill Gammage, *The Biggest Estate on Earth: How Aborigines Made Australia*, Allen & Unwin, 2012: 137.
10 Gammage: 281–304.
11 Nancy Cato, *Mister Maloga*, University of Queensland Press, 1976: 169.
12 Ibid.: 54.
13 Ronald Morgan, *Reminiscences of the Aboriginal Station at Cummeragunga and Its Aboriginal People*, a group of friends of the author, 1952: 5.

14 Cato: 15, 29.
15 See, for example, Gillian Hibbins, '"A code of our own"', *The Yorker*, 39, 2009: 8–9.
16 David Thompson, 'Aborigines were playing possum', *Herald-Sun*, 27 September 2007.
17 Gammage: Chapter 6.
18 Singh and Kershaw: 45–6.
19 M Perkins, 'Fire Today', *Sydney Morning Herald*, 31 December 2020.
20 Yorta Yorta Nation Aboriginal Corporation, *Joint Management Plan for Barmah National Park*, Yorta Yorta Traditional Owner Land Management Board, 2020: 30–2.
21 Wayne Atkinson, *'Not One Iota': The Yorta Yorta Struggle for Land Justice*, PhD thesis, School of Law and Legal Studies, La Trobe University, 2000: 33–4.
22 MH Monroe, 'Kow Swamp', Australia: The Land Where Time Began website, last updated 7 March 2013.
23 Yorta Yorta Nation Aboriginal Corporation, *Joint Management Plan for Barmah National Park*, Yorta Yorta Traditional Owner Land Management Board, 2020: 39–42.
24 J McLaurin, *Memories of Early Australia*, unpublished, 1888–89: 64.

Chapter 2 An Undeclared War

1 NG Butlin, *Economics and the Dreamtime: A Hypothetical History*, Cambridge University Press, 1993: 224.
2 'European discovery of the River Murray system: Charles Sturt and the discovery of the River Murray', State Library of South Australia website, last updated 2 March 2010.
3 Edward Curr, *Recollections of Squatting in Victoria*, Melbourne University Press, 1965 [1883]: 76–97.
4 Geoff Lennox, 'The Companion to Tasmanian History: Van Diemen's Land Company', Centre for Tasmanian Historical Studies, University of Tasmania, 2006.
5 Ibid.
6 Curr: 48.
7 Ibid.
8 Ibid.
9 Wayne Atkinson, *'Not One Iota': The Yorta Yorta Struggle for Land Justice*, PhD thesis, School of Law and Legal Studies, La Trobe University, 2000: 209.
10 Curr: 49.
11 Ibid.: 48, 49.
12 Rod Hagen, *Report to the Yorta Yorta Clans Group on Yorta Yorta Associations with the Claim Area*, unpublished, 1997: 19.
13 Butlin: 222; M Cannon, *Black Land, White Land*, Minerva Australia, 1993: 263–5.
14 Hagen: 19.
15 MF Christie, *Aborigines in Colonial Victoria, 1835–86*, Sydney University Press, 1979: 78–9, 206–7. Henry Reynolds, *The Other Side of the Frontier*, James Cook University, 1981: 98–9. See also Reynolds' evidence to the Yoorook Justice Commission, as reported by Kate Ashton: 'The British initially thought Victoria's rapid colonisation in the 1830s was illegal, and authorities were concerned by its violence', *ABC News*, 5 April 2024.
16 *Report from the Select Committee on the Condition of the Aborigines*, Government Printer Sydney, 1845: 41; Cannon: 139–42.
17 Ibid.; MF Christie: 63; Cannon: 137–42.
18 *Report of Inquiry into the State of the Public Lands and the Operation of the Land Laws: Instituted 8 January*, Government Printer Sydney, 1883: 7–8.

19 'Background', in Lyndall Ryan et al., *Colonial Frontier Massacres in Australia 1788–1930* [website], University of Newcastle, 2017–24.
20 'Definition' in ibid.
21 Ashton, *ABC News*, 5 April 2024.
22 Cannon: 141–2.
23 'Australian native police', *Wikipedia*, last edited 15 January 2025; CD Rowley, *The Destruction of Aboriginal Society*, ANU Press, 1970: 5, 37–9, 71.
24 Quoted in Lynette E Franklin (comp.), *Truth Telling: The Bangerang Tribes: Invasion or Peaceful Settlement 1838–1848*, self-published, 2020: 45. See also Cannon: 141–2.
25 Robinson, 3 January 1844, in Ian D Clark (ed.), *The Journals of George Augustus Robinson, Chief Protector, Port Phillip Aboriginal Protectorate*, Heritage Matters, 2000, vol. 4: 1.
26 Robinson, 5 January 1844, in ibid.: 2; Ryan et al., *Colonial Frontier Massacres in Australia 1788–1930.*
27 Ryan et al., ibid.
28 *Port Phillip Gazette*, 31 January 1844.
29 Broderick to La Trobe, 17 April 1844 in Franklin: 46–9.
30 Smythe to La Trobe, 26 April 1844 and statement by Edward Hogg, 5 June 1841 in Franklin: 54–9.
31 Colonial Secretary to La Trobe, 16 August 1844 in Franklin: 61.
32 Henry Reynolds, *Truth-Telling: History, Sovereignty and the Uluru Statement*, NewSouth, 2021: 74.
33 Ibid.: 73.
34 Ibid.: 70–5.
35 Curr: 93, 94.
36 Ibid.: 97.
37 See, for example, Robert Tonkinson and Ronald M Berndt, 'Australian Aboriginal peoples', *Encyclopedia Britannica* website, last updated 25 February 2025.
38 Curr: 89–97.
39 Samuel Furphy, *Edward M Curr and the Tide of History*, ANU E Press, 2013: 136.
40 Quoted in Ashton, *ABC News*, 5 April 2024.
41 Nancy Cato, *Mister Maloga*, University of Queensland Press, 1976: 51.
42 Christie: 68–9, 78–9; Reynolds, *The Other Side of the Frontier*: 99. See also Cannon: 12–14, 104, 165; K Cole, *The Aborigines of Victoria*, Keith Cole Publications, 1984: 25.
43 Rachel Perkins in her acceptance speech at the 2024 AACTA Awards: see AACTA, '"Stories that speak truth to power are made in this country"' [Instagram post], 9 February 2024.

Chapter 3 Moira Station and Maloga Mission

1 *The Wik Peoples v State of Queensland & Ors; The Thayorre People v State of Queensland & Ors* (1996) HCA 40; 187 CLR 1.
2 Wayne Atkinson, *'Not One Iota': The Yorta Yorta Struggle for Land Justice*, PhD thesis, School of Law and Legal Studies, La Trobe University, 2000: 61.
3 Nancy Cato, *Mister Maloga*, University of Queensland Press, 1976: 129.
4 Ibid.
5 Ibid.: 79–80.
6 Ibid.: 68–9.
7 Ibid.: 70–1.
8 Ibid.: 66–7.

9 Ibid.: 66.
10 Theresa Clements, *From Old Maloga*, Fraser and Morphet, 1930: 2.
11 'Aaron Atkinson (abt. 1854–1913)', *WikiTree*, n.d.; marriage certificate at Ancestry.com; 'John Oldbury Atkinson (1824–1883)', *WikiTree*, n.d.
12 'James Cooper (abt. 1831)', *WikiTree*, n.d.; B Attwood, *William Cooper: An Aboriginal Life Story*, Miegunyah Press, 2021: 5.
13 Cato, 1976: 104, 378; *Genealogical Data: Yorta Yorta Native Title Claim, 1994–2002*, Document Library, Yorta Yorta Nation Aboriginal Corporation website.
14 Nancy Cato, *Mister Maloga*, University of Queensland Press, rev. edn, 1993: 33.
15 Cato, 1976: 125.
16 Wayne Atkinson, *A Picture from the Other Side*, 1981: 108.
17 Cato, 1976: 387–8.

Chapter 4 Cummeragunja: Courage and Defiance

1 Nancy Cato, *Mister Maloga*, University of Queensland Press, 1976: 387.
2 Ibid.: 239.
3 Wayne Atkinson, *A Picture from the Other Side*, 1981: 97–8.
4 D Barwick, 'Coranderrk and Cummeragunja: Pioneers and policy', in TS Epstein and DH Penny (eds), *Opportunity and Response: Case Studies in Economic Development*, C Hurst, 1972: 51.
5 Atkinson, 1981: 74–5.
6 Ibid.: 78.
7 Aboriginal Community Elders Service and Kate Harvey, *Aboriginal Elders' Voices: Stories of the 'Tide of History': Victorian Indigenous Elders' Life Stories & Oral Histories*, Aboriginal Community Elders Service, Language Australia, 2003: 189.
8 See 'William Cooper—activist who helped found the Aboriginal rights movement', Solidarity website, 24 October 2020.
9 Wayne Atkinson, 'The Cummera walk off and the return to base camp politics', OnCountry Learning website, 2007: 1.
10 Atkinson, 1981: 128.
11 Ibid.: 114.
12 Ibid.: 128.
13 Rosalie Simkin and Lyn Loger, *Double ID: Life Story of Hilton Hamilton Walsh*, Prominent Press, 2001: 21.
14 Atkinson, 2008: 4.
15 Ibid.
16 Simkin and Loger: 21.
17 Barwick: 184.
18 G Tudor-Smith, P Williams and F Meakins, *Bina: First Nations Languages, Old and New*, La Trobe University Press in conjunction with Black Inc., 2024: Chapter 6.
19 Ronald Morgan, *Reminiscences of the Aboriginal Station at Cummeragunga and Its Aboriginal People*, a group of friends of the author, 1952: 23.
20 Ibid.: 2.
21 Elizabeth Hoffman, 'Cummeragunja' [video], Koori Oral History Program, 1988.
22 Simkin and Loger: 32.
23 Ibid.
24 Cato: 81; 'Maloga Mission (1874–1887)', William Cooper and the Australian Aborigines' League website.

Chapter 5 Riverbank Mooroopna

1 A bag humpy is a makeshift shelter made out of flour bags and sticks that Aboriginal people were forced to live under during the conditions of the fringe communities.
2 Wayne Atkinson, *A Picture from the Other Side*, 1981: 108.
3 Quoted in Aboriginal Community Elders Service and Kate Harvey, *Aboriginal Elders' Voices: Stories of the 'Tide of History': Victorian Indigenous Elders' Life Stories & Oral Histories*, Aboriginal Community Elders Service, Language Australia, 2003: 38.
4 Quoted in N Peterson and M Langton (eds), *Aborigines, Land and Land Rights*, Australian Institute of Aboriginal Studies, 1983: 253.
5 Parliament of Victoria, *Report upon the Operation of the Aborigines Act 1928 and the Regulations and Orders Made Thereunder* (McLean Report), Government Printer Melbourne, 1957.
6 'Brother's sister's keeper' is a common term used by Aboriginal people to mean looking after each other in solidarity.
7 Atkinson: 136–7.
8 SL James, letter to Minister for Home Affairs, 11 March 1932, National Archives of Australia, A659–1.
9 Atkinson: 138–9.
10 SL James, letter to JB Chifley, 2 April 1946, National Archives of Australia, PM's file B300–1.
11 McLean Report.
12 Parliament of Victoria: 7.
13 See 'Stolen Generations Reparations Package', Victorian Government website, last updated 25 September 2024.

Chapter 6 Off the Riverbank to Itchica

1 Wayne Atkinson *A Picture from the Other Side*, 1981: 88.
2 Ibid.: 89.

Chapter 7 The Journey of Education

1 See, for example, C Hawker, 'Why are blackfellas so darn good at footy?', research paper for Oncountry Learning Program, OnCountry Learning website, 2009.
2 Wayne Atkinson, *A Picture from the Other Side*, 1981: 83.
3 Neil Martin, 'Flying high! UNSW engineers help make David Unaipon's "helicopter" dream a reality', UNSW website, 7 July 2023.

Chapter 8 Working Man Blues

1 Wayne Atkinson, *A Picture from the Other Side*, 1981: 100.
2 Ibid.: 101.
3 Ibid.

Chapter 9 A New World in Adelaide

1 Saul Alinsky, *Rules for Radicals: A Practical Primer for Realistic Radicals*, Random House, 1971.

Chapter 11 A Picture from the Other Side

1 Nancy Cato, *Mister Maloga*, University of Queensland Press, 1976: 117–18.
2 Wayne Atkinson, *A Picture from the Other Side*, 1981: 65.

3 See Wiradjuri Condobolin Corporation, *The Yorta Yorta Dictionary App* [online app], 2022.

Chapter 12 First Nations Kinship

1 Wayne Atkinson, *A Picture from the Other Side*, 1981: Chapter 6.
2 Vine Deloria, *Custer Died for Your Sins: An Indian Manifesto*, Macmillan, 1969.
3 Ibid.: 83–5.
4 'Battle of the Little Bighorn', *Wikipedia*, last edited 22 January 2025.
5 'Not a discovery voyage', Australian Museum website, last updated 15 February 2024.
6 Wayne Atkinson, *A Look at North American Indian History Programs: Some Ideas for Aboriginal Programs in Australia, July–October 1981*, Australian Government Publishing Service, 1982: 18.
7 Ross L Jones, James Waghorne and Marcia Langton (eds), *Dhoombak Goobgoowana: A History of Indigenous Australia and the University of Melbourne, Volume 1*, Melbourne University Press, 2024: 249.

Chapter 13 Land Rights and Cultural Heritage Reform

1 *Numurkah Leader*, 'Land War: The Battle for the Barmah Forest', 17 August 1983 and 'Numurkah Joins Anti-land Rights Groups', 16 November 1993.
2 G Adams, 'Native Title Fears', *Shepparton News*, 10 August 1994; *The Age*, 29–30 June 1984.
3 *Numurkah Leader*, 17 August 1983.
4 *Numurkah Leader*, 17 August 1983 and 16 November 1993.
5 See Brett Nicholls, 'The communist empty signifier: The Australian League of Rights and the Voice to Parliament referendum', *Continuum*, 38(6), 2024: 915–33. Philippa Hawker, 'The Political War Over Land Rights in Rural Victoria', *The Age*, 25 May 1984.
6 Quoted in David Langsam, 'A nation fights for its heritage', *Herald-Sun*, 5 May 1986.
7 Langsam, *Herald-Sun*, 5 May 1986.
8 Quoted in Aboriginal and Torres Strait Islander Social Justice Commissioner, *Native Title Report: July 1994 – June 1995*, Commonwealth of Australia, 1995: 104.

Chapter 14 Bringing Koori Culture Centre Stage

1 The Koori Heritage Charter was published in *Koorier 2* in 1984.
2 Terri Janke, *Our Culture Our Future: Report on Australian Indigenous Cultural and Intellectual Property Rights*, Michael Frankel & Company, Solicitors, 1998.
3 UN General Assembly, *United Nations Declaration of the Rights of Indigenous Peoples: Resolution*, adopted by the General Assembly, A/RES/61/295, 2 October 2007: 8.
4 *Aboriginal Cultural Heritage: Victoria: Discussion Paper*, Ministry for Planning and Environment, Melbourne, 1985.
5 Greta Bird, *The Process of Law in Australia: Intercultural Perspectives*, Butterworths, 1993: 75–6, 136–7.
6 Onus v Alcoa *of Australia Ltd* (1981) HCA 50; 149 CLR 27.
7 Parliament of Victoria, Hansard, Legislative Assembly, 27 March 1980, p. 7576 (Race Mathews).
8 C Warren, 'Aboriginal Power Over Cultural Heritage', *Legal Service Bulletin*, 16(1), 1991–2.

9 Elizabeth Evatt, *Review of the Aboriginal and Torres Strait Islander Heritage Protection Amendment Act 1984*, Minister for Aboriginal and Torres Strait Islander Affairs, Canberra, 1996: 234.
10 H Fourmile, 'Aboriginal heritage legislation and self-determination', Australian Canadian Studies, 7(1–2), 1989: 47.
11 Jessica K Weir, *The Gunditjmara Land Justice Story*, Native Title Research Unit, AIATSIS, 2009; Peter Skehan, 'Noonkanbah controversy 1980', Western Australia Police Historical Society website, n.d.; Nick Everett, 'The battle for Aboriginal heritage on Perth's foreshore 30 years on', The Commons Social Change Library website, 2019; Garth Nettheim, 'The Hindmarsh Bridge Act case: *Kartinyeri v Commonwealth*', *Indigenous Law Bulletin*, 4(12), 1998: 18; Daniel Miles, 'Supreme Court dismisses Djab Wurrung fight to protect "culturally significant" trees', *ABC News*, 23 November 2021; D Kemp, K Kochan and J Burton, 'Critical reflections on the Juukan Gorge parliamentary inquiry and prospects for industry change', *Journal of Energy & Natural Resources Law*, 41(4), 2023: 379–402.
12 *Aboriginal Heritage Act 2006*: Authorised Version Incorporating Amendments as at 10 May 2023.
13 Celeste Liddle, 'If Australians knew the whole truth about Indigenous history, Lidia Thorpe's royal outburst would not have been a shock', *The Guardian*, 23 October 2024.
14 'Respecting those who came before: Ancestral remains', Victorian Aboriginal Heritage Council website, 2021.
15 Ross L Jones, James Waghorne and Marcia Langton (eds), *Dhoombak Goobgoowana*, Melbourne University Press, 2024: 138.

Chapter 16 Native Title or What?

1 William Cooper, Honorary Secretary, Australian Aborigines' League, to the Prime Minister, Joseph Lyons, 31 March 1938, National Archives of Australia, A659, 1940/1/858.
2 Commonwealth v. Yunupingu (On Behalf of the Gumatj Clan or Estate Group) & Ors (2025) HCA 6.
3 Aboriginal and Torres Strait Islander Social Justice Commissioner, *Native Title Report: July 1994 – June 1995*, Commonwealth of Australia, 1995: 104.
4 Wayne Atkinson, 'Mediating the mindset of opposition: The Yorta Yorta mediation process, 1995', *Indigenous Law Bulletin*, 5(6), 2002: 8.
5 G Adams, 'Native title fears', *Shepparton News*, 29 September 1994.
6 *Native Title Report: July 1994 – June 1995.*
7 Ibid.: 121.

Chapter 17 Nineteen-Second Judgment

1 Original phrase in *Mabo and Others v The State of Queensland [No. 2]* (1992) HCA 23; 175 CLR 1: paragraph 66; quoted in *Members of the Yorta Yorta Aboriginal Community v Victoria* (2001) FCA 45: par. 26.
2 Quoted in James Cockayne, 'Members of Yorta Yorta Aboriginal Community v Victoria: Indigenous and colonial traditions in native title', *Melbourne University Law Review*, 25(3), 2001.
3 Andrea James, *Yanagai! Yanagai!*, Currency Press in association with Playbox Theatre, 2003.

4 Geoff Lennox, 'The Companion to Tasmanian History: Van Diemen's Land Company', Centre for Tasmanian Historical Studies, University of Tasmania, 2006.
5 Wayne Atkinson, '19 Seconds of Djunguma Waala (Yorta Yorta word for big flood): Reflections paper on the Yorta Torta native title judgment', OnCountry Learning website, December 2000.
6 *Mabo and Others v The State of Queensland*: ibid.
7 Ibid.: pars 29, 40–3.
8 Wayne Atkinson, *'Not One Iota': The Yorta Yorta Struggle for Land Justice*, PhD thesis, School of Law and Legal Studies, La Trobe University, 2000: 123.
9 Ibid.

Chapter 18 Refusing to Yield

1 Wayne Atkinson, 'Uncle William Cooper and the spear of the pen', OnCountry Learning website, 2022: 4.
2 Quoted in Aboriginal and Torres Strait Islander Social Justice Commissioner, *Native Title Report 2009*, Australian Human Rights Commission, 2009: xii.

Chapter 19 Oncountry Learning

1 Alec Morgan (director), *Lousy Little Sixpence* [motion picture], Sixpence Productions, 1983.
2 Wayne Atkinson, 'Occasional address: Royal Exhibition Building, Thursday 14 December 2017', University of Melbourne, 2017.

Chapter 20 Andrew Bolt's Myths for Money

1 Quoted in Samantha Donovan, 'Aboriginal activist's anti-Nazi stand remembered', *ABC News*, 6 December 2012.
2 *Eatock v Bolt* (2011) FCA 1103: paragraph 406.
3 Ibid.: paragraph 452(ii).
4 Jerome Holleman, 'Perceptions of race and aboriginal identity in the Bolt case, 2011', Oncountry Learning website.

Chapter 21 Adventures Abroad: Travelling with Wayne

1 See Wayne Atkinson, 'Tracking the origins of the reserve system through the lens of Cummeragunja: The Irish connection', paper given at 20th Australasian Conference of Irish Studies, University of New South Wales, 4–7 December 2013.
2 A Mitchell, *Roger Casement: 16 Lives*, O'Brien Press, 2013.
3 Catherine Guinness, *Rubber Justice: Dr Harry Guinness and the Congo Reform Campaign*, self-published, 2017.
4 See Wayne Atkinson, 'Tracing the origins of Grandpa James: A journey of discovery' (typescript of family history project conducted in Mauritius, India and Sri Lanka, 2012–16), OnCountry Learning website, 2017.
5 'About Murujuga', Murujuga Aboriginal Corporation (MAC) website, 2025.
6 P Valde-Nowak, A Nadachowski and M Wolsan, 'Upper Palaeolithic boomerang made of a mammoth tusk in south Poland', *Nature*, 329, 1987: 436–8.

Chapter 22 Truth, Justice and Self-Determination

1 First Nations Constitutional Convention, *Uluru Statement from the Heart*, Central Land Council Library, 2017.

2 'Wamba Wemba to take up new seat in the First Peoples Assembly of Victoria', The Assembly website, 21 March 2024.
3 'Truth and justice in Victoria', First Peoples—State Relations website, updated 3 April 2024.
4 Victorian Government, Yoorrook Justice Commission letters patent [hereafter Letters Patent], published in *Victorian Government Gazette*, 14 May 2021: 2–3.
5 Wayne Atkinson, *A Look at North American Indian History Programs*, 1982; Wayne Atkinson, 'Treaty: Getting it right for a treaty now' (research paper, School of Social and Political Sciences, University of Melbourne), OnCountry Learning website, 2019.
6 Letters Patent: 1.
7 Ibid.
8 *Uluru Statement from the Heart*.
9 Ibid.
10 Lyndall Ryan et al., *Colonial Frontier Massacres in Australia 1788–1930* [website].
11 Wayne Atkinson, 'Chronology of inquiries reports and legislation: Victoria's First Peoples, 1836–2021', OnCountry Learning website, 2021.
12 Letters Patent: 3.
13 'Truth and Reconciliation Commission (South Africa)', *Wikipedia*, last edited 26 January 2025.
14 Maggie Walter et al.,'From dispossession to massacres, the Yoo-rrook Justice Commission sets a new standard for truth telling', *The Conversation*, 5 November 2021.
15 'Yoorrook report calls for self-determination to transform Victoria's child protection and criminal justice systems' [media release], Yoorrook Justice Commission website, 4 September 2023.
16 'Yoorrook laments major setback as government backflips on raising the age' [media release], Yoorrook Justice Commission website, 13 August 2024.
17 Jack Latimore, '"The embodiment of everything": Preserving the language of Indigenous Victorians', *The Age*, 13 October 2021.
18 Ibid.
19 Ibid.
20 Wayne Atkinson, '"Not to lose you my language": Working paper', OnCountry Learning website, 2022; Yoorrook Justice Commission, *Yoorrook with Purpose: Interim Report*, 2022: 9, 68–9.
21 First Peoples' Assembly of Victoria, *Tyerri Yoorrook 'Seed of Truth': Report to the Yoo-rrook Justice Commission*, June 2021: 4.
22 United Nations, *Declaration on the Rights of Indigenous Peoples*, 2007 (hereafter UNDRIP): 12–13.
23 Victorian Government, *Self-Determination Reform Framework*, Department of Premier and Cabinet, 2019.
24 Letters Patent: 2.
25 Yoorrook Justice Commission, Witness Statement of the Hon. Gabrielle Williams MP: 12.
26 Victorian Government, *Wirkara Kulpa: Aboriginal Youth Justice Strategy 2022–2032*, 2022: 11.
27 Yoorrook Justice Commission Hearing, 15 May 2023: 867.
28 Yoorrook Justice Commission, Witness Statement of the Hon. Natalie Hutchins MP: 60.
29 Yoorrook Justice Commission Hearing, 18 April 2024: 18.

30 Yoorrook Justice Commission, Child Protection and Criminal Justice Systems Hearing: Government and Departmental Day 10, 15 May 2023.
31 Yoorrook Justice Commission Hearing, 6 May 2022: 347.
32 Productivity Commission, *Review of the National Agreement on Closing the Gap: Study Report, Volume 1*, January 2024.
33 Ibid.: iii.
34 Letters Patent: 3.
35 Caroline Overington, 'Not so Black and White', *The Australian*, 24 March 2012.
36 Yoorrook Justice Commission, Witness Statement of Aunty Fay Carter: 13.
37 Australian Bureau of Statistics, 'Indigenous Status Standard, Version 1.5', *ABS website*, 2014.
38 See Yoorrook Justice Commission Hearing, 5 May 2022: 229.
39 Letters Patent: 4.
40 Bhiamie Williamson, 'The full truth of the past: Native title and the Yoorrook Justice Commission', *Arena*, 16 September 2021.
41 Yoorrook Justice Commission Hearing, 18 April 2024: 73.
42 See Chin Tan, 'Whatever the voice vote's result, Australia has a racism problem we must tackle', *The Guardian*, 6 October 2023.
43 See Marcia Langton, 'Truth-telling is one form of restorative justice, but more is needed to redress the wrongs done to Indigenous peoples', *Pursuit*, 28 May 2024.
44 Ross L Jones, 'Eugenics 1853–1945', in Ross L Jones, James Waghorne and Marcia Langton (eds), *Dhoombak Goobgoowana: A History of Indigenous Australia and the University of Melbourne, Volume 1*, Melbourne University Press, 2024: 188.
45 Ibid.: 182, 190–1.
46 'Conclusions' in Jones, Waghorne and Langton (eds): 489.
47 Personal briefing consultation with Yoorrook commissioners including Wayne Atkinson, 28 September 2021.
48 '2.11: Contact with the criminal justice system' in Australian Institute of Health, Welfare and National Indigenous Australians Agency, *Aboriginal and Torres Strait Islander Health Performance Framework: Summary Report August 2024*.
49 Rudi Maxwell, 'Indigenous children over-represented in juvenile detention', *National Indigenous Times*, 13 December 2023.
50 Royal Commission into Aboriginal Deaths in Custody, *National Report*, AGPS, 1991.
51 *Bringing Them Home: Report of the National Inquiry into the Separation of Aboriginal and Torres Strait Islander Children from their Families*, Australian Human Rights Commission, 1997.
52 'William Cooper petition (cabinet paper) 1938', National Archives of Australia website, n.d.
53 Chin Tan, *The Guardian*, 6 October 2023.
54 Joint Standing Committee on Aboriginal and Torres Strait Islander Affairs, *Inquiry into the Application of the United Nations Declaration on the Rights of Indigenous Peoples in Australia*, Commonwealth of Australia, 2023.
55 'Additional comment from Senator Lidia Thorpe', in ibid.
56 UNDRIP: 5–6.
57 Chapter 3, paragraph 3.111, in in *Inquiry into the Application of the United Nations Declaration on the Rights of Indigenous Peoples in Australia*.
58 'List of recommendations', in *Inquiry into the Application of the United Nations Declaration on the Rights of Indigenous Peoples in Australia*.
59 Anthony Albanese, 'Press conference: Parliament House, Canberra', 15 October 2023.

60 Kieran Rooney, 'Opposition dumps vow to back First Nations treaty process', *The Age*, 21 January 2024.
61 Editorial, *The Age*, 22 January 2024.
62 See Yoorrook Justice Commission, *Yoorrook with Purpose: Interim Report*, 2022: 86.

Chapter 23 Reflections

1 Irene Watson, 'First Nations and the colonial project', *Inter Gentes*, 1(1), 2016: 30.

Appendix

1 JC Altman and W Sanders, *From Exclusion to Dependence: Aborigines and the Welfare State in Australia*, Centre for Aboriginal Economic Policy Research, Australian National University, 1991.
2 *Bringing Them Home: Report of the National Inquiry into the Separation of Aboriginal and Torres Strait Islander Children from their Families*, Australian Human Rights Commission, 1997.
3 '"Protection" legislation introduced in Victoria', Deadly Story website, n.d.
4 *Report of the Board Appointed to Inquire into, and Report upon, the Present Condition and Management of the Coranderrk Aboriginal Station*, Government Printer Melbourne, 1882: 66–8.
5 '*Half-Caste Act*', *Wikipedia*, last edited 24 November 2024.
6 *Bringing Them Home: Report of the National Inquiry into the Separation of Aboriginal and Torres Strait Islander Children from their Families*, Australian Human Rights Commission, 1997: 51.
7 Parliament of Victoria, *Report upon the Operation of the Aborigines Act 1928 and the Regulations and Orders Made Thereunder* (McLean Report), Government Printer Melbourne, 1957: 6.
8 Ibid.: 19–22.
9 *Aborigines Act 1957 (Victoria)*, section 6.
10 'Aborigines Welfare Board', Find & Connect website, n.d.
11 Victorian Government, Yoorrook Justice Commission letters patent [hereafter Letters Patent], published in *Victorian Government Gazette*, 14 May 2021: 5.
12 Ibid.
13 Letters Patent: 2–3.
14 New South Wales Legislative Assembly, *Select Committee on Administration of Aborigines Protection Board: Proceedings of the Committee, Minutes of Evidence and Exhibits*, Government Printer Sydney, 1938.
15 *Aborigines Protection (Amendment) Act 1943 (NSW)*, section 2.
16 See Australian Law Reform Commission, *The Recognition of Aboriginal Customary Laws* (Report no. 31), AGPS, 1986, Chapter 3, paragraph 26.
17 *Bringing Them Home*: 28.
18 Paul Hasluck, *Native Welfare in Australia: Speeches and Addresses*, Paterson Brokensha, 1953: 16.
19 Royal Commission into Aboriginal Deaths in Custody, *National Report*, AGPS, 1991.

Index

THE MIEGUNYAH PRESS
This book was designed and typeset by Cannon Typesetting
The text was set in 11¼pt Adobe Caslon Pro
with 15 points of leading
The text is printed on 80 gsm woodfree
This book was edited by Katie Purvis

THE
MIEGUNYAH
PRESS